How to Get Rid of the Income Tax

With comments on political reform by Will Rogers

Books by Robert C. Hardy

Sick—published by Teach'em, 1978
Hero—published by the Oklahoma Health Sciences Foundation, 1985
One Hundred Years of Upstart Unitarianism—published by the First Unitarian Church of Oklahoma City, 1991

How to Get Rid of the Income Tax

With comments on political reform by Will Rogers

Robert C. Hardy

NPI

Northwest Publishing, Inc.

How to Get Rid of the Income Tax

Cover illustration courtesy of Billy W. Sandin

For information address: Northwest Publishing, Inc.
5949 South 350 West, Salt Lake City, Utah 84107

LC 1 19 94

First Printing 1994

ISBN: 1-56901-212-1

NPI books are published by Northwest Publishing, Incorporated,
5949 South 350 West, Salt Lake City, Utah 84107.

PRINTED IN THE UNITED STATES OF AMERICA.
10 9 8 7 6 5 4 3 2 1

WITH APPRECIATION TO:

DR. JAMES M. BUCHANAN, who won the 1986 Nobel Prize in Economic Science for his work applying economic principles to political decision making. His wisdom appears in Chapter Eighteen;

AND

PATRICK B. McGUIGAN, Chief Editorial Writer for *The Oklahoman,* who took an interest in these ideas and graciously reviewed the manuscript;

AND

FRANK C. STEWART, entrepreneur and ardent observer of the political scene, who contributed inspiration, ideas and information for this book.

PREFACE

Will Rogers had the Washington scene figured out in 1926 when he said,"Taxation is all there is to Politics."[1]

In the Will Rogers Memorial at Claremore, the Oklahoma humorist's den/study of his Santa Monaco ranch home is reproduced; the room in which he often banged out his weekly newspaper article; that is, when he wasn't roaming the world.

Today in that reconstructed room, you can hear a recording of his voice, talking about his favorite subject—politics. He said, "People often ask me, 'Will, where do you get your jokes?' I just tell 'em, 'Well, I watch the government and report the facts, that is all I do, and I don't even find it necessary to exaggerate.'"[2]

As you listen to his comments about the Congress, you could swear he was talking about what is going on in Washington today! It is absolutely uncanny the way he analyzed human nature, particularly the nature of politicians.

In these first years of Bill Clinton's new Democratic administration, many of the issues Will talked about are still around, and his comments are just as relevant today as they were more than half a century ago.

America has major problems—outlandish deficits, legislation by lobby, high taxes, the growing national debt, inferior education for our children, drug abuse and crime, unemployment, illegal immigration, environmental pollution, increasing numbers of bankruptcies, deteriorating city centers, skyrocketing health care costs, oppressive federal regulations, declining industry...

After a stumbling start, President William Jefferson Clinton was off and running. True to his promise to bring about change, he's doing that all right, but is it the kind of tax-and-spend change the American people want?

He firmly believes more government will solve the country's problems, including jump-starting the economy. But government's recent miserable record would indicate otherwise. Only private enterprise can create good, permanent jobs, because the more government drains off the incentive and money people need to improve the economy, the less our living standard will grow, and the less we shall prosper.

In the first months of the Clinton Administration, both political parties tried to convey to the President what the true interests of the people are. Senator Bob Dole said it best: "The people want more spending cuts, not more taxes."

Even his own Democratic leaders, like Senator David Boren of Oklahoma, fought to change the balance between new taxes and spending cuts.

But it doesn't help just to gripe about what's wrong.

Fortunately, there are many important ideas for sound, sensible, dramatic solutions to our difficulties, proposed by thoughtful people and reported in the newspapers. As Will said, "Well, all I know is just what I read in the papers."

This book is a collection of those ideas, and one or two of my own, to provide something other than the promises and rhetoric of the last Presidential election campaign as a basis for considering the reality of the issues facing America. Much of what Candidate Bill Clinton said he would do, President William J. Clinton backed away from, anyhow, so many of the problems remain.

This book was compiled as a source of information and opinion for further discussion, as these issues are either tackled or ignored by the President and the Congress. Clinton's goals for America are sound; the question remains whether his methods can achieve these goals. This book is intended as a checklist on Clinton's ideas and action to see if his vaunted "change" actually improves our standard of living, social conditions, and economic opportunity in America.

As you will see, Will Rogers had something to say about almost all of them!

INTRODUCTION

"Well, all I know is just what I read in the papers."
—Will Rogers[1]

Have you ever muttered to yourself, "If I were running America, things would be a whole lot different!"?

No single person, not even President William Jefferson "Bill" Clinton, is running America, thanks to the framers of the Constitution of the United States. America is run by the people and the people have a lot of different goals, values and ideas.

In America, there is opportunity for ambitious, industrious people who want to better themselves, gain security, get rich, make a contribution to others, improve their education and their skills...opportunity to do whatever they are motivated to do and are capable of doing. Will Rogers said:

America is a land of opportunity and don't ever forget it."[2]

More than half a century later, and despite industrial downsizing and increased job competition, I am convinced this is still true.

So why is America so screwed up today? Why are we the world's largest debtor nation, paying interest on more than four trillion dollars and going deeper into debt every day? Why are we flooded with foreign goods that other nations can produce better and cheaper? Why are our cities falling apart? Why did almost a million consumers and businesses, a record number, go bankrupt in 1992, up from 735,000 in 1983? Why do many Asian immigrants come over here and quickly become self-supporting, while our own poor, who've been here seemingly forever, are unable to break out of the poverty cycle? Why can't we and those who represent us get our act together?

All of us have a mental picture of the ideal America. When we look around, reality is a radically different picture. Crime, drug dependency, unwanted pregnancies, child abuse, savings and loan failures, homeless people, bond-trading and inside trader scandals, illiteracy, declining SAT scores, deteriorating cities, worn-out bridges and sewerage systems, mountains of waste we don't know how to dispose of...these are the realities of America in our recent past and today.

It is said that in America the people get the kind of government they deserve. Obviously, some of the problems we face are our own fault. As Will Rogers pointed out: "Shrewdness in public life all over the world is always honored while honesty in public men is generally attributed to dumbness and seldom rewarded."[3]

Sure, we elect the people we think can do the best job representing us, but none of them seems to know how to make America work anymore. Not since the tranquil Eisenhower years has the budget been balanced. We appropriate large sums of money, throw it at our problems, expand the already-bloated bureaucracy and often fail to make a dent in the trouble we had hoped to ease. It's been all downhill since the turbulent sixties, and it's not getting perceptibly better.

So, what would you do? Call in an expert?

You can find an expert on any subject you like; experts on the economy, on politics, on drugs, on crime, on education, on production, on child abuse, etc. They are quick to advise what should be done but so often the answer turns out to be that the "government," usually the Federal government, should supply more money. But America is broke; government doesn't have any more money, the federal government alone is already spending 24.9 percent of the annual wealth we produce (up from 20 percent in 1972), to say nothing about what states, counties and cities spend in addition. And even that isn't enough; witness escalating federal budget deficits. The FY 1991 deficit set a new record of $268.7 billion only to be exceeded by the FY 1992 deficit of $290 billion. Due to easing fiscal pressure, the budget deficit declined to $254.6 billion in FY 1993. These sums compare with the old record of $221.3 billion set in 1986.

President Bush submitted his FY 1993 budget to Congress with a built-in $400 billion deficit! President Clinton's original economic program proposed total outlays rising from $1,381.7 billion in 1992 to $1,612.8 billion in 1996. While he repeatedly contended this was a $500 billion deficit reduction plan, the net deficit reduction by the end of 1996 is expected to be only $84.9 billion below the $290.2 billion, 1992 deficit left by the Bush Administration. From then on, the deficit is projected to begin rising again.[4, 5, 6]

Some of the states are in a similar predicament; witness Governor Pete Wilson's effort to overcome California's $14 billion budget shortfall.

The trouble with experts is they fly in, proclaim their expertise, make a study, write a report that says what to do, and then fly out, assuming no responsibility for whether or not their advice produces the results they claim for it.

Oh, America isn't going down the tubes tomorrow. America still has a lot of enterprise, intelligence and guts. Like the British, we'll muddle through somehow, we hope. But just how much longer can we keep from sliding down this slippery slope?

I believe we could turn America around if we built in incentives and motivators to improve our deteriorating situation; if we took back much of the decision-making process from our elected politicians and from the lobbyists who control and contribute to them; and if we adjusted the American system so everyone had a compelling reason to work toward positive values and assure a brighter future for America.

I do not claim to be an expert—just a middle-class American who has lived here for seven decades and paid taxes for at least fifty of those years. I'm sort of like that other Oklahoman, Will Rogers; I get most of my information from the newspapers. And these days, what I read is not very encouraging.

On the other hand, a lot of good ideas about what to do are floating around in those newspapers, ideas that could improve the life of every American.

The purpose of this book is to react to the plight of America in the mid-Nineties, and, from the viewpoint of an ordinary citizen, put together these ideas which suggest solutions to some of our most pressing problems. And just perhaps, this book may stimulate the thinking of other citizens who believe our entire *system* of governance is moribund, in acute need of major surgery and prolonged intensive care. Will Rogers said, "I dident know before I got there and they told me all this—that Rome had Senators. Now I know why it declined."[7]

Some of these ideas will seem dumb and naive, impossible of accomplishment. Maybe they are, because the established power structure, those with vested interests (i.e., strong incentives to do so) will fight them vociferously. But, as I indicated, most of these possible answers have been expressed by other dissatisfied citizens. If there is a quote or a superscript referring to the source, you can be sure it's not my idea, only that I agree with it. I have selected those ideas that seem to me most effective and workable, the ones most likely to improve the future of America.

If I were running America, this is what I would do:

1. Eliminate the annual federal deficit
2. Free lawmakes from financial dependence on political action committees
3. Eliminate the income tax
4. Erase the national debt
5. Reduce the cost of elections and the length of election campaigns
6. Improve the quality of public education; teach values to our children
7. Reduce drug abuse and crime
8. Expand employment opportunities; reduce dependence on welfare
9. Control legal and illegal immigration into the United States
10. Export American know-how to developing countries
11. Reevaluate Environmental Protection Agency programs; balance short- and long-term benefits with people and animal concerns
12. Reduce credit abuses and bankruptcies
13. Revitalize the deteriorating centers of our cities
14. Control costs and expand the accessibility of health care services
15. Promote free trade; stimulate American technological innovation; recognize the reality of multinational companies
16. Change government regulation procedures to reduce paperwork for businesses and the cost to consumers

who ultimately pay the bill

17. Increase the retirement age: take advantage of the production of older Americans: "Work harder, save more, and pay the preacher."[8]

Who can do all this? We can…the caring, dedicated, taxpaying citizens of America. What's more, we'd better. When you stop to ponder our plight, it's us, the American citizens, against them, the rest of the American citizens who claim to represent us and who are on the government payroll at all levels.

Let's regain America for the common people who aren't paid by the government. Let's take the power back. Let's make America everything it must be if we are to continue to be the world leader we have been since World War II.

Chapter One

Incentive

We Americans have just witnessed the utter failure of communism in the Soviet Union after 74 years of experimentation with a system that left out the key ingredient of social organization—positive incentive. People can no longer be forced to work or perform for the common good; they must be inspired. By contrast, the American way of freedom—private enterprise and government of, for and by the people—is marvelous. But not as marvelous as it used to be.

Incentive incites or has a tendency to incite determination or action. However, incentive comes in two forms: 1. negative incentive—fear of punishment and 2. positive incentive—prospect of reward.

Actually, there is also a third form, prevalent in large, bureaucratic organizations like the government and the army. It is the neutral form, with just enough of both negative and positive pressures to neither strongly inhibit nor greatly inspire action in either direction. So things just seem to rock along. Neutral incentive slows progress because it attracts people who have a greater need for security than for accomplishment. They procrastinate, cover their posterior and otherwise make sure that they won't be fired. They also tend to devise laws, rules and regulations so that nobody can be fired. Unions and government bureaucrats are good at that.

Negative incentive was prevalent in the Soviet Union since 1917, enforced by the KGB. Until glasnost and perestroika were introduced by President Gorbachev in the mid-1980s, and the coup attempt by Soviet hard-liners was put down in 1991, the people had little hope of improving their lot in life.

Neutral incentive pervades American organizations which provide income based only on performance of described actions, not on the results of those actions. Example: While teachers grade their students on results, they are themselves rarely graded on their own performance, nor are they paid on that basis. Another example: enlisted army personnel do what they are told, rarely volunteer for anything, and take little personal responsibility for the results of their actions. Of course, there are the eager ones who rise in the ranks, but they are the exceptions. The table of organization severely limits the number of promotions, so there is little incentive for a soldier, sailor or airman to do more than wait in grade until eligible for the next step, keep his or her nose clean and float up with the tide.

Positive incentive, by contrast, inspires performance and rewards that performance with an increase in income, respect, adulation, fame, personal satisfaction, and the many intangible benefits of doing the job well. The people who become rich and famous in America have learned how to hustle. These entrepreneurs, movers, and innovators are those who continue to make America great. These people work long hours, measure their personal worth by achievement and aren't waiting just for the weekend and their paycheck. Some of these types are even employed in government, but they too are the exception. They are most likely found in small, wholly-owned businesses, in non-profit groups organized to pursue an idea like Right-to-Life, Planned Parenthood, Parents Against Drunk Driving, Alcoholics Anonymous and the like. It's a mindset, a way of life. As Patrick B. McGuigan, Chief Editorial Writer, *The Daily Oklahoman*, once observed to me, "For a true believer, a job is not what you *do*, it's what you *are*."

America has been famous for its entrepreneurial spirit and enterprise. We look down our noses at the Soviets whose Union has dissolved, whose economy, while improving, is still in danger of collapsing and who must look to the West for emergency credit to buy food and for financial as well as technical assistance to establish the market economy to which they now aspire.

But America has little reason to be smug. America is also struggling because it, too, has failed to use positive incentives to solve its increasingly difficult problems. For example, until now, when the fiscal situation reached the crisis level and voters insisted, Congress had no incentive to balance the budget because its members are reelected on the basis of what they can do for their constituents.

Privileges for congressmen are tilted to benefit the reelection prospects of incumbents and most of them return to Washington after each election. As Columnist Thomas Sowell observed, "The Franking Privilege alone guarantees that any member of Congress can maintain his name-recognition, at taxpayers' expense, simply by sending out tons of mail regularly to people in his district or state."

He went on to say, "We need to recognize that imposing a government policy is a lot like entering a Venus fly trap. It is easy to get in but almost impossible to get out. There may not be a lot that can be done about existing programs that have become entrenched. But before we go creating still more programs and more agencies, we need to understand that we are not making the kinds of decisions we make in our private lives. In private life, we can change directions...Government programs can be forever."[1]

This is the reason this nation continues to slip further into debt and can't seem to get out. If our representatives are assured of lofty position, why should they get exercised over a few trillion dollars of debt? They can always print more money or levy more taxes.

Senators and representatives must court or at least respond to political action groups to get enough money to finance their reelection, so we have government by lobby and special interest group rather than government for the ultimate good of the people. Special interest groups happily contribute to the election expenses of those congressmen who will support their interests. For example: Just one day after 22 people were slaughtered by a deranged gunman in a cafeteria in Killeen, Texas in October 1991, the House of Representatives rejected a proposed ban on assault weapons that was part of an anti-crime bill. The National Rifle Association, prime mover of the gun lobby, so influences the congressmen that they are afraid to go against this powerful political action group and risk the financial support they enjoy from that source.

So we have a reciprocal trade agreement in the formulation of the country's laws—a case of "You give me money to get reelected and I'll promote your interests, whatever they are." Quite a deal! Each party to this arrangement is dependent on the other, but the people who elect the congressmen and pay the nation's taxes are left out. Some people say, "So, throw the rascals out!" The problem is it makes no difference which professional politician we elect. As Will Rogers put it:

> *Most all new senators are earnest and mean well. Then the air of Washington gets into their bones and they are just as bad as the rest.*

Once in office, all of them are seduced by the lobbyists and quickly follow this behavior pattern to assure their continued incumbency.

This is just one way congressional action does not benefit the nation as a whole. To a large extent, congressmen get reelected because they are able to produce federal funds to benefit their district. Their incentive, therefore, is to tax everybody so they can get money for their district. And should the tax money run out, as it has been doing for years, and it's too risky to raise taxes, they can always borrow more money, i.e., sell government bonds to finance whatever they wish to do. That's why the national debt continues to rise.

You and I can live on borrowed money, too, as long as the bank, credit union or Savings and Loan company will loan us the money, but we have to pay it back! The Congress feels no such obligation when it borrows to spend. Proof? This nation has gone from less than one trillion to well over four trillion dollars deeper in debt in less than a dozen years. As a result, in 1991, we taxpayers paid more than $280 billion in interest—24 cents of every tax dollar—to service our huge and growing debt. The Tax Foundation estimated this cost the typical family of four $2,238 that year.

So what's the answer? We must create incentives for our representatives not only to balance the budget but to look at the broader, long-range picture and, in a statesman-like manner, devise answers to the many problems which beset America.

It's obvious the current system is out of control...our control!

The people we call our representatives represent themselves first; they are career politicians, in it for the long haul. After them, we come first as long as their own position is not threatened. If this were not so, why would so many of our representatives be accused of ethics and law violations? Why did so many members of the House run up a $300,000 tab at the House restaurant? Why did the House members write 8,331 hot checks in a single year at their private bank? Why are our congressmen exempt from the rules their constituents must abide by?

The following chapters will examine in detail each goal listed in the introduction and suggest ways by which the system can be remodeled to build in the motivation necessary to accomplish these goals. Of course, in a free society, if the reader should not agree these are worthwhile goals, the methods suggested for achieving them are pointless. I believe, however, that most of these goals are like apple pie and motherhood—most Americans would approve them.

Chapter Two

Eliminate the Annual Federal Deficit

We will never get anywhere with our finances till we pass a law saying that every time we appropriate something we got to pass another bill along with it stating where the money is coming from.

—*Will Rogers*[1]

Is it impossible to eliminate the annual federal deficit?

No. President Dwight D. Eisenhower managed to balance the federal budget in the 1950s, but it hasn't happened since, a period of more than three decades. President Kennedy, a Democrat; Johnson, a Democrat; Nixon, a Republican; Ford, a Republican; Carter, a Democrat; Reagan, a Republican; and George Herbert Walker Bush, another Republican, were unable to inspire or control the Congress sufficiently to keep the nation from going from the world's largest creditor nation to the world's largest debtor nation. This, of course, presumes these presidents were interested in balancing the budget, a dubious assumption. As Will Rogers observed more than half a century ago, "Taxation is about all there is to government. People want just taxes more than they want lower taxes."[2]

There's something wrong when our lawmakers continue to spend more money than America has and the annual budget deficits continue to climb. This is not because nobody in the Congress remembers a balanced budget. Seven representatives and five senators have been up there long enough to have experienced or at least remember the Eisenhower years quite vividly.

They are:

Representatives	*Elected in*
Jamie Whitten (D., Miss.)	1941
Jack Brooks (D., Texas)	1952
William Natcher (D., Ky.)	1953
John Dingell (D., Mich.)	1955
Bob Michel (R. Ill.)	1956
Dan Rostenkowski (D., Ill.)	1958
Neal Smith (D., Iowa)	1958
Senators	
Strom Thurmond (R., S.C.)	1956
Robert Byrd (D., W. Va.)	1958
Claiborne Pell (D., R.I.)	1960
Edward Kennedy (D., Mass.)	1962
Daniel Inouye (D. Hawaii)	1962[3]

With this kind of senior leadership, one would think the Congress could understand the concept of a balanced budget and the utter waste of the $280 billion in interest we paid in 1991 on the national debt which was then $3.7 trillion and will continue to pay on the debt which is now well over $4 trillion.

The inability of the Congress to manage the nation's funds became more clear when it was revealed in 1991 that 355 members of the house had written 20,000 hot checks in only three years at their private bank. What incensed the newspaper-reading public was that the lawmakers were not charged the usual $15 fee ordinary depositors must pay when they write a hot check. What's more, the members took an average of seven days to cover these checks; some took up to four months. Just considering checks written for $1,000 or more, 134 legislators cashed 581 checks which were returned for insufficient funds. Some 200 members overdrew their accounts by more than their next paycheck, about $5,000.

A few days later, the General Accounting Office revealed that some 300 current and former House members owed the House restaurant system more than $300,000.

Within the week, the House voted 190 to 8 to shut down the members' bank, hoping the scandal would be quickly forgotten and damage to the legislators' reputations could be controlled. But these examples of profligacy and personal mismanagement paled to insignificance when compared to the $268 billion deficit in the nation's finances at the end of fiscal year 1991.

How does this happen? How does the nation run up such horrendous deficits? Simple. If any proof of the propensity of our representatives to spend were needed, it was supplied by the National Taxpayers Union Foundation, which asked how every bill introduced in the first eight-and-a-half months of 1991 would affect spending if they were all passed. The result: spending would go up nearly half a trillion dollars! Of course, no one would expect that to happen, but the Foundation chairman, James Davidson, said the lopsided nature of the bills introduced is "dramatic evidence of a dynamic that is propelling Congress toward ever higher levels of federal spending."

The Foundation found that in the entire 435-member House, only one lawmaker—Herbert Bateman, R-Va.—sponsored bills that would result in a net decrease in government spending. No senator did that. Senate Democrats sponsored 65 spending-increase bills for every spending-cut measure. For Republicans the ratio was 23-to-1. House Democrats offered 12 increases for every cut; House Republicans proposed six increases for each reduction.[4]

So why aren't Americans a lot more concerned? Elayne Boosler, the popular stand-up comic, says:

> *I have a whole theory on why people aren't crazed from the deficit. It's because they don't relate to the amount. It's a grillion dollars now. I looked it up and that is a thousand flillions. And most people never see that much money. So it's a billion dollars, so it means nothing. I do believe that if the deficit was $842, people would burn the White House down. Because you would have every man and every woman who makes a buck a day, they would march on Washington, zillions of people. They would say, 'Eight hundred and forty-two dollars! You lost our tax money? You lost $842? What are you, an idiot? Where were you yesterday? What stops did you make? Do you know what I could do for my family with $842?' And then the government would say, 'No, no, it's a billion dollars.' And the people would go, 'Oh, a billion. Well that sounds like a lot of money.'*[5]

Obviously, our learned representatives in the Congress might as well be talking about grillions or zillions or flillions, since they apparently don't fully understand what a billion or a trillion is, either.

James M. Buchanan, Ph.D., who won the 1986 Nobel Prize in economic science for his work applying economic principles to political decision-making, says, "I don't think we can justify deficit spending on any grounds. One of the reasons we aren't saving more now is because of the gross dissaving the government is doing. That's what reduces our net savings rate down so low compared with other countries and compared with our own historical experience. In that sense, if you think of ourselves behaving publicly, through our representatives who are creating the deficits, we are grossly immoral and unethical. In a way, voting for a congressman who generates that dissaving is analogous to negative saving, violating the norm of the saving ethic rather blatantly, rather grossly."[6]

Several conditions contribute to the professional congressmen's attitude they are above the law. In fact, they are, as a result of their own action. They decide which laws of their own making they will and will not be subjected to. Since 1935, they have exempted themselves from:

Social Security Act 1935
National Labor Relations Act 1935
Minimum Age Act 1938
Equal Pay Act 1963
Civil Rights Act 1964
Freedom of Information Act 1966
Age Discrimination Act 1967
Occupational Health and Safety Act 1970
Equal Employment Opportunity Act 1972
Title 9 of Higher Education Act Amendment 1972
Privacy Act 1972
Rehabilitation Act 1973
Age Discrimination Act Amendments 1975
Ethics in Government Act 1978
Civil Rights Restoration Act 1988[7]

Nor has the Congress quit exempting itself from laws everybody else has to obey. In October, 1991, while the Senate included itself under coverage of the anti-discrimination laws when passing a new civil rights bill, it exempted itself from the legal procedures to which everyone else is subject. Senator Warren Rudman (R-N.H.) said, "We should be subject to the same laws, but hardly the same enforcement mechanism." Senator Pete Domenici (R-

N.M.) observed, "Frankly, this [the United States Senate] is a rather special place. There is no doubt about it, the Constitution intended it to be a very special place."[8]

The Senate then proceeded to kill an amendment by Senator Don Nickles, a Republican from Oklahoma, which would have made this exclusive club and their brothers and sisters in the House subject to both the Occupational Safety and Health Act and the Fair Labor Standards Act.

Every auditor/accountant in America would call any business to task if it failed to have appropriate internal financial controls. Example: The employee who writes the company checks may not authorize changes in his own salary. But the Congress can. All they have to do to raise their own salary is to take a vote among themselves. This process is made easy because there is no debt control; when the congress exceeds the latest debt ceiling, all they do is raise it. Nobody seems to worry if there is no money in the till. They merely borrow it or print it.

> *I wish America could get some of the political bandits that live off this country to come in and give up. Then we would know just what we are paying them to live on, instead of the present system of letting them grab what they can.*
>
> *—Will Rogers*[9]

In an article in the July, 1993, issue of *The Atlantic Monthly* magazine entitled, "It's not the economy, stupid," Charles R. Morris said Bill Clinton was elected on an untenable promise; that it is the job of the president to manage the economy. The author went on to explain how the American economy is too colossal to be managed. However, he gave the president great credit when he appealed to citizens to do the right thing—to endure some pain in order to bring the appetites of government back into line with its resources, and to forgo some personal benefits for a greater good.

Morris warned, though, "If taxes go up and the deficit does not go down, it will be a breach of trust not likely to be forgiven or forgotten, and the backwash of voter cynicism could poison the political system for years. Unfortunately, as the specifics of the Clinton program become clearer, the danger of precisely such a result seems very real."[10]

Probable miscalculations, inadvertent or intended, in the Clinton economic plan and congressional disregard for the importance of fiscal responsibility, both personal and on behalf of the nation, call for forceful action. Because the congressional incumbents have proven beyond all reasonable doubt their inability to govern the nation's fiscal affairs, the length of time a legislator can fail to do the job and still remain in office should be limited. While Will Rogers was talking about the office of the president, (reelection of incumbents was unlimited prior to 1944; after Franklin Delano Roosevelt was elected to an unprecedented fourth term that year, presidents were limited by law to two, four year terms) the Oklahoma humorist's idea was to:

> *Elect 'em for a six-year term; not allow 'em to succeed themselves. That would keep their mind off politics.*[11]

Term limitation is hardly a new thought. Will Rogers saw the wisdom of it more than half a century ago, long before the United States presidency was limited to two terms. He died in an airplane crash in Alaska in 1935.

Today, 70 percent of the American public believe that term limitation is an idea whose time has come. Even Democrats, following the tradition of Presidents Truman and Kennedy, support term limits for Congress by 71 percent. Women favor the idea more than men. While some people think it is a "meat-ax approach," could it be that's all the professional politician understands?[12, 13]

Confidence in our lawmakers has slowly eroded since the 1950s as public-spirited, part-time representatives and senators have been replaced by professional politicians proficient in the art of winning elections and working full time at their craft. Unfortunately, the skills it takes to get elected to a job in Congress are not the skills necessary to govern wisely.[14]

Each member seems to have an agenda of his own so that concerted effort by either party tends to be ineffective. This is because politicians nominate themselves. There is no longer a smoke-filled room in which the experienced party leaders screen ambitious, would-be nominees. The party no longer decides who is qualified to run so the party no longer influences those who are elected to Congress. In 1925, Will Rogers recognized the problem that now seems even greater. "Slogan: Be a politician; no training necessary."[15]

Self-preservation is the major motivation of today's politician. Example: In mid-July, 1991, the senators voted themselves a $23,200 pay raise. In addition, the staffs of the House and Senate have quintupled since 1945, growing from 2,400 to 12,000.[16] As Will Rogers lamented:

> *Lord, the money we spend on government and it's not one bit better than the government we got for one third the money twenty years ago.*[17]

Keep in mind that Will Rogers made this observation more than half a century ago.

In order to discourage a permanent congressional bureaucracy, the people on the staff of each lawmaker should be required to relinquish their job when their boss has completed his six-year term. And like their boss, they should be ineligible for employment in the congressional bureaucracy ever again, either in Washington or in the fifty states.

A single, six-year term should apply to all congressmen, senators and representatives. Six years is long enough to learn the system and accomplish worthwhile goals; Short enough not to become stale and self-serving in the job. Without reelection to worry about, they can concentrate on the needs and desires of the American people. Said another way, they can function as statesmen, taking the long view and casting their votes for the benefit of all Americans.

A third of each house should be elected every two years to assure congressional continuity. Thus, at any point in time, every senator and representative would have no more than four years' seniority over his colleagues who were elected later. As for congressional staff, they too would learn rapidly from the experienced staff people how the system works. Hopefully under the constraint of term limitation, it will work a lot better than it does today.

Columnist and one-time presidential candidate Patrick J. Buchanan believes that "eight years is long enough for congressional boodlers."[18] Will Rogers would not have given them that much time!

Term limitation has been gathering momentum. Colorado has imposed limits on the terms of members of Congress; Oklahoma on state officials. The California Supreme Court ruled 6-to-1 that voters can enact strict term limits for elected officials. In California, this means officials may serve only two, four-year terms. Citing term limits on the presidency and half of the governors in the United States, the court ruled against state senators who had brought suit, claiming Proposition 140, the term-limit law passed by the voters in 1990, unfairly restricted legislators' and voters' rights. Proposition 140 does not restrict politicians' opportunity to be elected to a higher office. In March, 1992, the U.S. Supreme Court decided not to rehear this California case.

What's more, cities have gotten into the term-limitation act. San Antonio, Wichita, Jacksonville, San Jose and Kansas City all restrict the terms of municipal officials. Similar bills have been introduced in the legislatures of 45 states. In 1992, this issue was on the ballots in 14 states and before the election, according to *The Wall Street Journal*, proponents predicted term limits would carry in a dozen states.

Two weeks before the Washington State vote on term limitation, which occurred on November 5, 1991, Governor Booth Gardner announced that he would not be a candidate for a third term. Mr. Gardner said he was leaving because "politics shouldn't be a career." Other incumbents in the state took the opposite point of view. They vowed that the first bill to be introduced in the 1992 legislature would limit terms of state Supreme Court justices, a warning to them not to declare term limits constitutional.[19]

While the term limitation question was defeated in the Washington State referendum, there were practical problems with the measure which won out over the philosophical concept. First, the bill would have applied to sitting congressmen, essentially destroying any seniority-based clout the state had. It would have meant that the powerful and popular House Speaker Tom Foley would have had to retire in three years. Foley didn't like that idea at all and campaigned against it throughout the state.

The second effect would have been to give seniority and power to the massive California congressional delegation which could then perhaps push through legislation redirecting Washington State water into parched California. The voters considered this intolerable. Still, the vote was close, 54 percent to 46 percent.[20]

But in other states, the sentiment was "throw the rascals out." In Worcester, Massachusetts, an advisory term-limit initiative for Congress won with 74 percent. Local term limits passed in Cincinnati, Houston, Rockville, Maryland; Palo Alto and Sunnyvale, California. The issue failed in White Plains, New York.

The proponents of term limitation were more clairvoyant than even they imagined. On election day November 3, 1992, congressional term limits were approved in a 14 state landslide—no exceptions—and by an average of two-thirds of the voters. This happened in Arizona, Arkansas, California, Florida, Michigan, Missouri, Montana, Nebraska, North Dakota, Ohio, Oregon, South Dakota, Washington and Wyoming. To be sure, 11 of those 14 states are west of the Mississippi. In Arkansas, 60 percent of the voters approved term limitation; Bill Clinton himself got only 43 percent of the vote nationwide.

Will Rogers commented about how people regard their elected representatives: "You remember...I wanted to have the home folks meet their Senator? You would be surprised at the amount of resentment that has come to my roll top desk...They all claim they don't want to see their Senator. That's why they elected him—was to get rid of him. If they had wanted him at home, they would have kept him at home."

Politicians having served in one house of Congress should not be eligible for election to a six-year term in the other. In addition, the presidency should be limited to one, six-year term. Moreover, a life term for United States Supreme Court justices seems greatly excessive. A twelve-year term for these appointees should be ample to assure stability and avoid stagnation of the highest court in the land. Thomas Sowell commented, "If federal judges were appointed for a fixed term, instead of for life, or if they could be impeached more readily for violating the Constitution by creating new "rights" to sue on ever more tenuous grounds, then maybe the many counterproductive effects of easy lawsuits would be curbed."[21]

Will Rogers pinpointed the basic problem. "The trouble with senators is the ones that ought to get out don't."[22]

Would a single, six-year term for senators and representatives solve all of the nation's problems? Obviously not. It would, though, make Congress attractive once more to Americans who want to serve their country for a few years and then return to the career in which they have already achieved success. Conversely, it would discourage career politicians who want to get in and never get out.

A limited tour in Congress would attract mature people with experience in the real world; people who are better able to understand what makes America work. In fact, a better balance of talent in Congress should be a goal of our political parties. It is now top-heavy with lawyers who have little expertise in the productive aspects of the American culture. Sixty-four of our one hundred senators are attorneys. There are only five businessmen in the entire group. The others include a banker, a publisher, seven teachers, a social worker, a restaurateur, a farm broadcaster and a radio broadcaster, two astronauts, two basketball players, one farmer, one rancher, four state and federal employees, a naval officer and a newsman. We should set some realistic requirements, through party persuasion, about the backgrounds which qualify people to serve in Congress. Does knowledge of the law automatically equip a person to make new laws in the best interest of the greatest number of people in America? [23]

Senator Phil Gramm of Texas heads the GOP's senatorial campaign committee. He has a Ph.D. in economics so his "profile of the perfect candidate" contains some rigid specifications. The perfect candidate for the Senate would be:

> *Male or female, about 51 years old, handsome or pretty, very successful in business, made lots of money, steady progress starting early in life as an Eagle Scout or the Girl Scout equivalent, and going through to building up a Fortune 500 company, involved in politics as a person who has been finance chairman for various people running but never run, been involved as the kind of person that when the city got into trouble they came to help, head of United Way, pretty spouse, three pretty children, active in everything, all-American type, with good political judgment, who understands they need to hire good people and listen to what they've got to say—that candidate is unbeatable.*[24]

Such a candidate would be hard to stop, but how many of the people who now represent us have such outstanding experience?

Gramm said he gave a sales pitch recently to someone closely fitting that description and the response was, "Why should I give all that up and run for the Senate?" Perhaps if such ideal candidates saw that other community-minded people were making similar sacrifices, and they would not be competing with "professional, career politicians," they would not be so reluctant to serve their country the way our founding fathers once did. Many employers would be happy to give a six-year leave of absence to a congressional aspirant and hold their job for them until they returned. The current group of professional politicians in the Congress, people who have never had to meet a payroll and who have always lived off the government, have dramatically demonstrated their inability to manage the nation's business.

We need people with mature judgment in the Congress, people from every background, not just lawyers. Perhaps the minimum age limit should be increased so candidates would bring a track record other than government service, law school and lawmaking to the election process. Greater maturity would not rule out innovation and idealism; it would merely balance these qualities with reality.

This is not to say that there are not a few statesmen in the Congress who recognize the problems and are trying to do something about them. Will Rogers had his idea about just what a statesman is:

> *A statesman is a man that can do what the politician would like to do but can't, because he is afraid of not being elected.*[25]

Notable among statesmen in the Senate is Rhodes Scholar and former governor of Oklahoma, David Boren. Under the current system, Senator Boren is at absolutely no risk of losing reelection. A Democrat, supported by Sen. Pete Domenici, R-N.M. and Reps. Lee Hamilton, D-Ind., and Willis Gradison, R-Ohio, Boren finally got Senate leaders in November, 1991, to agree to a hearing on his ideas for streamlining the legislative process. He said, quite accurately, "There is a cancer eating away at this institution, and we must treat it now before it does damage that can never be repaired to the heart and soul of the Democratic process "[26]

According to Boren, there are only two things that can be done.

> *1 The public is so fed up that they're going to have term limits or something if Congress doesn't get its act together...The feeling is that people may get so mad that they'll totally turn over the membership.*
> *2 The frustration level of the good and responsible members may reach such a high level that Congress begins to reform itself.*

In 1947, Mike Monroney (D-OK) and Robert LaFollette (R-Wis) restructured the Congress so that it was down to 17 or 18 standing committees in each house. Now there are 301 committees and subcommittees, all overlapping jurisdictions, in the House and Senate. Boren says, "I have been in conferences where we've had as many as 11 different...committees represented on the same bill. We've had as many as 200 conferees. There's no way the system can work."[27]

The Senator went on. "...the staffs have grown. So, you've gone from about 2,000 staff members after the Monroney-LaFollette reforms up to 12,000 now...We've also gone to a smaller and smaller percentage of bills being passed...It's like 7,000 bills, out of which we act on 250. Bills are eight times longer than they were even ten years ago."[28]

Senator Boren did not expect the restructuring he proposed to solve the nation's problems. "It's not going to fix everything. This doesn't mean that Congress is going to reduce the deficit, come up with a national health-care plan, do what we need to do in education, change tax policy, that sort of thing. What I think it does is it makes a more orderly process that gives us a better chance of doing those things."

Now, he is quite frustrated with the system. "The average member belongs to 12 committees. I come up here some days and it's not at all unusual for three or four of my committees to be meeting at once. I race from morning to night from one committee to another just keeping track of it all. At the end of the day you say, 'What have I really done about the big problems, like economic policy, educational policy, things that are really going to matter in terms of whether this country is going to be a leader in the next century?' And you think, 'We haven't really done anything on the important things.'"[29]

It is easy to see why Senator Boren feels dissatisfied.

Senator Boren is indeed a career politician. Highly regarded in Oklahoma, he is a very articulate advocate of improved education in America. But he's always been in politics with the single exception of four years as a teacher in the Department of Government at Oklahoma Baptist University (1970–74) and even then he was serving in the Oklahoma House of Representatives (1967–75). Next, he became governor (1975–79), and is now in his third term in the U.S. Senate. He turned 50 years old in April, 1991.[30]

The senator is now asking himself if he wants to continue as a senator after his current term which he will complete in 1996. He may run for president that year or he may follow Senator Henry Bellmon's lead and try for another term as governor of Oklahoma, but he has no plans for the latter at present. Bellmon resigned after two terms, saying he missed the power of being a chief executive when he was senator. So does Boren. "As governor, I could sit down with the chairman of the Appropriations Committee...and I could reach an agreement and get things done," he said, implying agreement was not all that easy to achieve in the Congress. He reiterated that senators are spread too thin to give enough attention to the most pressing issues.[31]

Adding to the Senator's frustration is the opinion of the American people. A January, 1992, poll found that 71 percent disapproved of the way Congress was handling its job, while only 21 percent approved. This trend has continued since 1988, when only 32 percent were disenchanted by the Congress. This downhill slope became significantly steeper in 1989–90, when Congress voted itself a pay raise, House Speaker Jim Wright resigned, and the Keating Five scandal surfaced. Now, 37 percent blame Congress for the nation's problems. It would be difficult for any dedicated Senator to sustain his enthusiasm for the job under these circumstances.[32]

However, there is one encouraging sign on the horizon. A bill was introduced in November, 1991, which would limit the amount of money congressmen could spend for election campaigns. This effort also supports Boren who has been trying for several years to change campaign financing laws. While this is a small step in the right direction, it isn't enough [see the next chapter).[33]

Despite the frustration level in and reputation of the Congress, there is considerable opposition to the idea of term limits among career politicians now in office. House Speaker Tom Foley has said he will carry the case against term limits to the Supreme Court, and there's speculation it will take to the turn of the century to see if the state laws mandating limitation of federal terms are constitutional. This argument could keep congressmen and attorneys busy and prosperous for the next six years. On the other side of the question, the proponents of term limits are also organized. The National Term limits Campaign, based in Denver, provides information about the movement. The Term Limits Legal Institute in Washington is headed by Cleta Deatherage Mitchell, an attorney and former state representative in Oklahoma.

As more states limit the terms of their representatives in Washington, there will be a greater congressional incentive to pass federal legislation limiting the terms of all senators and congressmen to even the playing field. After all, with reelection odds greatly favoring incumbents, seniority is a dominant factor in this power game. Those congressmen whose terms are limited will no doubt try to get the same rules applied to everyone on Capitol Hill.

In fact, sentiment in the U.S. Senate is slowly changing in favor of term limitation. When it was first voted in 1948, the idea won only one vote. In 1991, it lost 68 to 30. But in May, 1993, 39 senators voted in favor of the bill, while 57 were still opposed. Slowly, the idea is winning converts, even among the incumbents.[34]

Chapter Three

Free Lawmakers from Financial Dependence on Political Action Committees

Lobbyists in Washington are reaping a harvest. A Lobbyist is a person that is supposed to help a politician to make up his mind, not only help him, but pay him.

—*Will Rogers*[1]

A clue to national lobbying efforts is found in Oklahoma's weak lobbying law. In October, 1991, the Oklahoma Ethics Commission began considering proposed changes that would "make the state lobbying law one of the strongest in the nation."

The commission started out to prohibit county or state officials from accepting gifts of any kind or "anything of value." The chairman of the Ethics Commission, Jon Ford of Enid, said, "You're dealing head-on with government by special interests." The existing law put no limit on how much lobbyists could spend; only made reporting requirements above $42 on one occasion or $300 in 12 months. The law allowed a special interest group to spend $45,000 a year on the 149 members of the Oklahoma Legislature without reporting any of it.

Oklahoma Legislators certainly liked that system. One former legislator said, "That is what the lobbyists do up here. Feed me pretty good…I eat with them every night, just about…I grab one of them for lunch too," Thus it didn't cost that legislator much to live while the legislature was in session.

Another member said the Legislature "is apt to throw up" if a rule is adopted aimed at banning the practice of lobbyists wining and dining legislators and from giving them Christmas gifts.[2]

Will Rogers had something to say about politicians:

Once a man holds public office he is absolutely no good for honest work.[3]

But the lobbyists are always the people most opposed to change. Opponents of the proposed ethics rules in Oklahoma dubbed these changes as the "No-cup-of-coffee" rule. That rule would have barred lawmakers and others in state government from accepting anything of value from a lobbyist—Christmas gifts, lunches, dinners and the like. One lobbyist told the Ethics Commission strict interpretation of the proposed rule would mean neither lobbyists nor their children could give Christmas presents to relatives employed by the state. The lobbyists' objective was to concentrate on the "No-cup-of-coffee" idea in order to build public sentiment against the proposed rules, an indication that the lobbyists were afraid of the outcome of the public hearings.[4]

Moving up to the federal level, the big problem is special interest contributions to the reelection campaigns of our senators and representatives. It should be against the law for any individual or group to donate anything of value to a lawmaker: money, trips, hotel accommodations, meals, gifts…anything! These are bribes by any other name.

But allowing the responsibility to rest entirely with the lobbyist is unrealistic. It should also be a felony for any lawmaker to accept anything of value from any individual or group while he is in office. The limitation of a congressman's term to a single, six-year period would take away his incentive to accept campaign contributions. This suggested felony law would be a negative incentive, reducing the congressman's propensity to accept for any purpose money or other things of value "under the table."

The cost of the lawmaker's original election to congress is discussed in Chapter Six.

The problem which exists on the state level expands exponentially on the federal level. The special interest dollars floating around Washington are in the millions. Contributions by Political Action Committees (PACs) to Congressmen rose from $12.5 million in 1974 to $150 million in 1990, according to Congressional Research Service and Federal Election Commission.[5] Will Rogers talked about these lobbyists more than half a century ago. "All the 'lobbies' are gathered in there [Washington] to see that the tax is put on somebody else's business, not on theirs."[6]

Common Cause, a nonprofit, nonpartisan, citizens' lobbying organization, calls government by special interest group a disgrace, a threat to our system of government. Archibald Cox, chairman of Common Cause, says PACs are blocking government from helping to solve the country's problems. "For example, over the past decade, when health care costs more than doubled and prescription drug prices increased by 152 percent, medical industry PACs poured $60 million into the campaign coffers of 41 congressional candidates. These are the same PACs that are out to block reforms of our health care system."

As Cox points out, "Most scandals involve broken laws. In the case of the congressional campaign financing system, however, the laws themselves are the scandal—they must be changed."

Here is what happened in 1990:

- Special interest PACs gave House and Senate incumbents $121.1 million for their campaigns, eight times the $15.3 million they gave to challengers.
- Successful candidates for the U.S. Senate in 1990 raised, on average, nearly $4 million each. That means to win a Senate seat a candidate had to raise an average of $12,000 a week for six years!
- Nine out of every ten House incumbents seeking reelection in 1990 were in financially uncompetitive races—that is, their opponents lacked the resources to run competitive campaigns.

Common Cause is hardly a voice crying in the wilderness. The *Charleston* [West Virginia] *Gazette* warns, "Disguised bribery has grown like a cancer in Congress, corrupting the lawmaking process, making 'bag men' of most senators and representatives."

The New York Times wrote, "The need to restore integrity to political life is obvious. And the best place to begin is at the top, with a massive overhaul of Congress's odious system of campaign financing."

The Dallas Morning News observed, "As important as all the other issues of the nation are, this one cries out for immediate attention. Upon it rests the people's confidence in government."[7]

And Will Rogers summed it up:

If we could just send the same bunch of men to Washington

for the good of the nation and not for political reasons, we could have the most perfect government in the world.[8]

In a *Wall Street Journal* editorial, the writer observed, "There was a time when political analysts said Congress was merely trying to hold its ground against an expanding executive branch. By now, it's obvious that Congress has come to regard much of the structure of government as a personal kingdom. A Charles Keating and even less notorious visitors from beyond the Beltway purchase congressional safe passage through the kingdom. Executive-branch officials who resist this declaration of congressional sovereignty get prosecuted and bankrupted. The resulting government remains a powerful kingdom, but it is neither efficient nor very productive of anything useful to the people. To Congress it is Utopia.

"But many in Congress, upset at their battered public image, wish to enact some form of campaign-finance reform. We find it inconceivable that Congress would pass reforms that would strengthen challengers at the expense of incumbents, a goal of real change. Also, the most frequently-cited reform—public financing—is overwhelmingly opposed by Americans. Only 21 percent use their tax forms to check off a mere $1 contribution to a presidential election fund."[9]

Perhaps the voting public previously has not been sufficiently stirred up about congressional behavior to take action. But that's changing. The results of the 1992 election showed that reforms are now on the mind of the electorate, and voters want their representatives to heed Senator Alan Cranston's message.

Senator Cranston of California was reprimanded by the Senate Ethics Committee in November, 1991, for being one of the infamous "Keating Five" which accepted a large amount of campaign money from Charles H. Keating, Jr. in exchange for intervening with thrift regulators on behalf of the failed Lincoln Savings and Loan. Cranston had received more than $900,000 to support his reelection campaign and other causes. The senator said his fund-raising efforts and the easy access he granted to constituents such as Keating were no different from the behavior of other senators:

So let me ask: Since I have been singled out for a reprimand on access today, who among you can be sure you will not be singled out tomorrow? Here, but for the grace of God, stand you.

There is only one way out: Get money out of politics. Enact public financing and enact it now.[10]

But getting money out of politics is easier said than done, as forcefully demonstrated in Oklahoma. While the Oklahoma Ethics Commission aspired to make the state lobbying law one of the strongest in the nation, what it came up with fell far Short of that target. The campaign rules were stiffened to require:

1. Candidates, state officials and top state employees must disclose by name any source of income in excess of $1,000.
2. State officials and top state employees have to report monthly on any gifts received from lobbyists.
3. Any candidate receiving a contribution in excess of $200 from an anonymous donor must give the money to the ethics commission.
4. No cash contribution to a campaign shall exceed $100.
5. Any contribution of $500 or more immediately before an election must be disclosed within 24 hours.

Under these new rules politicians may still be wined and dined regularly by lobbyists, public officials and legislators may receive gifts, and huge amounts of campaign contributions may still be funneled to politicians through the speaker of the house and the senate president *pro tempore*.[11]

While these new rules are a small step in the right direction, they are still being contested by the legislature. In addition, the new reporting system creates a review procedure which the ethics commission must go through periodically. As one member observed, "Cheaters are going to cheat and there is nothing we can do to stop that." Another said, "This certainly will not be an incentive. It will be a disincentive for honest people."[12]

These "stiffened" rules for Oklahoma politicians and state employees do not "get the money out of politics." They do not even spell out any responsibility for the lobbyist, although the panel voted 3–2 to ask the legislature to grant the commission the same rule-making authority over lobbyists as it has over state officials and state employees under the Constitution. Still, it remains for the politician to reject any contributions which exceed the limits. There is no provision at present for the lobbyist to lose his privileges if he exceeds the limits. And who checks up when cash is passed from hand to hand?

The Ethics Commission chairman, Jon Ford, said these rules will provide Oklahoma "with a set of rules for ethical conduct second to none in the nation." The commission is now staffed with an investigator, a former prosecutor, five staff members and an executive director who is an attorney. This budding bureaucracy will no doubt shuffle a lot of paper and look into a lot of rumors, but it is doubtful it will change much of the conduct of the legislators, state officials, state employees or the lobbyists. As long as a lobbyist may give something of value to a politician, that lobbyist will have better access to his representative than the ordinary citizen who does not contribute. And those who wish to subvert the rules can find ways around them. Meanwhile, more report forms will be generated, checked, rechecked and filed by eight more state employees.[13]

It now appears that Oklahoma will continue to have legislation by special interest groups for some time to come. What's more, if the new rules are flouted to the extent the old limitations were ignored, there will be more grand jury investigations of campaign financing similar to the protracted inquiry into Governor David Walters' 1990 campaign. A number of felony indictments were handed down to contributors who gave more money to Walters than the rules permitted.

Back to the federal level and the Clinton Administration. In his acceptance speech at the Democratic convention, Bill Clinton said, "He (Bush) won't break the stranglehold the special interests have on our elections and the lobbyists have on our government. But I will."

How will he accomplish this radical change? While he talks about an ethics code for his administration, all the while he's beholding to all sorts of contributors who poured a record $71 million into his campaign, particularly those 62 who gave more than $100,000 each. He depended heavily on lobbyists to help him develop policy positions for his campaign.[14]

Will Rogers said, "Any person that can't spot a propagandist and lobbyist a mile away, must be a person so blind that they still think toupees are deceptive and can't tell a hotel house detective from a guest."[15]

Certainly, Bill Clinton is neither dumb nor blind. Immediately following the election, hundreds of lobbyists flooded Little Rock. They were not just trying to get their nose under the Clinton tent; they were angling for a cushy job on the inside where they could mold policy to their own special interest. This, according to *The Wall Street Journal*, is the "ultimate insider's goal."

Some lobbyists were already ensconced on the transition team. Vernon Jordon, the co-chair, is a partner in a Washington law firm heavily involved in lobbying. During the campaign, Clinton depended for advice on the American Bankers Association, the Direct Selling Association, the American Society of Travel Agents, the Association of Trial Lawyers of America. The travel industry, the health care industry people, and others helped the Clinton team put together papers on policy issues. A former Carter White House aide, Ann Wexler, head of Wexler Group, a lobbying firm, was being pushed by other lobbyists for a high-level appointment such as secretary of commerce.

Those already inside the Clinton tent were heavily courted. Gloria Cabe, in charge of congressional relations for the Clinton campaign, said, "I haven't bought my own lunch or dinner in three or four weeks. There are a couple of really nice restaurants I haven't been to yet."

Clinton's ethics code for the transition team members barred them from lobbying during the transition period and for six months thereafter. They also had to fill out financial disclosure forms, disqualify themselves in the event of conflict of interest and never in their lifetime use for private gain non-public information obtained during the transition. Again, these are steps in the right direction but hardly adequate to inhibit the activities of entrenched political action groups. Besides, many of the advisors called on were exempt from these "strict" ethics rules.[16]

How many of these lobbyists have disappeared within the Clinton Administration as officials who can mold policy inside the tent? Their influence will be much harder to trace because it's easy to forget their previous connections with special interest groups. A blatant example of saying one thing and doing another is the appointment of Ron Brown as Secretary of Commerce. As chairman of the Democratic National Committee and "consummate Washington insider," he was a powerful lobbyist for Haiti and for Japan Air Lines. How many special inside deals will he make in his cabinet position?[17]

If the attitudes of Michael Berman, of the Duberstein Group, and Peter Kelly, of the lobbying firm Black, Manafort, Stone and Kelly, are typical, the lobbyists are not concerned. Berman sees no major changes in store for his firm; Kelly doesn't worry about new lobbying laws. "There will always be lobbyists," he said.[18]

On the other hand, how much freedom will they retain? In May of 1993, President Clinton proposed the most serious overhaul of campaign financing in two decades, providing public money for candidates who agree to abide by spending ceilings. His solution would also limit PAC campaign contributions to $1,000, limit "soft" money contributions that now let companies and individuals give unrestricted amounts to political parties, end tax deductions for lobbying expenses, and end the "lawyers' loophole" that lets lawyer-lobbyists avoid disclosing their activities on behalf of foreigners.[19]

Obviously, incumbent lawmakers hate these proposed restrictions and the effect they would have on reducing the tremendous financial advantage seated senators and representatives have over political upstarts who would challenge them.

Unfortunately, the Clinton program does not go to the heart of the problem; it merely scales down the magnitude and scales up the difficulty of control. If and when passed, which may occur in 1994, this proposal would leave intact the current system of legislation by lobby, still fortified by the powerful influence of money.

The effect of the lobbyists' support of incumbent congressmen in 1988 was consistent with the 1990 result detailed above. In that presidential election year, of the $156 million in PAC dollars that went to congressional candidates, more than $118 million went to the campaigns of incumbents. Only $18.9 million went to candidates in races for open seats and $18.8 million was given to challengers.[20]

As John L. Jackley, a former staff man for Representative Thomas A. Luken (D-Ohio) and later for Representative Ronald Coleman (D-Texas), stated in his book, *Hill Rat: Blowing the Lid off Congress*, "To be successful, politicians need more than a message; they need muscle, and in this town, muscle means money. Lots of it." Jackley was hired as press secretary and legislative assistant to Representative Luken in late 1978, after having "long dreamed about the first Hill job that would propel me into the corridors of power." Seven years later, after he became a father for the first time, his values changed remarkably.

The difference was that I now had a real flesh-and-blood purpose in life against which my Capitol Hill existence did not measure favorably. A baby—a new person, a new soul, a new world—was something to stand for, to die for, if necessary. More than anything else, my child made me realize that we had come to stand for nothing in the Capitol Hill of the 1980s. We worked for a single purpose—ensuring that our congressman survived and flourished. Issues, ideals, principles, even the Democratic party—all these were of secondary concern.[21]

Obviously, the ambition and the opportunity to carve out a professional career in a congressional seat, and the necessity to raise large sums of money to finance periodic reelection have helped to bring the U.S. Congress to its present state of ineffectiveness and to perpetuate legislation by lobby. The combination of term limitation and "getting the money out of politics" is necessary for effective reform of the lawmaking process in America.

If we finally get laws which effectively prevent legislation by lobby, it might not be too bad for our representatives. As Will Rogers said many years ago:

That's one thing about these politicians, when they can't make politics pay, they can always fall back on the honest profession of Law.[22]

Chapter Four

Eliminate the Income Tax

Well, the good old days with most of us was when we didn't earn enough to pay an income tax.

—*Will Rogers*[1]

The income tax system is now so complex and expensive and unevenly administered that it is a burden on everyone. Even the Internal Revenue Service itself is complaining. In the 1990 annual report of the agency, the IRS noted that the Internal Revenue Code had been changed more than 100 times since 1980. The report went on to say, "The IRS has not kept pace with the growth of the taxpayer population and workload." One reason had been a hiring freeze in 1989 and 1990. "Another reason why enforcement levels are too low is the impact of the increasing complexity of the tax system." Audits were down from an average of 92 percent in 1989 to 80 percent in 1990. The decline has been significant:

Approximate percentage of Returns Audited

Year	*Individual*	*Corporate*
1980	2.0%	6.4%
1985	1.2%	2.1%
1990	.9%	2.2%[2]

In 1992, however, the combined audit rate jumped to three percent, up from 2.4 percent in 1991.[3]

The statistics are enough to boggle the mind. In 1990, the IRS:

1. Processed 202 million returns, up from 199.6 million in

1989. Of these, 4.2 million were filed electronically.
2. Handled in excess of one billion information documents—W-2s and 1099s—sent in by employers and investment brokers.
3. Processed 85 million refunds totaling almost $100 billion, up from 82.6 million in 1989 totaling $94 billion.
4. Assisted 63 million taxpayers to fill out their returns, 56 million by telephone, 7 million who visited an IRS office. In addition, 75,000 citizen volunteers helped 2.8 million struggling filers. This means about a third of the filers couldn't complete their returns just by following the written instructions. In addition, the international program assisted 300,000 taxpayers in 73 countries around the world.
5. Receipts grew 4.2 percent in 1990, reaching $1.1 trillion, exceeding 1989 revenue by $43 billion. IRS enforcement measures added $51 billion to the total.
6. It cost 52 cents to collect every $100 the IRS takes in.[2]

That last statistic is misleading because it cites only what it cost the IRS, and of course the taxpayers who fund the Internal Revenue Service. New research now establishes this cost at 65 percent of the revenue collected, in which case the cost to collect $560 billion in individual and corporate income taxes is $363.5 billion, not $5.44 billion. Our income tax system is a "do it yourself" enterprise. We "volunteer" (under irresistible pressure, of course) to collect from ourselves and remit the taxes to the IRS.

American business spends more than $100 billion a year to collect taxes for the IRS, hiring lawyers and accountants to minimize their tax bills, keeping records for each employee and remitting withholding taxes to the government.

According to studies paid for by the IRS, individual Americans spend $262 billion on compliance costs. The study estimates that in 1985 Americans spent 5.4 billion hours on tax compliance, the equivalent of 3 million Americans working full-time on taxes.[4]

As previously noted, W. Kurt Hauser of the Hoover Institution, said, "the cost to the economy of the current tax system is six billion hours and $600 billion to $1 trillion annually." That adds up to at least 10 percent of the GDP.[5]

I still figure out my own tax returns because I do not believe any taxpayer should need an attorney or a CPA to interpret the law for him. I may not get all of the deductions to which I am entitled, but it's the principle!

There have been proposals to simplify the income tax system but they have been totally ignored by the U.S. Congress. Perhaps the most notable plan was the 1981 "Postcard Tax Return" idea advanced by Robert E. Hall and Alvin Rabushka of the Hoover Institution at Stanford University. It was based on four principles:

1. All income should be taxed only once, as close as possible to its source.
2. All types of income should be taxed at the same rate.
3. The poorest households should pay no income tax.
4. Tax returns for both households and businesses should be simple enough to fit on a postcard or one page.

Essentially the plan provided that all individual and corporate taxpayers would pay 19 percent of their gross income to the federal government. The system would remain progressive insofar as the dollars paid;(i.e., the more the corporation or individual took in, the more they had to pay) but the tax rate would not increase as income rose, as reflected by our currently progressive rates of 15, 28, and 39.6 percent increased in 1993 by the Clinton tax program.

There would be only one deduction, a personal allowance:

Married couples	$5,000
Single people	$3,000
Single head of household	$4,500

Thirteen years ago, the authors observed, "Political promises of real simplification and reform remain unfulfilled." Unfortunately, the numerous changes that have occurred in the system since 1981 have taken the system in the opposite direction, making it ever more complicated and costly. On December 9, 1992, *The Wall Street Journal* reported that, "The IRS has a large backlog of regulations to be written. As of October 31, IRS specialists were working on 574 regulation projects. That was up from 571 a month earlier.

"The average American worked 81 days this year (through April 24) just to pay federal taxes, up from 75 days (through April 16) in 1985 the Tax Foundation said."[6]

Hall and Rabushka pointed out that the income tax "attenuates individual incentives to work, save and invest." This happens because individual savings are taxed twice; once when they are earned and a second time when those savings earn interest.

Likewise, corporate profits are taxed twice; first as profits and then as dividends on which the stockholders are taxed. As a result of this double taxation, people perceive that saving a dollar in taxes is worth more than earning another dollar in income, only to have it taxed at an ever-increasing (progressive) rate.

The tax system also gives people strong *incentives* to conduct their business in cash, and sometimes by barter, in what is known as the "underground economy," roughly estimated to range from tens to hundreds of billions per year.

As a measure of the proliferation of government activity and expense, prior to the 20th century and before the 1913 enactment of the income tax law, federal revenues made up just 3 percent of the GNP, collected largely from custom duties. This modest percentage has since multiplied about seven times to 20 percent of GNP.[7]

One time presidential contender Jerry Brown, former governor of California, picked up on the flat rate tax idea and advocated it in his 1992 primary campaign. Instead of 19 percent, he said that a rate of 13 percent, levied against individuals and corporations, would bring in the same revenue the current system yields. Brown's campaign feature verified Will Rogers' observation six decades previously:

> *When a party can't think of anything else they always fall back on lower taxes. It has a magic sound to a voter, just like Fairyland is spoken of and dreamed of by all children. But no child has ever seen it; neither has any voter ever lived to see the day when his taxes were lowered.*[8]

Any simplification of the tax code would bring welcome relief to millions of people, but the trend is in the other direction. Effective January 1, 1992, the IRS installed new regulations which bar giving high-paid executives unduly richer benefits than lower-paid employees. Employers say the rules are hopelessly complex and costly. "A Philadelphia lawyer can't even figure these out," complained one employee benefits manager.

A major oil company representative said, "It's dismaying that an employer should be required to waste so much time and money." The company has the problem of trying to match home-nation pension accruals for foreign nationals reassigned to the U.S., as well as adjusting the pension accrual of a woman executive drawing leave-Shortened salary after returning from a long maternity leave. To come up with 600 pages of complicated, non-discrimination rules took the IRS three-and-a-half years, but the agency gave employers less than four months to digest and comply with them.[9]

President Bush's out-going Secretary of the Treasury Nicholas Brady called for tax reform on December 10, 1992. His plan would:

- Drastically boost standard deductions so that more than half of all individuals would effectively be removed from the tax rolls.
- Integrate the corporate and individual tax systems to eliminate double taxation of corporate profits.
- Eliminate the corporate alternative minimum tax and business preferences from the individual AMT.
- Reform international tax rules to simplify the regulations by which multinational businesses are taxed.
- Introduce a broad-based levy on consumption, known as a business transfer tax.
- Provide a refundable credit to low-income families.

Of course, with a Democratic administration now in place, backed by a Democratic majority in the Congress, Brady's ideas may be merely academic. Ironically, many of these issues are those Mr. Brady pledged to take up when he first arrived at the Treasury in 1988.[10]

Perhaps simplification of the income tax utilizing the Flat Tax/postcard return system or Treasury Secretary Brady's proposals just do not go far enough. Regardless of the system's simplicity, we'd still have to pay Uncle Sam our hard-earned money for our representatives to mismanage. Total *elimination* of the individual and corporate income tax would have all the advantages of the Hall and Rabushka simplification plan and Mr. Brady's ideas plus many more. It would:

1. Release many of the IRS's 116,425 people (as of 1990, up from 115,798 in 1989) for productive work and allow reduction and redirection of its $5.44 billion

budget for better uses. In addition, elimination of the income tax system would also reduce expenditures such as an $8 billion modernization effort which includes a $1.4 billion computer contract.[11]

2. Save thousands of hours of the employers who withhold taxes and the employees who must spend days preparing their income tax returns. Because benefits such as stock-option plans are complicated from the tax standpoint, companies like Texaco and Waste Management provide tax counseling for more than just their top executives. 56 percent of all employers now give some tax counsel, up from 38 percent in 1985. Proctor and Gamble staffers can select tax and financial advice for $235 from a benefits menu. As an indication of the cost of such advice, KPMG Peat Marwick charges $5,000 for a basic, one-day finance and tax seminar for up to 30 employees, which works out to a minimum of $166 apiece.[12]
3. Save hundreds of thousands of dollars taxpayers now spend to have a tax attorney or accountant prepare their return for them. Thus, thousands of CPAs and tax attorneys could turn their attention to other, more important matters.
4. Stabilize the amount of GNP the federal government could absorb.
5. Eliminate the annual deficit by placing a control on the fiscal affairs of the nation.
6. Stimulate economic growth gradually over several years, thus raising the standard of living while avoiding inflation. Most importantly, just as the simplification plan would have done, elimination of income tax would give Americans the *incentive* to work, save and invest.

Our current income tax mess doesn't have to be this way. For 80 years we've lived with a tax system which has grown ever more complicated. Again, Will Rogers had something to say about it:

> *The income tax has made liars out of more Americans than golf...Even when you make one out on the level, you don't know when it's through if you are a crook or a martyr.*[13]

Here is how the income tax system could be eliminated.

We should retain the present federal income tax system, both individual and corporate, with *no* changes except, beginning the first year this program can be passed by the Congress, reduce withholding and estimated tax payments by 2 percent per month. At the end of the first year, each taxpayer, whether an employee, sole proprietor or corporation, would file the usual return but take a 25 percent deduction in the calculated tax he or she or the corporation owed Uncle Sam. The second year the process would be repeated, but the taxpayer would take a 50 percent deduction in the tax owed. The process would go on the third year with a 75 percent deduction. At the end of the fourth year, the taxpayer would owe only the amount estimated or withheld on the declining percentage described above. The individual or corporation would not have to file a return at all unless the IRS determined this final amount did not reflect the previous pattern of income. Then the burden of proof the individual's or corporation's income had indeed changed would rest with the taxpayer.

Thus, in four years, the entire income tax system would be just a memory. This action would stimulate the economy in a gradual, non-inflationary fashion. The money freed for use by the citizens would slowly generate more jobs, reduce unemployment, get people off welfare and reduce the need for many social programs now supported by federal funds. The next step would be to establish a percentage of the GNP as the appropriate amount available to the federal government to operate the bureaucracy, providing needed services. At first this could be the approximately one-fourth of the GNP which the federal government now uses, enacted into law by the Congress. During the four years the income tax was being eliminated, the maximum the government would be allowed to spend would be reduced each year by one-fourth of the deficit. After four years of identical reductions, annual expenditures would no longer exceed income. This would also mean a gradual reduction of the percentage of the GNP Congress could spend. From that point, the percentage could be adjusted downward by the Congress as the expanding economy permitted but any upward adjustment would require a vote of the people. While the amount of money would rise with the GNP, the percentage of GNP used by government would remain the same or float downward. Under this system, the only way the money available to Congress could grow Short of a vote of the people would be for the economy to grow. This would create the incentive for the Congress to pay attention to the health of the economy, seeking ways for it to thrive.

The deficit at the end of FY 1992 was $290 billion. President Clinton's economic program proposed to reduce the annual deficit to a net of $205 billion by the end of his first term in office. Because it is impossible to tell what the deficit will be, the calculations which follow were based on the 1992 deficit of $290 billion.

When I first put down this idea in October, 1991, I had never seen it in print. On January, 21, 1992, another version of using incentive to improve the performance of Congress was advanced by Joseph A. Grundfest, associate professor of law at Stanford University. He wrote an article in *The Wall Street Journal* entitled "Incentive pay for Politicians." Here is what he said:

> *Congress.*
>
> *At first blush, the idea of incentive compensation for members of Congress sounds totally impossible. How would we even begin measuring congressional performance? How would we measure the value of egalitarian goals, of civil justice, of the environment, of national defense? And how could we fold all of these objectives into a single incentive plan?*
>
> *But this makes the problem overly complex. There is a broad consensus that the U.S. is better off with a strong and growing GNP. A growing economy creates jobs and generates revenues that can be used to support social programs. Tying congressional pay to real GNP growth over a suitably long period, adjusted to correct for the effects of deficit financing could have several benefits.*
>
> *Incentive for Cooperation*
>
> *First, it could create an incentive for cooperation among members of Congress and reduce the energy now devoted to special interest measures that benefit specific groups at the expense of society as a whole. Second, it could cause Congress to pay increased attention to the cost of regulation. Third, it could induce Congress to consider more carefully the economic costs of social programs that would otherwise be adopted on the basis of wishful projections.*

The Shortcomings of even such a plan would be legion. The GNP does not calculate the value of clean air, of quality of life, or of a scenic vista. But the question is not whether we can design a perfect incentive plan. We can't. The question is, can we design a plan that works better than the one we now have in place? That is a far easier hurdle to clear.[14]

The third step in my plan is to require the Federal Reserve to create the necessary funds (in cash or credit) according to this formula, in quite the same fashion it now increases the money supply. By using the Gross National Product as the standard for the increase in the money supply and allocating the voter-authorized portion of it to the Federal government, the Congress would have the positive incentive to pay attention to the economic health of the nation.

For years I wondered just how the Federal Reserve (the Fed) managed to expand the money supply—how the money just seemed to appear like magic—out of thin air. Of course, if the government mints in Philadelphia and Denver merely print more currency, that's easy to understand. But the currency, that is, paper money and coins, is only a small part of the money in circulation. The rest of the money supply is in the form of credit. This, the Fed creates out of thin air. A banker friend explained it this way:

Banks operate on a partial reserve system. That means that a bank which takes in a million dollars in deposits can loan out all but a small percentage of that amount and collect interest on those loans, at a higher rate than it pays interest to its depositors. The difference is the bank's profit. That's how banks stay in business.

The amount the Federal Reserve requires the bank to retain in order to pay depositors who come in and demand their money is called "non-borrowed reserves." This partial reserve banking system is based on the idea that all of the bank's depositors won't come in the same day and demand their money. There just has to be enough on hand so that when a depositor wants to take his money out of the bank, he can get it. If all the depositors storm the bank on the same day, as happened during the Great Depression, we have a "run on the bank." Then the bank must "go under," i.e., close its doors, or borrow money from the Federal Reserve or other banks to pay off their depositors. The required amount of reserves the bank must have is dictated by the Fed.

Keep in mind that money merely represents something of value—a bushel of wheat, an hour of labor, a meal at a restaurant, a new tire; any object we may possess for exchange or any service we may render for pay. Money is an exchange medium that permits us to trade without bartering, i.e., seeking someone who has what we want and in turn wants what we have to exchange.

Now, if the Fed wants to expand the money supply to serve an expanding economy, it purchases securities from any seller and pays for it by issuing a check on itself. The seller's bank, on receipt of the check, presents the check to the Federal Reserve for payment and the Fed, in return, honors the check by increasing the reserve account at the Federal Reserve bank of the seller's bank. Thus, the reserves of the seller's bank rise with no offsetting decline in the reserves elsewhere. Consequently the total volume of reserves magically increases.

Suppose, now, the security the Fed purchased was for $1,000 and the required bank reserve was 20 percent. A multiplier effect then begins to operate as this $1,000 is circulated through the economy.

The seller's bank, with $1,000 additional reserves, loans out $800, retaining $200 in its Fed-required reserves. The person who got the $800 loan puts it in another bank, his bank. This second bank then retains $160 in its reserves and loans out $640. Already $1,440 has been loaned out from the original $1000. As this process continues, the money circulates through the banking system, the original $1000 grows to $5000. So the supply of credit (another form of money) has increased five fold. See how easy that was? When the Fed thinks there is too much currency and credit in circulation, it reverses the process by selling securities. The payment results in a reduction in the reserve account of the buyer's bank at the Federal Reserve Bank with no offsetting increase in the reserve accounts of any other bank. Thus, the total reserves in the banking system decline.[15]

In step four, the Federal Reserve would be required to be the government's banker. If the Fed can create credit for use by the banking system for the general economy, it can do the same for a special bank to supply credit (money) for the federal government to replace the $560 billion lost as the income tax is eliminated. No longer would our representatives and senators be permitted free reign over fiscal policy. They could not "put it on the tab" anytime they felt like spending more money than the 25 percent (or lower authorized percentages) of the GNP (based on the statistics of the preceding year). When the government ran out of money, it would have to shut down. Of course, this would mean that congressmen's salaries, low cost meals and haircuts, free transportation, staff services and other emoluments would screech to a halt. In contrast to Mr. Grunfest's plan for incentive pay, this is a negative incentive that would quickly get their attention.

Congress would then be under the painful obligation of deciding what government services had to be shut down until the beginning of the new fiscal year, or perhaps permanently, a process which would not endear them to their constituents. This would be a totally new experience. Until now, when federal spending bumped up against the congressionally-decreed debt ceiling, all Congress had to do was go deeper into debt by raising the ceiling. Convenient!

Thus, the federal government would no longer be able to go into debt and only the independent Federal Reserve, governing monetary policy and managing fiscal affairs, would be in full control of the nation's finances. Fiscal policy would no longer be in the possession of the professional politicians but would be dependent on the state of the economy.

And the people would decide what percentage of the GNP the Congress could spend!

This really wouldn't be as hard on our representatives as it first appears. Since the Congress now has the *incentive* to spend in order to keep in the good graces of special interests that contribute to their reelection war chest and with the voters back home, it is extremely difficult for them to sponsor any legislation that would reduce spending. This new system, which includes term limitation, no reelection to finance, and fiscal control by the Federal Reserve based on a percentage of the GNP, means our representatives would not have to accept any blame for the spending cuts. When criticized, they could legitimately pass the responsibility on to their banker, the Federal Reserve, and ultimately to the voters who would decide if the percentage of the GNP the federal government was authorized to spend should change. After all, they would be making judgments based on the needs of the entire country, not just their home state, and would not have to think about running for national office again. Our representatives could begin working with each other again and become true statesmen in the process.

In 1991, the Heritage Foundation, a conservative think tank, came up with a whole list of budget deductions the Congress could make by abolishing 117 federal programs. Their ideas included reducing Rural electrification loans, eliminating federal water subsidies, imposing user fees on special weather services, prohibiting payment of agricultural subsidies to individuals with gross farm incomes above $100,000. They would also cut agricultural research, postal subsidies, and effectively kill the Small Business Administration. In addition, they would end grants to Amtrak, cut funding to mass transit, cut funds for the National Institutes of Health, eliminate the Interstate Commerce Commission, and end funding for public broadcasting.

The last proposal would repeal the Davis-Bacon Act that mandates high-priced union wage scales on federal construction.[16] None of these suggestions was designed to make heroes out of our senators and representatives except to the rare taxpayer who did not benefit by any of these targeted programs.

Under the present system of career representatives, abolishing any federal program would be tantamount to committing political suicide. With term limitation in place and no opportunity for reelection, our congressmen and senators could proceed with full immunity from everything except a terrorist attack by a disgruntled bureaucrat.

The Federal Reserve, established in 1913, the same year the income tax was enacted, is the handmaiden of the Congress. It is supposed to fight inflation, avoid recessions and otherwise look after the economic health of the nation but can control only the monetary aspects of this equation: the supply of money and credit. It cannot control the national debt built up over decades of irresponsible deficit spending by the Congress. The Federal Reserve must borrow or print money whenever the Congress votes to spend more than it takes in.[17]

The situation we are in today is analogous to a struggling middle-class family in which both the father and mother work, trying desperately to make ends meet, to stay afloat financially, while their teen-age children have credit cards without limits and are allowed to spend freely. Anyone can clearly see this is a no-win scenario.

A kind parent knows that it does a child no service to give him money whenever he whines for it. The wise parent gives the kid an allowance and doesn't give him more if he spends it before it's time for the next week's installment. That parent also teaches the child to open a savings account at the bank and put some of his money away for another day, so the child learns fiscal responsibility. What the Congress needs is a wise parent. In this sense, the Federal Reserve could be the mother and father our representatives so obviously and desperately need.

History has demonstrated that confiscatory taxation has strangled the economy and as income taxation has been reduced, prosperity has increased. This proposed system would also stimulate the economy without piling up debt for our grandchildren to pay. In addition, this principle would be an example for those who abuse credit and declare bankruptcy. The question then is how would this proposed system work. Let's look at the figures, which come from the *Statistical Abstract of the United States.*[18]

Total Federal Revenue-1992	$1,154.6 billion
From individual and corporate income taxes	$560 billion
Gross National Product-1990	$5,248 billion
GNP in 1987	$4,545 billion
GNP in 1988	$4,908 billion
Growth in one year	$363 billion
Percentage growth in one year	7.98 percent
One-quarter of the income tax revenue, 1992	$140 billion

The following illustrates how the deficit might be eliminated in four years while the process of eliminating the income tax is under way. President Clinton promised to eliminate the deficit in eight years, so it is a matter of judgment and the will of our representatives in Congress how rapidly spending could be cut.

Here is a "best case scenario," obviously impossible under the Clinton administration, but an illustration how the country's fiscal house could be placed in order. Had the Senate passed on June 23, 1993, the Republican alternative economic plan that relied on spending cuts rather than tax increases, we would now be well on our way to eliminating the budget deficit.

Based on the 1992 Gross National Product of $5,900 billion, the federal budget would be frozen at $1,445 billion, the FY 1992 deficit was $290 billion and federal revenue would also remain flat at $1,155 billion, spending would have to be reduced $72.5 billion each year for four years in order to eliminate the deficit. This also assumes there would be no new spending and no increase in taxes. Expenditures would thus decrease as follows:

Fiscal year expenditures (billions):

1992	Year 1	Year 2	Year 3	Year 4
$1,445	$1,372.5	$1,300	$1,227.5	$1,155

Thus, in Year 4, expenditures would match today's federal income. The percentage of the Gross National Product allocated for use by the federal government, based on the 1992 GNP, would decline as follows:

24.49%	23.26%	22.03%	20.81%	19.58%

The Year 4 revenue, expressed as a percentage of GNP, would be approximately the same as it has been every year since 1960 (20%), when the top tax rate was 91 percent![13]

The combination of freezing the growth of current programs, savings in the military budget and the elimination of waste as proposed by the Grace Commission ($922 billion during the next five years or $184 billion per year) could give the Congress resources with which to achieve these savings. The changes detailed above will be possible only when the Congress has the will to protect the long range future of this country and accept the fiscal responsibility this entails.

As the burden of personal and corporate income taxes is gradually lifted during these same four years, and assuming the economy expands at a reasonable rate of 4 percent, well under the 7.9 percent growth rate of 1988, the GNP would rise as follows assuming this program was made effective in 1993:

	1992	Year 1	Year 2	Year 3	Year 4
(Billions)	$5,900	$6,136	$6,381	$6,636	$6,901

After the budget is balanced in Year 4 and government expenditures are reduced to 19.58 percent of the previous year's GNP, spending in Year 5 could then rise to $1,351 billion or $196 billion over the level of FY 1992. A major portion of this increase should be applied to retirement of the national debt to decrease the growing cost of interest.

As a result of the 1991–1992 economic downturn, growth was significantly depressed. President Clinton's economic plan was to spend more *federal* funds to stimulate the economy. By contrast, a $140 billion shot in the private sector's arm for each of four years, coupled with specific spending cuts to decrease the deficit, would accomplish economic stimulation in a gradual, Federal Reserve-controlled, non-inflationary fashion. It is not unreasonable to speculate that the growth in GNP would quickly exceed the four percent used in the above illustration.

History has shown that if the prospects of lower taxes are good, people increase their spending in anticipation of having more money in their pocket. Conversely, if higher taxes are in the offing, consumers tend to hang on to their money, as very modest economic growth in the first half of 1993 showed.

If the federal income tax were completely eliminated, as this new purchasing power was used *by the public*, federal revenues from other sources would also grow making up in part for the loss in individual and corporate income taxes. Also, as the economy improved, such expenditures as unemployment compensation and welfare would automatically decline.

With a tight, Federal Reserve rein on fiscal policy so the Congress could not spend more money than it takes in, the voter-approved, percentage-of-GNP expenditure lid enforced by the would keep the free spenders in Congress from indulging in fiscal fantasy and the economy could then follow an inflation-free course. The federal government could promptly regain its Eisenhower-era level of fiscal responsibility.

Should the reader have the impression that the idea of total elimination of the federal income tax is original with the writer, this is also the central theme of the Libertarian Party, whose 1992 candidate was Andre Marrou. This minor but perennial political party believes that the income tax and the Internal Revenue Service must be abolished. Columnist Joseph Sobran points out that "government can't do one citizen a favor without doing proportional harm to another. If it pays you a dollar, it has to take that dollar from someone else. This means that every politician's promise to one group is an implicit threat against the rest of us. But politicians want to disguise the force nexus.[19]

The newest political party on the horizon is the Taxpayers Party, the brainchild of Howard Phillips, founder of the Conservative Caucus. Phillips headed the Office of Economic Opportunity for President Richard Nixon, but when he tried to dismantle his own agency, he was promptly fired. He is now working to build a vehicle for his principles.

The Taxpayers Party advocates the immediate reduction of

the top income tax rate to 10 percent, with the ultimate goal of abolishing income tax altogether. It also wants to slash the $1.45 trillion dollar annual federal spending level to $300 billion and to confine it to purposes clearly authorized by the Constitution.

Reaching back 45 years for a benchmark, Harry Truman's 1948 budget was $38 billion. Sobran points out that Article I, Section 8 of the Constitution (plus a few amendments) enumerates the powers of Congress and says, for example, "the National Endowment for the Arts is unconstitutional, for the simple reason that Congress has no authority to subsidize the arts, any more than it has the authority to censor them.

"Government is not a charitable organization, but a monopoly of coercive powers, beginning with the power to tax. This is the point that always gets disguised.

"The Constitution was written on the presumption that there are precious few things the citizens should be forced to pay for. This is the presumption the U.S. Taxpayers Party wants to reanimate. It doesn't promise 'no new taxes.' It promises to get rid of all but a few of the old ones."[20]

Herbert Stein, a fellow of the American Enterprise Institute and former chairman of the president's Council of Economic Advisers, predicts that "the decision to raise taxes in 1990 will turn out to be the fatal blow to capitalism, free markets and conservatism." He dates the decline of capitalism from 1913, with the adoption of the 16th Amendment, authorizing the federal government to impose an income tax. The first such tax was only 2 percent and applied only to the wealthiest Americans. Soon thereafter, when America got into World War I, there was an enormous increase in rates of income tax.

In the 1920s, Andrew Mellon, secretary of the Treasury, was smart enough to see that a 10 percent cut in tax rates would reduce revenues somewhat less than 10 percent because the economy would be stimulated and the national income would rise. Sixty years later, Arthur Laffer showed that tax revenues would actually rise when taxes were cut. Mellon did bring income tax rates down substantially in the 1920s.

But in the ensuing downturn, President Hoover didn't follow Mellon's advice; he proceeded to raise taxes, thus converting an ordinary recession into the Great Depression. Whether or not he knew this would bring about a permanent weakening of capitalism is unclear.

Conservatives elected President Roosevelt and thought they could establish a corporate state on the model of Mussolini's in Italy, where the economy would be run by committees of CEOs and trade union leaders. It started out all right with the National Recovery Administration, the NRA, but in 1935 and the two following years, FDR turned to soak-the-rich tax increases. During World War II, he raised taxes again.

In 1962, John F. Kennedy proposed a big tax cut; he had learned the virtues of free enterprise from his father. While there was opposition to the forces of tax reduction, the years 1948 to 1973 were to see the most rapid increase of productivity in American history.

But the anti-capitalist forces controlled real tax rates through the maneuver of "bracket creep." By causing inflation they forced people up into higher and higher tax brackets of the progressive tax system, even though the rates stayed the same or were falling.

When Ronald Reagan became president in 1981, he delivered on the promise he made during his campaign—a big tax cut. Intimates said he had never really believed that cutting taxes would raise revenue; he went along with tax increases every year of his administration except the first.

In 1990, George Bush shocked conservatives by reneging on his "read my lips" promise not to raise taxes. The economy promptly went into recession. Looking at all of this history, Herbert Stein saw the Republicans being ejected from the White House in the 1992 election and death of capitalism which will follow. While others will cite different reasons for continuing recession and its effects, Mr. Stein believes, "It is taxes that make the world go round, or keep it from going round."[21]

Mr. Stein might also have said, "It's taxes that make the family go down." According to the Tax Foundation, based in Washington, D.C., a typical, two-earner family with two dependents took in $54,926 in 1992. Out of each dollar, 30.2 cents disappeared in Federal taxes and another 9.5 cents was swept away by State and local taxes, almost 40 percent of their income. After current expenses, this family had only 2.3 percent left to assure their future with payments on insurance protection and a pension fund. It is not difficult to understand why Americans don't save more of their income.[22]

The White House budget office predicts that if these trends continue your descendants yet to be born will pay nearly three-fourths of their income in federal, state and local taxes.[23] In January, 1992, *Barron's*, the financial weekly, did not go so far as to suggest all income tax should be eliminated but recommended that the corporate income tax should be abolished. The magazine predicted that little revenue would be lost to the government because eliminating the tax would "add to the store of capital of every profitable business. It would sweep away the need for corporate lawyers and accountants that attempt to reduce tax bills to the lowest amount and it would sweep away the IRS lawyers and accountants that attempt to audit the work of the first group. This army of two million could find productive work at last."

According to an editorial in *The Daily Oklahoman*, the result of this change would "jump start the American economy—creating additional jobs, additional buying power, lower prices and additional revenue to run the government."[24]

Eliminating the individual income tax would, over time, have four times the effect of abolishing only the corporate income tax. It would also settle continual arguments over the capital gains tax, an integral part of the income tax. Why settle for a minor improvement when a bold, dramatic change bringing relief to every taxpayer in the country is past due?

Chapter Five

Erase the National Debt

All I know is just what I read in the papers. In fact, all I know is what I read about criminals and Congress.

Congress has been getting more money out of us lately than the criminals. The criminals don't take it until after you get it, but Congress is making us all sign I.O.U.s for all we will ever get during our lifetime.

—*Will Rogers*[1]

Any self-respecting corporation with a debt more than four times its annual income would have considered bankruptcy years ago. But the United States government doesn't seem to be concerned that interest on the national debt cost $286 billion in fiscal year 1991, up from $264 billion the year before. In 1993, the payment rose to $292 billion.

The interest bill eats up 22 percent of annual federal outlays, and the national debt itself had increased to $3.7 trillion as of February, 1992 from a measly one trillion in just 11 years. By October 29,1993, it was $4,326,795,000,000.

In the first half of the calendar year, deficit estimates were different. Receipts through May, 1993, were $730 billion but government spending during the same period was galloping ahead at $942 billion, projecting a deficit of $322 billion for FY 1993

But suddenly in mid-July, the Congressional Budget Office revealed that "the deficit will actually be $50 billion smaller than expected," about $285 billion. The actual deficit turned out to be $254.9 billion. This was due to unexpectedly lower spending on bank bailouts, Medicare and other programs, but primarily to lower interest and inflation rates achieved by the Federal Reserve, plus increased economic activity as the business cycle turned slowly upward. The new CBO deficit estimate for FY 1998 was $200 billion but was expected to rise rapidly to $359 billion in FY 2003.[2]

This means each family's share of the current debt is more than $50,000 and will continue to rise as annual deficits pile up. The national debt changes at the rate of *$8,000 a second,* reflecting the interest cost and the growing rate of deficit spending.[3]

Will Rogers was talking about the national debt back in the 1930s when FDR was president:

> *I never thought we would live to see a Democrat that would put down that many figures and get 'em right. Well it goes for relief, and there is nobody can legitimately kick on that. By the end of next year, 1936, our per capita debt will be $270 each. Course, if you think that's too high, you got a perfect right to die and beat it.*[4]

The income tax elimination system described in the previous chapter would place fiscal affairs under sufficient control that the deficit would be eliminated and money could then be applied to the national debt.

Unfortunately, the federal debt we have created over the years has been caused by spending for the country's operating expenses; welfare payments, entitlements, unemployment benefits, S and L bailouts, and the like. Will Rogers said:

> *It must be nice to belong to some legislative body and just pick money out of the air.*[6]

We spent little of the money represented by the national debt for investments such as roads, sewers, dams, bridges and other long-term capital improvements in the infrastructure that would have added to the country's wealth and well-being. Our national accounting system has no way of telling us how many dollars we invested and how many dollars we spend for current operations.

We should specify a schedule for the repayment of our $4.3 trillion national debt. The following suggestion was calculated in early 1992 when the debt was just $3.7 trillion. Because deficits grow and interest rates change, no payback schedule remains accurate for long. If our debt were still $3.7 trillion and we had begun then to pay $400 billion on the debt each year, applying $286 billion to the interest and $114 billion to the principal the first year, it would have taken 17 years and three months, until the year 2011, to rid the nation of this huge debt. Each year the interest would decline and payments on the principal would increase, assuming we did not spend more money than we took in. Of course, at the deficit rate of $255 billion in fiscal year 1993, the current national debt would take somewhat longer to amortize. Despite declining interest rates, the 1993 debt service totalled $292 billion, six billion more than it was in 1991, when the national debt was $3.7 trillion.

However, if the economic plan President Clinton has presented works out as originally projected, deficit will decline to $205 billion by FY 1996, a net deficit reduction of $85 billion after four years in office.[6]

If we fail to understand where continuing budget deficits are leading, the debt hole we have been digging for ourselves will become ever deeper until we can no longer climb out of it. The United States then will be totally

and none of our representatives will be able to deny it. Worse, the countries which now purchase U.S. bonds, as well as our own citizens, will think twice before continuing to bail America out.

The plan to eliminate the income tax detailed in Chapter Four can bring this problem under control because there will be a surplus in Year 5, a portion of which can then be used to pay on the principal of the national debt.

In addition, with government spending finally under control and more money available to individuals as a result of eliminating the personal and corporate income tax, the economy would boom, increasing the GNP, unemployment would decline and the standard of living would rise. The federal government's share of the increased Gross National Product would make payments on the national debt easier and 20 or 25 years later we would no longer have to pay billions of dollars in interest each year.

With such a system in place, the nation would not, as Tennessee Ernie Ford used to sing, "become another day older and deeper in debt."

Chapter Six

Reduce Cost of Elections and the Length of Election Campaigns

> *The Democrats are having a lot of fun exposing the Republican campaign corruptions, but they would have a lot more fun if they knew where they could lay their hands on some of it themselves next November.*
>
> —*Will Rogers*[1]

Today, the cost of elections virtually eliminates any candidate of modest means who does not accept contributions from individuals and groups seeking favors. Certainly Bill Clinton depended heavily on lobbyists and special interests to finance his $71 million campaign. Incumbents have a particular advantage over challengers because they not only have closer relationships with PACs and other special interest groups but have a longer period of time in which to collect contributions for reelection. Besides, they are a known quantity with a historical election advantage which makes them the best possible bet for PACs which want to gain legislative influence.

President Clinton produced a voluntary campaign reform plan which would limit spending to $600,000 for House races and allow senators and their challengers to spend $1.2 to $8.5 million. Originally, the president proposed using taxpayer money to provide complying candidates with up to 25 percent of the limits in the form of vouchers that could be used to pay for postage and advertising. After consideration by the Senate, however, the bill was changed so public money would be given only to candidates whose opponents exceed these limits. The subsidies would be financed by a 30 percent tax on the campaigns which exceed the limits and by repeal of the current tax deduction for lobbying expenses.

But this is just another half-way measure akin to the president's program to restrict lobbyists. It does not "get the money out of politics," as Senator Cranston recommended. Bill Clinton said, "Unless we change fundamentally the way campaigns are financed, everything else we seek to do to improve the lives of our people will be much harder to achieve." What he proposed and the Senate passed is hardly fundamental. The influence of special interest money would remain as would the necessity for vigorous fundraising efforts by the candidates.[2]

All elections should be financed by the political subdivision for which it is held: national, state, county, municipal. Expenditures should indeed be limited by law, allowing enough to inform the voting public about the positions of the candidates. In addition, the period for campaigning should be reduced from lengthy endurance contests to a period just long enough for voters to understand the issues and evaluate the candidates. Great Britain manages to compress election politicking into a couple of months. Thomas Sowell suggests "we need a constitutional amendment that says no state can hold a primary election for any federal office more than two months before the federal election. After all, in the television-dominated culture in which we live, those who profit most from our current system are the ones who operate the communication media."[3]

Now, the millions of dollars spent on national elections tend to generate more heat than light and primarily enrich the media. Fortunately, two trends evident in the 1992 presidential election bode well for change in the right direction. Ross Perot led the other candidates to multiple appearances on network news and talk shows. He also invented the "infomercial" for political purposes, a presentation welcomed by the electorate interested in understanding the candidate's stand on the issues.

Then the debates featuring the three presidential candidates, shown on the networks and public television, were highly useful to voters trying to make up their mind. Still, there were the ubiquitous, derogatory and expensive 30-second "sound bites" which did little to clarify the issues. With public financing in place, the focus should be on debates on the issues, what the candidates intend to do about national problems if elected to office. With campaigning time limited by law, they would be pressured to concentrate on the real issues, leaving little time to snipe about the Short-comings of their opponents.

As a condition for license renewal, the television networks should be required to devote their public service time to programs such as debates and infomercials which will enlighten the voting public on the issues during the limited campaign period. Broadcasting is a licensed privilege; the air doesn't belong to the media who use it.

If qualified congressional aspirants no longer had to spend time raising money for their election, they could concentrate on national issues and serving the public. And when they became senators or congressmen, with no reelection to think about, they could keep their mind off politics, just as Will Rogers suggested.

In any track event or horse race, all of the entrants come off the starting line or out of the gate at the same time. Not so politicians. Those who make a career of gaining elective office may campaign for years.[4] Limiting the time of the public campaign before an election would reduce both the cost of taxpayer-financed elections and the difference between "professional" politicians and those who aspire to office primarily to serve their country. As a result of term limitation, fewer elected officials would ask what their country could do for them. Remember what President John F. Kennedy said about that.

This system of election would allow less affluent people to compete for public office, do their civic duty for the people and derive their satisfaction from a statesman's service to the nation. It would also level the election playing field between the two parties, since the Republicans usually have greater financial resources than the Democrats.

In 1928, Will Rogers commented on the cost of elections. While he was talking about the presidential contest between Herbert Hoover and Al Smith, the principle applies to all elections even more so today:

> *So much money is being spent on the campaigns that I doubt if either man, good as they are, are worth what it will cost to elect them.*[5]

Chapter Seven

Improve the Quality of Public education; Teach Values to Our Children

Say, any of you that have kids in school, either grammar, high or college, it don't make any difference, but can any of you parents get head or tail of what they are doing, what they are taking, what they are learning? All the kids I know, either mine or anybody's, none of 'em can write so you can read it, none of 'em can spell so you can read it. They can't figure and don't know geography, but they are always taking some of the darndest things, political science, international relations, drama, buck dancing, sociology, Latin, Greek art.

But us poor old dumb parents, we just string along and do the best we can, and send 'em as long as we are able. We don't know what it's all about. We just have to take the teacher's word.

—*Will Rogers*[1]

Improved education for the upcoming generation is a must in order to reduce unemployment and compete in the global marketplace. The high-paying, union-protected factory jobs we got used to in the forties, fifties and sixties were reduced by overseas competition in the seventies and the eighties, so here we are in the nineties with a growing number of young people under-educated to take their place in the world of work.

Many of the manufacturing jobs which are left are either performed by robots or call for technical skills which the average high school graduate just doesn't have; the drop-out is even more handicapped. So those without further education must work for minimum wage at McDonald's or Burger King, sit around drawing unemployment insurance or welfare, or, they like to think, the only thing left is to sell drugs or engage in other criminal pursuits. There is no question their employment opportunities are severely limited and today's fast-paced, high-tech world is passing them by.

So what's wrong with the public educational system? Probably the basic problem is that the system is a monopoly, run by professionals who form a powerful lobby to increase funding from the public but who are not held to elevated standards of accomplishment. The Educational Unions are able to influence the reelection-sensitive state legislators to provide ever-increasing amounts of tax money to "improve" the existing system. Education is a principal if not the major item in every state and municipal budget.

As in many bureaucratic systems, educators tend to measure inputs—number of students, dollars spent, teacher salaries compared with those in other states. There is less attention to outputs—the percentage of students who graduate, the number who qualify for college entrance, their SAT test scores, the number of students who go on to productive careers versus the students who wind up in criminal court, and other measures of the results of the teachers' efforts. The bottom line is that old adage, "If the student hasn't learned, the teacher hasn't taught."

Albert Shanker, president of the American Federation of Teachers, says, "we should realize that the overwhelming majority of American children, perhaps 90 percent, are not learning much. Middle class parents are happy with the education their children get because they go on to college. They don't realize that most of these youngsters would not be admitted to a university in any other industrialized country. Their kids are getting their junior high and high school educations in college."[2]

The Educational Testing Service of Princeton, New Jersey, surveyed children ages nine and thirteen, finding that though American nine-year-olds managed to rank third in science skills measured against students in nine countries, they were next to last in math. American 13-year-olds hovered near the bottom in both science and math compared with students in 14 other countries.

ETS President Gregory R. Anrig said, "If a Korean 13-year-old can do something, there's no reason for an American not to be able to. But we've got to figure out how to do that." South Korean children scored the highest in all categories. Children from Taiwan, Switzerland, Hungary and the former Soviet Union were consistently in the top five.

A National Science Foundation study concluded that throwing money at education is not a cure-all. The U.S. spends 7.5 percent of its Gross National Product on education, compared with South Korea's 4.5 percent.[3]

Shanker says American students lag behind because they don't work hard. "We know what would happen to our economy if we announced that, starting tomorrow, work was voluntary and every adult was going to get the same wages. That's exactly what we say to our students. In other countries, there are reasons for students to work hard. If they don't, they won't qualify for university. Here, only students who want to get into elite institutions have to apply themselves. The rest know there is some college that will accept them if they have a diploma." Shanker thinks the simple, but difficult, answer is to re-establish standards and insist that students meet them. In other words, he would outlaw all social and athletic promotions.

Shanker suggests the federal government make grants and loans contingent on colleges demanding that students meet world standards for admission. This could be phased in over ten years and include an incentive program that offered to pay a much higher proportion of college expenses for students who met world-class standards and pay full costs for students who met these standards but could not otherwise afford to go to college.

In other countries, students who do not aspire to college are required to meet high school standards in order to get into high-quality apprenticeships which prepare them for real jobs. Even the slow learners are followed up with continuing education programs that allow them to make up what they have missed in high school so they do not remain unemployable and a ward of the government for the rest of their lives.[2]

Money is not the total answer. During the last decade, spending for education has increased 33 percent but Americans realize they have little to show for it. This situation is not totally the fault of the teacher; much of it has to do with the changes in the nuclear family and how much help and encouragement kids get at home. This is evidenced by the difference in the progress Asian immigrants make in school compared with Americans who are just as poor and don't even have the language handicaps the Asian newcomers have. To be sure, some Asian parents are too strict on their kids who consequently suffer in other ways.

In Kansas City, though, there is hope that money is the key to the improvement of urban schools. In 1984, a judge had the idea that schools within the city—where the general population is heavily white but the school population is three fourths non-white—should be made so attractive that whites as well as blacks would want to attend city schools. Kansas City is betting $500 million in construction costs alone on Judge Clark's idea about how school integration should be accomplished. Of course, the city fathers and the taxpayers didn't have much choice after the court decision to go this route.

The city is trying to lure whites back out of their private schools with Olympic-size swimming pools, field trips to distant states, and teachers imported from Belgium. The question is whether nearly five dozen "magnet schools," together representing almost every conceivable approach to teaching, can succeed where more traditional efforts have failed. The jury is still out. Kansas City has the chance to turn urban education around but, according to the district superintendent, Walter Marks, "If Kansas City fails, then I think it's questionable whether it can be done in any setting."

Opponents of this grand plan see it as a money-eating machine but Judge Clark's order to remedy the segregation problem despite the cost has survived state appeals to federal judges and the U.S. Supreme Court. And the State of Missouri must pick up the rest of the tab if the school district runs out of money, a sum which may eventually total $1.2 billion. White flight has been arrested, the percentage of white pupils rising to 25.8, in contrast to the goal of 40 percent prescribed by Judge Clark. While some white parents vow never to send their kids to public school, others have taken a second look.

The question remains: Can the fanciest of schools and the best intentions, supported by blank-check financing, improve public-school education? Nobody yet knows. Superintendent Marks recently told a gathering of parents and taxpayers, "The dilemma is, how do we make all this work?"

In a Columbus, Ohio, middle school, significant non-academic improvements have been made without a lot more money. Led by a determined principal and faculty, Eastmoor was able to overcome the handicaps of students from low-income families by stressing discipline and peer pressure. The school became drug-free in 1990 because Phillip Hobbs, a strong principal who took over in the fall of 1986, and some committed faculty members emphasized discipline and created reverse peer pressure. They used a program called Youth to Youth which made it cool to shun drugs.

Previously, the kids in the neighborhood were into gangs, graffiti and dope. Hobbs forbade students from wearing the colors of a dozen gangs. He outlawed other trappings like bandannas, jean jackets with writing on them and T-shirts promoting beer and drugs. He expelled 18 or 20 youngsters over the objections of their parents. And this was a tough district in which two-thirds of the students came from broken homes and 22 percent of them said someone in their family had a drug problem.

In 1986, one of the teachers posted a notice: Anyone interested in a drug-free group should come to room 207. She didn't expect many to come because she knew it wasn't cool. But it was standing-room only! They came for a number of reasons: to get out of class, because their friends did, or just out of curiosity. That was the beginning of the school's chapter of Youth to Youth and the start of positive peer pressure. Of course, others stayed away, saying that the program was for "nerds." Youth to Youth sponsored dances, pizza parties, skiing trips, so it became the social center for the school. These events were open only to members but each could bring one guest.

Now it is obvious that this program does not guarantee academic success but Eastmoor found it is important to give students a way to express their feelings, discuss their concerns. Years ago, this kind of program wasn't necessary but times change, values have changed, drugs have become a way of life for a lot of kids, and schools must create the learning environment and enthusiasm which was previously taken for granted.[5]

William Tucker, a writer for *Forbes* magazine, commenting on a book by Edward B. Fiske, *Smart Schools, Smart Kids*, believes the teachers' and administrators' unions and educational bureaucrats are "ferociously defending their 'one best system.'" In Tucker's opinion, "the basic problem of the schools is not that they are 19th-century factories or that they don't have telephones, but that they are 20th-century government monopolies. Every factory is ultimately accountable to its customers, no matter how efficiently organized. Schools remain unaccountable for one reason—because year in, year out, they know an assigned allotment of pupils will be at their doorsteps. Take away this captive constituency and the public schools would become wholly different—and probably much better—institutions." Tucker believes "School choice emerges as the 'one best system' for reforming American education."[6,7]

Others think so too. J. Patrick Rooney, the president of Golden Rule Insurance Company in Indianapolis, was attacked for giving poor, inner-city kids a chance at a better life. He funded a $1.2 million voucher program to let low-income parents send their kids to private schools. He did it in 1991 after the Indiana Legislature refused to pass a School choice program. The voucher would pay up to 50 percent of the costs at a private school, with a maximum of $800. Most Indianapolis private schools charge less than $1,600 a year; public schools there spend an average of $4,000 a year per student.

Who could be against such a generous program to benefit low-income families? Public-school hard-liners, school-board members and the president of the NAACP set up howls of protest, saying the money should be given to the public school system. "We need to support the public schools. To do anything else will be disastrous."

But Bill Crawford, a state legislator who represents the 70 percent black Indianapolis district, thinks giving low-income kids a choice of schools will force the public school system to improve. He noted that 54 percent of the city's elementary school students score below grade level on national tests.

"Public schools give up on students more easily than private schools. They are unwilling to discipline students.

"Parents see choice of schools as a way of empowering them to give their children a chance at upward mobility," Representative Crawford went on to say. "Teachers are the only ones really upset by choice here."[8]

In Poland, private education was suppressed for 45 years under communism. Since that country has been liberated, 250 new private schools have sprung up because the new Solidarity government lifted the restrictions on them. In addition, Katarzyna Skorzynska, a 30-year-old activist, convinced the Parliament to reimburse private schools for up to 50 percent of what it would have cost the state to educate their students. And who opposed that idea? The same people who oppose choice of schools in the U.S.:

the trade unions and the education bureaucrats. However, in Poland those groups have been completely discredited because of their failures. Ms. Skorzynska says, "We have learned that competition is indispensable in providing quality education."[9]

Another innovative development has given the educational establishment cause for nervous laughter. Christopher Whittle, the Knoxville entrepreneur, introduced Channel One into public schools, exchanging television receivers and educational programming for the privilege of limited advertising beamed to the students. Now, he wants to commercialize America's classrooms further by opening 200 "profit-seeking instructional concerns," i.e., a chain of private schools which would charge tuition, make money for investors, and conduct experimental programs in education. He proposes to keep these schools open 12 hours a day with a staggered schedule to assist working parents. What's more, they would operate nearly year-round. Whittle says his program is the "private research and development end of the public schools."[10]

In May, 1992, Whittle Communications, Inc. recruited Benno C. Schmidt, Jr., who was president of Yale University for six years, to be president and CEO of the Edison Project, as this new venture was named. The idea is to get talented people to think about problems of the schools. The plan is to design these 200 schools for 100,000 students and have them up and running by 1996. Whittle says, "Our biggest breakthroughs will be ones you don't see in the physical sense. For example, we want to find the key to motivating kids." His system seems to hinge on finding the incentives which will make students want to attend, learn, and stay in school. If the first 200 schools do well, Whittle's goal is 1,000 such units nationwide.[11]

Dr. Schmidt believes "the problem lies not in the people who teach in our public and private schools, or even primarily in the financial resources at their disposal. The problem, I think, is the system itself." The Edison Project, a private project with a public mission, aims to create a new conception and model of education for children from the earliest years through high school. Edison wants to provide a laboratory of innovation, new models of schools that public schools can emulate if they wish.

Schmidt says that evidence of trouble in the schools has been growing for the past 20 years, and while many devoted people have tried to improve things, real progress is hard to find. We have doubled per-pupil spending (after inflation) since 1965, trained teachers better and toughened high school graduation requirements, but drop-out rates remain distressingly high and SAT scores of today's high school students are lower than a generation ago. Schmidt asks these provocative questions:

> What if children came to school as toddlers or even earlier, rather than five-or six-year-olds?
> What if parents were systematically involved and actually worked regularly in schools?
> What if students taught other students much more? What if schools were open 12 hours a day, 12 months a year?
> What if, for the first time in history, a school system across the nation was tied together technologically, and could take advantage of system-wide experimentation, teacher-training and economies of scale, but free of the weight of political bureaucracies?
> What if, also for the first time, adequate financial resources were invested in educational innovation?
> What if pioneering-creative thinkers were free to break through the inherited mold of our schools?[12]

Columnist Cal Thomas points out that latest national SAT scores are at their lowest level in history, while spending on education reached $413.8 billion in the fall of 1991, of which $248.6 billion went to public primary and secondary education, making the average per-pupil investment just under $6,000, an increase of nearly $3,000 in ten years. In other words, it cost twice as much to get poorer results. In contrast, independent private schools registered a combined SAT average score of 994, 100 points above the national average. Thomas believes School choice is the answer and "the public ought to demand...the acceptance by Congress of freedom of choice in education."[13]

If parents received vouchers for their children to attend the best school, there would be waiting lines at the good ones and the poor ones would have to close for lack of students. Freedom of choice is the American way; forcing kids to go to bad public schools is the Communist way. The Indianapolis example demonstrates that money is not the major missing ingredient in our educational system.

Pennsylvania may become the first state to enact a true

educational choice program, granting parents up to $900 a year if they choose to send their children to a public school outside their district or to a private school. Choice proponents were able to bypass the Education Committee, long a graveyard for school-reform proposals, and bring the issue directly before rank-and-file legislators, where it passed the Senate in December 1991 by a 28 to 22 margin. Of course, the 100,000 teachers in the Pennsylvania State Education Association opposed this legislation

A black state legislator in Wisconsin, Polly Williams, pushed through a choice bill that awards 500 of Milwaukee's low-income students a $2,500 voucher to attend private schools. The Wisconsin State Supreme Court upheld the Williams plan.

Vermont has had a program similar to Pennsylvania's for years. In addition, there have been experiments in East Harlem, N.Y., Cambridge, Mass. and Minnesota. It may well be that choice is an idea whose time has come.[14]

An idea whose time has gone is that kids need a vacation that lasts the entire summer. America is no longer a collection of farm dwellers who need all their kids home to help out during the growing and harvest seasons. One of the reasons the Asians who come to America do so well is they are used to going to school year 'round. Japanese students, for example, attend school an average of 240 days a year, fully sixty days more than American students. When an Asian student has that much more exposure to the learning process, it doesn't take a Ph.D. to understand why they learn more and progress faster. Again, a lot of teachers are not crazy about the idea of working in the summertime and certainly the Travel Industry Association was dead set against it when suggested for Oklahoma. This industry does 80 percent of its business during the three month school vacation. Perhaps that's another good reason to change the system.

In Texas, one district tried a year-round school calendar in 1990 and the next year, nineteen districts were using it. Texas officials expect the trend to continue. One advantage is that learning retention rates are usually much better for students who have been away for three or four weeks, as opposed to those who have been off for three months. Another advantage is financial. With some of the district's students gone all of the time, fewer classrooms are needed, with savings in construction and operating costs.[15]

With more time spent per year in elementary school, students would be better prepared to meet higher standards in junior high and high school. According to the National Academy of Sciences (NAEP) that tests students at ages 9, 13, and 17 years, all 17-year-olds can do basic arithmetic and nearly all can read simple materials. But only 6 percent of students are in the top category in mathematics, which does not go beyond first year algebra. Only two to four percent reach top categories in reading and writing. Less than 30 percent of students produce what NAEP calls an "adequate" paragraph. And NAEP's definition of "adequate," which permits spelling and grammatical errors, is not very demanding.[16]

Despite all of the evidence of the need for change and choice, the education establishment is not about to relinquish its power without a battle. Signs of this conflict were evident in 1992 elections, when Colorado voters rejected a ballot item that would have created the first statewide school voucher program. Detroiters threw out school board members who had spearheaded bold reforms. Michigan and Pennsylvania returned to Capitol Hill members of the House Education and Labor Committee, men who had blocked efforts to create national standards, national tests and a (pilot) federal voucher program.

While Governor Clinton appeared to be for School choice in the public school system, Chester E. Finn, a former assistant secretary of education, claims he "is so heavily in thrall to the teachers unions that their leaders are boasting of the influence they will wield." Thus the battle is joined and only time will tell how it will all come out.[17]

Values

If the American public/private education system could become the year-round, integrated, full choice, drug-free, high academic standard-achieving, non-monopoly it ought to be, how would our kids then fare in the real world? Parents naturally expect their children to become industrious, responsible, well-adjusted, sensitive adults, able to make their way in the world. Would an improved education system, working with parents, help achieve their expectations for the next generation? Hopefully.

But growing up is hard and there are many temptations, detours and hazards along the way. In just one day in the lives of American children:

2,795 teens get pregnant
1,106 teens give birth
10 children are killed and 30 children are wounded by gunfire
16 youths commit suicide
135,000 bring a gun to school
7,742 teen-agers become sexually active
211 children are arrested for drug abuse
437 children are arrested for drinking or drunken driving
1,532 teen-agers drop out of school
3,288 children run away from home
1,629 children are in adult jails
2,556 are born out of wedlock
2,989 children see their parents divorced.[18]

William J. Bennett, Secretary of Education from 1985 to 1988 and now co-director of Empower America, in a *Wall Street Journal* editorial, cited these eight cultural indicators:

1992 Average Daily TV Viewing—7.04 hours, from 5.06 in 1960
1992 SAT scores—899, down from 975 in 1960
1990 Percent of Illegitmate births—26.2 percent, 5.3 in 1960
1990 Children with Single Mothers—22 percent, from 8 in 1960
1990 Children on Welfare—11.9 percent, from 3.5 in 1960
1990 Teen Suicide Rate—11.3 percent, from 3.6 percent in 1960
1991 Violent Crime Rate (per 100,000)—75.8, from 16.1 in 1960
1990 Median Prison sentence—8 days, from 22.5 days in 1960.[19]

With these hazards to appropriate development, one could conclude that American families are often dysfunctional. How then can values be instilled and reinforced in the lives of today's children? If the typical American family cannot or will not accept the responsibility of teaching basic cultural values to their children, can this challenge be picked up by the nation's schools?

By necessity or preference, parents turn over early child-rearing to day care centers and nursery schools, to Head Start programs, to nannies. This is reality. Parents already leave crucial value concerns for others to teach.

Instruction in "basic cultural values" does not mean teaching religion in the schools, although most American values are also found in most religions—the Golden Rule, the Ten Commandments. It does mean that teachers as well as parents should communicate American values to their students throughout their entire educational experience. If the parents and the schools will not assume this responsibility early on, the corrections and welfare departments of cities, counties, states and the Federal government must do it later, after the results of such neglect surface. But by then, success may be impossible.

Today's kids are getting negative messages daily from television and movies and most kids spend at least as much time watching the tube as they spend in the classroom. The things which happen to children daily (see the list above) involve sex, weapons, violence, drug abuse, parents getting divorced, dropping out of school, running away from home. TV programs, both the news and "entertainment," saturate kids' minds with these kinds of behaviors until the results, happening to other people, are trivialized or ignored. Kids become convinced that "It can't happen to me!" But the statistics show otherwise.

How do we convince kids that it's not cool to get pregnant, to get hooked on drugs, to carry a weapon and shoot people, to drop out of school, to get drunk, to cheat, steal, to deface or destroy other peoples' property, to solve their problems with violence?

The effort must begin early, and the pre-school educators have the opportunity to mold the youngest minds with gentle guidance. The appropriate values can be communicated to the very young and the process continued by weaving these ideas into the curriculum and into the discipline each succeeding school must sponsor in order to teach at all.

In addition, the television media and Hollywood should accept their responsibility. Some may claim that any de-emphasis of violence in the television news is censorship and an infringement on the right of the public to know. But the TV does not graphically present pornography or sexual abuse when a person is accused of these crimes; some rules of propriety are followed. But crime saturates the news daily; the sensational sells!

Also crime and sex dominate network television and movie entertainment, becoming increasingly graphic and pervasive, so that children have easy access to the examples these presentations set. Unfortunately, their ability to distinguish fantasy from reality is not fully developed, nor are they able to delay the gratification this entertainment urges them to experience.

Fortunately, a ray of reason has entered the television networks and a turnaround may yet occur. ABC, CBS and NBC have agreed on standards governing television violence that could influence the fall, 1993, programming. A voluntary agreement sponsored by Senator Paul Simon (D-Ill.) gave the networks an antitrust waiver so they could plan together to dampen the now prevalent depictions of violence. The new principles would require that violence:

1. Be relevant to the plot
2. Must not be gratuitous or excessive
3. Must not be glamorous or a solution to conflict
4. Must not shock or stimulate
5. May not show excessive gore or pain
6. Must not show how to use harmful devices or weapons
7. Should include consequences to victims and perpetrators
8. Should be used with exceptional care when children are portrayed as victims and should be eliminated from children's programming if it would unduly frighten them
9. Should only involve animals if needed for the plot
10. Must not be mixed with sex as erotic.[20]

If similar rules could be applied also to the explicit sex scenes shown in the movies made for television and big-screen feature films which are eventually shown on the tube, perhaps this too would influence impressionable teenagers in a direction better for their health and social well-being.

At hearings before the Senate Judiciary Subcommittees on the Constitution and juvenile justice in early June, 1993, Hollywood executives argued that "prime-time TV shows are much less violent than their critics claim." Nevertheless, Jack Valenti, President of the Motion Picture Association of America told the senators he would hold a series of meetings over the next few months with representatives of the Directors Guild of America, the Writers Guild, program producers, agents and others to discuss TV violence. Maybe Hollywood is finally getting the message.[21]

So what else should we do? We should insist on working values education into the curriculum K through 12. It should be sufficiently explicit to make kids understand the importance of American values and the threat which abandonment of these values holds for them and their country. We should set up the opportunity for kids to discuss their concerns as Principal Hobbs and his teachers at Eastmoor did, providing programs that make appropriate behavior cool. It *will* be cool if the kids believe it is and they say it is.

We should continue to pressure TV stations, networks and cable companies to soft-pedal crime, give upbeat news more time and emphasis. President Bush , the advocate of a kinder and gentler America, protested against the "filth and indecent material" to which the public is exposed through televised trials. He said the "American people should be protected against some of these excesses."[22]

We should further pressure television stations to reduce the daily menu of sex and violence in the entertainment they program. Pressure comes by refusing to buy the products of companies sponsoring objectionable entertainment.

We should support laws which curb access to adult films by non-adults—people under 21. This would not inhibit speech, art and/or freedom; it would merely use reason to determine when our kids are ready for adult themes. Liquor stores and bars do not allow minors in; narcotic drugs are illegal; similarly, "R" and "X" rated movies should be confined to adult theaters and all ticket buyers suspected to be underage should be carded. Just the fact that certain movies could be shown only in adult theaters would probably inhibit their patronage and Hollywood might just get this message, as well. What's more, when such films are converted to videotape and rented at Blockbuster and other video stores they should not be permitted for checkout by underage customers. While there is a lot of sex and violence in today's literature, the problem of such books readily obtainable in libraries and legitimate bookstores is probably not as acute because reading is not teenagers' favorite form of recreation.

The open culture of America generates problems which other cultures do not experience. China, for example, requires that women must be 23 and men 26 before they can get a marriage license, and the Chinese culture does not condone living together prior to marriage. Thus they avoid single parent households, now nine percent of the households in the U.S., the complications of teenage pregnancies and many of the problems we in America try to cope with daily. Perhaps, more emphasis on appropriate values would prevent these and other problems which are making America more dangerous and certainly less attractive as a place to live.[23]

And just maybe the process would eventually reorient our

culture toward that kinder and gentler America President Bush once talked about. Joseph W. Gauld, president of the Hyde Foundation and head of the Hyde School, a boarding institution in Bath, Maine, is convinced that character development is a school's primary task. He said, "The educational Mafia has never understood that all learning begins with the development of character and a sense of purpose. Take World War II, when Congress voted a free college education for returning GIs. Academia was horrified; no less than the president of the University of Chicago darkly warned that these obviously academically unprepared vulgarians would turn our universities into "educational hobo jungles." In fact, the GIs ended up being hailed as the best students in our collegiate history.

> *Hyde assumes each youngster to be gifted with a unique potential, thus making our boarding school's mission to help each student develop the necessary character—courage, integrity, concern for others, curiosity, leadership—to fulfill this larger purpose of life.*
>
> *The 25-year-old experiment has prepared youngsters for life. And over 97 percent of Hyde's graduates have gone on to four-year colleges.*
>
> *We at Hyde are now setting up public-school models, one of which opened in September, 1992, in Gardner, Maine. Similar models are expected to open, probably in September 1993, in high schools in Washington, D.C., Indianapolis, Winston-Salem, and Springfield, Massachusetts. Each will require a commitment from student, parent and teacher alike to honor Hyde principles at home and at school."*

Said in a single paragraph, Mr. Gauld's idea is: "Address the entire character of youngsters; reinvolve the family; create a dynamic parent-teacher-student partnership; then teach academic subjects. This approach will help move American students to first place in the world."[24]

Chapter Eight

Reduce Drug Abuse and Crime

Do you know what has been the cause of the big increase in murders? It's been the manufacture of the automatic pistol. The Automatic pistol is as much more dangerous and destructive than the old Six-Shooter, as poison gas is over perfume. In the first place there is no skill or nerve required in using it. You just touch a trigger and aim the thing around like you would a sprinkling can or a hose.

They should advertise those guns—'Killing Made Easy.'

—*Will Rogers*[1]

Today, firearm technology has advanced so that Will Rogers would be talking about AK-47s and other assault rifles the Congress may yet ban. Back in Will's time, there was plenty of crime but it appeared to be a gentler time when crime affected fewer people. Today crime affects everyone. Those gentler times seem to have passed into history, replaced by gangs, drive-by killings, rape, robbery, assault and murder which daily fill the headlines and the evening television news. Now all Americans must take precautions to protect their personal safety.

As Will Rogers recognized, alcohol and other drug abuse begets crime. People hooked on crack cocaine and other illegal drugs have a *biological incentive* to find ways to support their habit. The profit available to those who deal in drugs provides a monetary incentive to perpetuate the market.

Several years ago, about three blocks from our home there was a crack house, run by teenagers. It operated with an increasing volume of business for many months because the police were waiting until the main pusher turned eighteen and could be arrested as an adult. During that time, our home was broken into twice and items with street value were also stolen from our garage. When the crack house was finally shut down, we had no more problems.

Unfortunately, more and more people are getting hooked on cocaine and other addicting substances, as the arrest rates for drug abuse violations attest. The increase in arrest rates per 100,000 inhabitants in the U.S. are:

Year	Arrests per 100,000 inhabitants
1980	256
1985	346
1988	423
1989	526

For 1989, the rates varied as follows:

Male	905
Female	167
Northeast	622
Midwest	312
South	440
West	769[2]

Tragically, so many drug abuse victims are the minorities whose opportunities for legitimate employment are severely limited. They are often handicapped by unemployment, broken homes, discrimination, and lack of education, making them an easy mark for drug dealers who offer them easy money.

If the U.S. were suddenly invaded by military force from another country, we would immediately defend ourselves, carrying the fight to the invading country. But we have been invaded by drugs instead of soldiers, drugs which are causing death, crime, and effectively turning addicted Americans into dependent zombies. And we do little to force the supplying countries to cease producing and shipping in drugs.

While the Pentagon is increasingly involved in the drug war, with a $1.2 billion budget for 1992, the efforts of our armed forces do not include combat and thus are singularly ineffective. There is too much political corruption in the producing countries' armed forces at the sites of origin and too little effectiveness in interdicting the supplies as they penetrate the U.S. border, by air, sea or land. In view of rising rates of arrest for drug abuse, our coastline presents a veritable sieve to smugglers.

In this situation, U.S. drug enforcement faces the almost impossible task of finding and arresting—coast to coast—hundreds of thousands of pushers whose war chests amount to dozens of billions of dollars a year, the revenue from their sales. The Drug Enforcement Agency's ineffective efforts cost the U.S. taxpayers $20 billion a year.

Although we already have 500 American soldiers on the ground in Central and South America, working in counterdrug training and intelligence, just helping the producing countries' armed forces to fight the drug lords isn't working.

According to *Newsweek*, "the basic problem for U.S. efforts in Peru, Bolivia and Columbia is that drug consumption is not a serious social problem in those countries, while exports are a source of hundreds of millions of badly needed dollars for hundreds of thousands of people, many of them farmers, in remote areas."[3]

While we are now trying to control the crack cocaine invasion, the Columbian drug pushers are developing a "new" product which may be even more profitable—heroin. Columbian intelligence authorities have discovered large stretches of agricultural land sown with poppy, the plant that provides the chemical base for both opium and heroin. The peasant who grows the plant gets about $3,000 per hectare (2.47 acres) for his crop. Two hectares of poppies can be processed into 2.5 kilos of heroin, worth about $125,000 on the U.S. market. A like amount of cocaine fetches no more than $37,500. The drug dealers are likely to cut their selling price in order to get people hooked on heroin and then take advantage of them by raising the price.[4]

Most of the coca originates in the growing areas of Peru and Bolivia and is bought by drug traffickers in Columbia, processed and shipped to markets worldwide. It is important to understand that the coca farmers are poor people with a per capita income between $400 and $600 a year. Like addicts and the urban poor in developed countries, they are victims of society and drug traffickers. Government regulations have prevented coca farmers from growing and marketing alternative crops.

The drug traffickers, on the other hand, are wealthy criminals who are into smuggling, money laundering and other well-known illegal activities, to say nothing of their immorality.

Hernando de Soto was the personal representative of Peru's President Alberto Fujimori for various issues including drugs. He is now president of Institute for Liberty and Democracy, author of *The Other Path*, and an entrepreneur in Lima. He reports that: "On May 14, 1991, enlightened U.S. authorities signed an agreement with Peru accepting for the first time that coca growers were not to be considered criminals; that their organizations would be recognized as legitimate intermediaries, capable of negotiating with governments and business; that they would participate in creating new legal institutions to remove the barriers to other opportunities in the market economy; and, if they eradicated coca, their property rights would be legalized. To demonstrate their support—and despite intimidation and the assassination of their principal leader, Walter Toca—every one of the 180 identifiable coca-growing organizations signed commitments to switch from coca to other crops, providing markets could be guaranteed."

These 250,000 farmers had previously formed alliances with drug traffickers to defend their property against trespassing and violent incursions by authorities. Now they welcome an alternative. Because Peru's coca crop has an annual market value of $160 million, it is less than one percent of the U.S. drug enforcement budget.

While military people do not comprehend this approach, opting for bigger and better drug busts, European multinational corporations understood it as a business deal and, with Peru, began to develop plans for creating alternative opportunities for the growers. By drying up the supply side of the drug flow, the traffic would be controlled peacefully. When the traffickers can no longer buy what they would smuggle to the U.S. and other markets, they will be out of business.

When market-economy and private-property institutions are introduced in Peru, coca farmers are willing to switch and private business will play its part in the war for the environment and against drugs. When it was suggested that drug traffickers would just raise the price for coca, competing with alternative crops, a coca grower replied, "Look, surely a successful drug dealer earns more than you in Washington. If you don't push drugs, it's because you have decent alternatives, you know drug dealing brings violence and corruption. You don't want to raise your family in hell. Why should I be any different, given the chance?"[5]

The United States should give favored-nation status to all drug-crop-growing countries for importation of non-drug products which the United States can appropriately use. The U.S. should help the coca and poppy growing countries find and develop such products to substitute for the drugs they now produce. It would be significantly less expensive for the U.S. to guarantee the market for these alternative products than continue ineffectively to interdict the illicit drugs as they flow across our borders. The economies of these cooperating countries will improve as legitimate job opportunities expand and the cost of controlling drug trafficking within their borders declines.

In addition, the United States should cooperate, preferably under the umbrella of the United Nations, with European countries which have taken the lead in this effort to dry up the supply of drug crops. This would take the "war" on drugs direct to the source, just as the drug lords have tried to confine the drug battles to the United States.

Our allies and the world should recognize that traffic in illegal drugs is a hazard to the well-being of *all* countries and that cleaning up this kind of crime should be part of the "New World Order," just as promoting peace is a part of the effort to mold the planet's future. Europe, Great Britain and Japan are ready markets for the drug lords; it's just harder for them to deliver the stuff over such a long distance. However, traffickers have recently been diverting increasing amounts of crack cocaine to Europe where the price is higher. Thus, many members of the United Nations have a vested interest in getting control of illegal drug traffic.[3]

When the supply of drugs has been eliminated at the source, using this business approach, and the flow of illegal drugs into the United States has stopped, we can then turn all of our drug enforcement resources to the task of rehabilitating the victims of drug abuse. Only then will the drug war begin to subside.

Most of the marijuana used in the U.S. comes from Mexico, which produces 90 percent of the world supply. Only 2 percent comes from Southeast Asia. But *cannabis* cultivation in the U.S. is a growing industry, partly because the quality is better. In 1982, the federal government destroyed 2,250,000 plants; by 1990 that number increased to 125,876,000 plants.[6]

While cannabis cultivation and use has been illegal since 1937, perhaps America should reconsider decriminalization of the drug, exercising the same level of control over it that the government maintains over alcohol. There are differing opinions about marijuana's harmful effects and whether or not it leads to the use of hard drugs. The budget of the Domestic Cannabis Eradication/Suppression Program is $3.5 million a year. If the drug were controlled and taxed like alcohol, it might become less sought after and be used by people primarily for occasional social purposes.

In April 1992, Peru's President Alberto Fujimori suspended democracy as usual by closing Congress, suspending the Constitution, and calling on the military to intervene in order to control violence, terrorism, corruption and unrest. While U.S. Secretary of State James Baker reacted by saying "you cannot destroy democracy in order to save it," 70 percent of the Peruvians agreed with or accepted the president's action.

The Peruvian Congress had a history of voting for pay raises every year and now members earn $2,000 a month in a land where the minimum wage is $50 a month. congressmen also have immunity from criminal prosecution and enjoy other privileges. The Peruvian constitution is a highly ambiguous and technical document which many feel is understood only by the ruling elite and the politicians. Violence and corruption were practiced by a terrorist group, *Sendero Luminoso* or "Shining Path," led by Abimael Guzman Reynoso, which constantly attacked citizens who could expect no protection from a corrupt police force nor did they receive justice under the existing legal system.[7]

This situation changed dramatically when Guzman and his henchmen were arrested on September 12, 1992 and less than a month later were sentenced to life imprisonment.[8] Robert J. Barro noted that "the key source of Shining Path's economic power was the U.S. Government's drug policy. The Peruvian terrorists obtained most of their income from the protective services they provided to local drug traffickers. American aid to Peru, earmarked mostly for drug interdiction, created more demand for these services and thereby added to the Shining Path's income."

He went on to say, "More fundamentally, the problem stems from the demand for drugs by U.S. residents in conjunction with the U.S. government's policy of curtailing the supply of drugs by making the trade illegal and dangerous. If drugs were legalized, then the demand for protection services would vanish along with its income (as would the incomes of many criminals in the U.S.)"[9]

Manuel S. Klausner of Los Angeles took the same position in a letter to *The Wall Street Journal.* "It is becoming increasingly clear, just as with prohibition of alcohol, that the most egregious costs of drug abuse are those that result from criminalization. And despite its vaunted 'war' on drugs—a massive multi-billion-dollar program in the tradition of the *biggest spenders* on the left—the government has been unable to keep drugs out of prisons, let alone off the streets. Why should we begin to 'concede the ruination' of any nation or U.S. city because of the costly failures of the counterproductive 'war on drugs'?"[10]

The notion of decriminalization of drugs sparks emotional arguments on both sides and it is difficult to know what would happen if hard drugs were made legal through channels similar to those used to control the sale of alcohol. Certainly, crack cocaine and heroin present different problems than does marijuana.

The alternatives facing President Clinton are to continue President Bush's cold shoulder to Fujimori because of the Peruvian president's authoritarian methods, or sit down with him to resume dialogue about getting the peasants of the Upper Huallaga out of coca production. Currently, the attempt to interdict 60 percent of the world's cocaine production from a U.S.-built military base in Santa Lucia is only one percent effective. In November, 1992, Fujimori told columnists Evans and Novak he "wants to see Clinton [in order] to develop a plan to eradicate Peru's poison."[11]

On November 22, 1992, when 90 percent of the Shining Path leadership had been jailed, Peruvian voters braved guerrilla threats and ignored appeals to spoil the election, handing Fujimori a solid victory. All of this demonstrated a "degree of independence, determination and attachment to democracy that confounds sophisticated observers."[12]

Even back in Will Rogers' time, guns were a problem, but he probably never imagined how acute it would become. He said:

> *This gun thing is getting pretty serious here around New York. Everybody that doesn't have a gun is being shot by somebody.*[13]

The gun thing is getting even more serious in the 1990s. The Coalition To Stop Gun Violence, based in Washington, D.C., cites these facts:

1. Guns kill their owners and family far more often than criminals. Handguns purchased for home protection are 43 times more likely to be used to kill the owner, family member or friend than it is to be fired in self-defense.
2. More than 24,000 Americans die from handgun violence each year. Handguns kill the same number of Americans every two years as were killed in the entire Vietnam War.
3. More than 135,000 students carry handguns to school every day and another 270,000 have carried a gun to school at least once.
4. The sale of dangerous assault weapons is on the rise, weapons which are ten times more likely to be used in crime than other firearms.
5. In Stockton, California, a lone gunman murdered five schoolchildren and injured 30 others and a teacher with an AK-47 in less than two minutes.
6. Gun dealers are virtually unregulated. Anyone who sends in $30 to the U.S. Bureau of Alcohol, Tobacco and Firearms can obtain a three-year license for selling guns, often a violation of local law.
7. America is the world's most violent nation. The chance that you will be gunned down in America is 55 times higher than if you lived in Great Britain, which has a virtual ban on handgun sales.[14]

A recent study by the University of Maryland shows that a handgun control law in Washington, D.C., which went into effect in 1976, reduced the average monthly deaths from gunfire by 25 percent. The law affected both suicides and homicides by prohibiting the purchase, sale and possession of handguns by civilians, although residents who owned guns when the law became effective were allowed to register and keep them.[15]

The National Rifle Association characterized this report as "pure science fiction," a reaction which was not unexpected. In 1987, firearms accounted for nearly 33,000 deaths in the U.S.—18,000 suicides and 12,665 homicides. Captured as the Congress is by the NRA, the prospect for fully effective gun control legislation is dismal.[16] However, when congressmen no longer stand for reelection and when giving anything of value to a senator or representative is a felony, the National Rifle Association will itself be appropriately disarmed.

Robert A. Goldwin argues that the Second Amendment, the right to bear arms, is not a barrier to gun control legislation. A resident scholar in constitutional studies at the American Enterprise Institute, he claims that the right to bear arms protected in the Second Amendment has to do directly with "a well-regulated militia." The Militia Act of 1792 said, "Every free able-bodied white male citizen" was required by the act to "enroll" in the militia for training and active service in case of need. When reporting for service, every man was required to provide a prescribed rifle or musket, and ammunition. This is the link between private and public aspects of bearing arms. The expectation was that every man would have his own firearms. But the aspect that was raised to the level of constitutional concern was the *public* interest in those arms. Today, this means that Congress has the constitutional power to enact a Militia Act of 1994, to require every person who owns a gun or aspires to own one to "enroll" in the militia. In plain 1990s English, if you want to own a gun, sign up with the National Guard.

Goldwin further suggests that requiring every gun owner to register with the National Guard would provide the information about gun owners sought by the Brady and Staggers bills, and much more. Standards could be set for purchase and ownership of guns, and penalties could be established. He pointed out that there is no time to dawdle. Americans now own more than 200 million guns, and opinion polls show that Americans want gun control. This Second Amendment remedy is available now.[17]

When the Los Angeles riots began on April 29, 1992, because a jury acquitted four policemen of beating Rodney King, looters seized 4,000 guns from pawn shops and gun stores. Then, hours later, law-abiding citizens swamped gun stores to buy weapons to defend themselves. The *Los Angeles Times* estimated that more than 8,500 people were hit by bullets in Los Angeles County in 1991, or about one an hour, and that was before the rioting began.

A *Wall Street Journal*/NBC News poll in May, 1992 showed that 87 percent of registered voters nationwide favor a seven-day waiting period before the purchase of a handgun.[18] The congress finally passed the Brady bill in November 1993.

Strangely, West Virginia, despite having the highest unemployment rate and the lowest per capita income, had the lowest crime rate in the nation. In a book entitled *Take Back Your Neighborhood*, written by West Virginia Supreme Court of Appeals Chief Justice Richard Neely, the author advocates self-help and neighborhood crime prevention because "regular police are incapable of protecting law-abiding citizens."[19] He demonstrates how a few communities already have organized "community policing…with the same seriousness, professionalism and attention to detail that we now find among our volunteer fire departments. In 1975, there were 4,000,000 uniformed, full-time police officers at the state and local level…and roughly the same number of security guards. By 1988, however, there were 6,000,000 officers and 1.4 million private security guards!"

Private security guards are simply "vigilantes for the rich." Private guards devote over 90 percent of their time to patrolling and crime interdiction: People who are paying for their own protection want to prevent crime in the first place, not apprehend criminals after the fact.

But persons who live in most neighborhoods and can't afford to hire security guards can take back the streets themselves. Community patrol efforts have developed in Washington, D.C., St. Louis, Dallas, Seattle and New York City. In some ways, the inner city community crime patrols that have emerged are organized peer pressure, an attempt to replace social sanction which died in the 1960s as the collapse of the family and the advent of the drug culture changed the folkways of America.

Unarmed but uniformed citizen patrols, exercising when necessary and possible the ancient right of citizen's arrest, could provide the manpower and visibility to take back America's streets. Chief Justice Neely does not pretend his recommendations will serve as a panacea but he presents a detailed examination of the volunteer approach to crime control. He believes this alternative is important because the economy cannot bear the tax increases that would be needed to put regular police in every neighborhood in the country.

Patrick B. McGuigan, chief editorial writer for *The Oklahoman*, hails Neely's book as "a ray of light, a practical, hopeful look at a 'new' idea as old as the medieval 'hue and cry'—a call for average citizens to accept personal responsibility for the peace in our streets."[20]

But then the question arises, how do you punish criminals once they are apprehended? A new study by the National Center for Policy Analysis, reported in December, 1992, said one of the main reasons crime is so rampant in the United States is criminals can expect little if any punishment. By averaging sentences of criminals who go to prison with those who don't, Texas A&M economist Morgan Reynolds found the "expected punishment" is only 23 days for robbery, 125 days for rape, 4.8 days for burglary, 1.8 years for murder and 1.5 days for auto theft. "From the criminal's point of view, crime definitely pays," Reynolds concludes. "If you expect to spend only a day and a half in prison for stealing a car, you have to ask whether the car is worth a day and a half of your time. Potential criminals compare the cost of crime with the benefits. When the cost goes down, there is more crime."[21]

Chapter Nine

Expand Employment Opportunities: Reduce Dependence on Welfare

Our principal worriment in this country is our unemployed, and it's the only problem I see we have in this country. But if it's any consolation to the unemployed, I've been in countries where our unemployed would be arrested for being Capitalists!

—*Will Rogers*[1]

While everyone in the former Soviet Union under the communist system had a job, the workers used to say, "We pretend to work and they pretend to pay us." This was a complaint about the lack of goods in the stores. The people had the rubles but there was little to buy with their money. Today, of course, Russia and the other Independent States are having great difficulty converting to a free market system.

In the U.S., the prospect of getting rich in our free enterprise system has provided strong incentives to entrepreneurs to produce the goods and services people need and want. In fact, this system cannot sell all of the products it manufactures and imports. During the recession in 1991, employers such as General Motors, General Electric, Bridgestone/Firestone and Pratt & Whitney offered early retirement to blue-collar workers. This is an indication of a future problem as well as one brought on by the economic downturn. Automation, computers, robotics and other technical innovations mean that fewer and fewer people, particularly the unskilled, will be needed to produce the goods and services Americans need and want. Today's jobs require the education to carry out technical and sophisticated tasks, for which adequate salaries are paid. But service work which may be learned quickly on the job generally pays only minimum wages set by the government, locking the unskilled into poverty-level jobs.[2]

With the elimination of the income tax, the economy would be restored to full productivity, absorbing the unemployed who have the skills necessary to produce modern goods and services. But this will not solve the problem of the under-educated who have no skills to sell. Millions will still be dependent on government welfare programs. At least fifty-eight years ago, Will Rogers had an idea about how the welfare system ought to work:

> *If you could in no way find a job, you could go to some State or National, or City or County Public work, that would give you say four hours a day work, instead of the usual eight. You wouldn't be accepting Charity. But you would be doing honest work for it, until you could get employment in some line that was not public work, and at a regular wage. It wouldn't cheapen labor; it would only cheapen Public works, the thing that belongs to all the people, and the thing they would like to have cheapened. But it would be an Insurance against not having anything to do. It might not be a great plan, but it will DAM sure beat the one we got now.*[3]

This approach parallels President Clinton's proposed program for stimulating the economy by creating jobs with federal money. It also echoes Marvin Olasky's observation that "when financial aid is given in a way that makes the poor lose all initiative to help themselves, it can produce pauperization. Nothing creates pauperism so rapidly as giving relief to persons without requiring them to earn what they receive by some kind of honest labor." With the growth of government, the 19th-century charity worker gave way to the 20th-century "social worker," armed with a portfolio of abstract social causes and attached to the taxing power of the state. Indiscriminate bureaucratic giving replaced the old effort to save individuals. As Mr. Olasky puts it: "Bad charity drives out the good."[4]

On January 7, 1992, Senator David Boren (D-OK) proposed a sweeping national plan to put welfare recipients to work. His idea, adopting Will Rogers' philosophy, was patterned after the Works Progress Administration (WPA) and the Civilian Conservation Corps (CCC) which operated during the Great Depression of the 1930s.

"It is high time we changed our welfare system to give people a chance to work instead of simply giving them handouts," Boren said. "I think most Americans would be shocked to learn that we spent over $210 billion last year [1991] on welfare programs, almost 4 percent of our total GNP [Gross National Product].

"The current welfare system is a complete failure. No one doubts it. Both taxpayers and the welfare recipients are victimized by the current system." Boren said his program would exempt the disabled and mothers with children under 3 years old.

He noted that nearly 40 million Americans are receiving some kind of public assistance. About 8 million get unemployment benefits. In Oklahoma, DHS spokeswoman Pam Williams said the state's program to train welfare recipients for work got nearly 6,000 people off the welfare rolls in fiscal year 1991.

Boren would create within the U.S. Commerce Department the "Community Works Progress Administration." Those without jobs could work for the state or cities in construction and maintenance programs, in parks and law enforcement. There would also be two youth divisions. Beginning in the seventh grade, students could work up to 200 hours per year and earn up to $10,000 in college vouchers, or take $3,300 in cash. The second youth division would cover people ages 18 to 22 who could earn another $10,000 for college. Other incentives would help school dropouts work in such a program while earning a GED (high school diploma equivalent).[5]

Senator Boren's plan for a return to the WPA and the CCC has built-in limitations. Many of those receiving welfare are not able-bodied people, free to take a job in public service. Assuming Oklahoma welfare rolls are typical, most of American welfare dollars are distributed to families with dependent children. The money in Oklahoma is divided this way:

Recipients	Average Monthly Supplement
30,867 elderly	$47.25
662 blind	$57.49
29,545 disabled	$57.18
37,000 families with 82,000 children on AFDC	$284.37

Nationwide in 1992, there were 4.6 million families on AFDC, each receiving monthly payments averaging almost $400.[6] Many of the families on Aid to Families with Dependent Children (AFDC) have only one parent in the home, making it difficult for that parent to accept a job outside the home. To do so would require the use of government-subsidized day care for children.

In addition to cash subsidies, AFDC families in Oklahoma get an average of $150 in food stamps and $225 in Medicaid services each month, which means Oklahoma taxpayers provide $660 per month or almost $8,000 per year to support each of 37,000 families, a total of $296 million a year, or 80 percent of the welfare department's direct payment expenditures.[7]

What's more, this group of welfare-dependent people is growing rapidly. In 1991, the Oklahoma Department of Human Services (DHS) closed 1,500 AFDC cases but opened up 31,583 new AFDC cases. These figures reflected not only the lack of employment for the under-educated during the recession but point up the changing lifestyle of the young poor who can create families a lot faster than they can learn to support them.

Louis W. Sullivan, Secretary of Health and Human Services in Washington, D.C. during the Bush Administration, gave a speech to the Council on Families in America in January, 1992, in which he identified "male absence from family life" as the greatest challenge of our generation. One-third of the nation's children live apart from one biological parent and 60 percent will spend part of their childhood in a single-parent household.

"These children," the secretary said, "are five times more likely to be poor and twice as likely to drop out of school as those from intact families. Approximately 70 percent of juveniles in long-term correctional facilities did not live with their father growing up."

Almost every vexing social problem is related to family dissolution. Fully one-third of all female-headed families are in poverty. Their children are far more likely to fail academically, commit crimes, use drugs and become sexually active at an early age. What AFDC has done for the underclass, no-fault divorce is doing for the middle class. Nearly two-thirds of today's marriages will end in divorce or separation. According to columnist Don Feder, "To avoid social chaos, we must engender responsibility. Men must be made to want to marry the mothers of their children and not cast off their families. This will require nothing less than a total reorientation of current governmental policy and societal attitudes."[8]

Wisconsin has launched an effort to cut massive AFDC costs while increasing the beneficial results. Governor Tommy Thompson wants to recreate the family unit in impoverished areas by removing from welfare rules the disincentives to marriage. He says, "Our first task is to rebuild the system on a basis that encourages people to find work, and to re-establish two-parent, self-sufficient families as the norm, not the exception, in poor neighborhoods."

Under the system in Oklahoma and most other states, an unemployed man will actually make the mother of his child worse off if he marries her because both would then become ineligible for welfare. The Wisconsin plan would allow young married couples to continue to receive limited welfare, but they would be required to enter educational, parenting and work-training programs.[9]

In Oklahoma, similar changes, including a possible two or three year time limit on AFDC, are being considered. The concept is to encourage welfare mothers to get a job and supplement their income with welfare so that going back on total welfare would not pay more than working.[10]

Medicaid in Oklahoma is a growing item in the DHS budget, whose director is once more asking the legislature for a supplemental appropriation, another bailout. In a state of three million people, 426,119 received payments for physician services, 153,931 received psychiatric and/or hospital services, 212,000 were granted prescription drugs and 28,000 received nursing home care.[11]

The tremendous cost of these benefits is the result of this combination:

1. The poor get sick more often because they don't or can't organize their lives to avoid preventable illness. Often, putting food on the table has a higher priority than taking one of the kids to the doctor.
2. The cost of health services is galloping ahead of the general cost of living.
3. Eligibility rules for welfare benefits are loose, and
4. Exotic medical procedures are approved for taxpayer funding.

The Boren workfare plan will not reduce the cost of welfare. Only better economic times, improved training and education, as well as a major change in the social values and lifestyles of the poor will effect such reductions. These are long-term efforts calling for key policy changes by the Congress and by state legislatures. But workfare could reduce the cost of the public works the country needs and help restore the work ethic and pride of those now on welfare who are able to work.

California has such a high level of welfare aid (maximum: $663 a month) that people come from other states to take advantage of it. In December, 1991, there were 2.2 million people on welfare compared to about 1.5 million less than three years previously. Governor Pete Wilson proposed cutting welfare 25 percent and using the state's resources to improve education. Bill Jones, the Republican leader of the California State Assembly thought Governor Wilson's plan "a good idea." He said, "The concept is sound because we're looking at trying to move people off welfare and still allow the program to do what it's supposed to do—be a place for transition, either for immigrants or for those who are out of work."[11,12]

As the economy recovers and the deficit is brought under control, the federal and state governments should use the money saved as a result of declining welfare expenditures to increase job opportunities for the hard-core unemployed in programs like those proposed by Senator Boren. The country's deteriorating infra-structure, i.e., roads, bridges, sewerage systems, etc., could be improved as a recently-passed piece of legislation provides. Jobs in this program should go first to those on the welfare rolls, so the net increase in government expenditures would be minimal.

But to expect government to do it all is not realistic. An editorial which appeared in *First Things* in April 1992, a monthly publication of the New York-based Institute on Religion and Public Life, declared, "The efforts required to reconstruct inner cities lie outside the competence of government. For the most part, the only available institutions for taking the lead are churches."

This editorial pointed out that a bloated and bureaucratic welfare system, spending $184 billion a year, has only exacerbated the problems of poverty. "Black and Hispanic churches may seem like a very slim reed on which to lean, and they are that...However, a growing number of inner-city clergy are preaching a different message; they call upon their people to take moral charge of their own lives.

"Policy changes are required to empower poor people to break out of dependency. Genuine reform requires a careful rethinking of attitudes and policies across the board. Peter F. Drucker urges that the time has long since come to recognize that 'government has proved itself incompetent at solving social problems. The answer is to look to the voluntary organizations. There are now some 90 million people—one out of every two adults—working as volunteers in nonprofits for an average of three hours a week.'"[13]

Bill Clinton, campaigning for president, promised to "end welfare as we know it." His idea was to "provide people with the education, training, job placement assistance and child care they need for two years—so they can break the cycle of dependency. After two years, those who can work will be required to go to work, either in the private sector or in meaningful community service jobs." Whether or not President Clinton can effect such change in the cumbersome, bureaucratic system now in place may depend entirely on the availability of tax money to finance it, hemmed in as he is by the public cry to reduce the federal budget deficit.

Irving Kristol, writing in *The Wall Street Journal* on Flag Day, 1993, said, "What conservatives ought to seek, first of all, is a welfare state consistent with the basic moral principles of our civilization and the basic political principles of our nation...This means we ought to figure out what we want before we calculate what we can afford, not the reverse, which is the normal conservative predisposition."

He went on to say that the problem with our current welfare programs is not that they are costly—which they are—but that they have such perverse consequences for the people they are supposed to benefit. The emergence of a growing and self-perpetuating "underclass" that makes our cities close to uninhabitable is a demonstrable consequence of the present, liberal-inspired welfare system. The system breeds social pathologies—crime, juvenile delinquency, illegitimacy, drug addiction and alcoholism, along with the destruction of a once functional public school system. He called Mr. Clinton's neo-liberal response, "two years and out," a fantasy which will not happen. He said the general rule has to be: If it is your own behavior that could land you on welfare, then you don't get it, or you get very little of it.

Mr. Kristol said the key to a conservative reform would be (a) to discourage young women from having an illegitimate child in the first place, and (b) discriminate between "welfare mothers" and "mothers on welfare." He emphasized that such discrimination must have a clear moral basis.

"Mothers on welfare" includes married women with children who have been divorced or widowed or abandoned by their husbands. For the most part, they have middle-class aspirations, subscribe to "family values," and create no intergenerational class of welfare dependents. They are not a problem population and deserve our generous assistance as well as our sympathy.

"Welfare mothers," on the other hand, usually end up on welfare as a result of their own actions. Young girls permit themselves to get pregnant, and to bear a child, because the prospect of going on welfare does not frighten them. Welfare permits them to leave homes that are often squalid or worse. It provides them with support, in cash and in kind (food stamps, housing allowances, Medicaid), that is in many ways superior to what they could earn working at the minimum wage.

Mr. Kristol said these girls should be made to look upon welfare not as an opportunity, but as a frightening possibility. They should receive no housing allowance; living with your child in your parents' home is a lot less alluring than having your own apartment. Only the child should be eligible for food stamps and Medicaid—not the mother. The net effect would be to reduce the mother's income by 30 percent to 50 percent.

In addition, able-bodied men and mentally healthy men would have no entitlement whatever to welfare. If necessary, they would have to rely on private charities.

A "phasing out" procedure would have to be invented but, Kristol argues, it is crueler to entice people into the blind alley of welfare, where their very humanity is dissipated and degraded, than to sternly warn them off.

A conservative welfare state should express conservative moral values, just as a liberal welfare state tries to impose liberal moral values on us. It should discriminate in favor of satisfactory human results, not humane intentions.[14]

Chapter Ten

Control Legal and Illegal immigration into the United States

Any cause is a lost cause without a reduction in population.

—*Negative Population Growth, Inc.*[1]

Will Rogers was silent about the population explosion because at the time he was writing, during the twenties and thirties, the population of America was about 125 million, half of the quarter of a billion people in the United States today. Nobody thought about a possible population explosion and its effect on the environment back then. There was plenty of space for everybody.

You would expect any group advocating Negative Population Growth to make a blanket statement like the one above. But other thoughtful observers now concur:

The environment is the first and most obvious casualty of the population explosion. I wouldn't want to say that God wills it this way, but in one way or another, it will be limited—there's no doubt about that. I remember visiting Riding Mountain National Park in Manitoba. The great elk herd there, I was told, (then) numbered four or five thousand. Previously, it was much larger and then came one bad winter and three-quarters of them died. The herd got down to two thousand and was gradually building up again. I think the same forces will operate on the human population as well.

We have an opportunity that no other species has: to

try to plan and manage the relationship between our species and the planet in such a way as to maximize the opportunities, not only for ourselves but for future generations and for other species as well. In fact, we are the only advocates that other species have. Somehow a religious ethic that is focused at that point...that's not answering any specific issue or taking any policy stance.[2]

This is the view of the Reverend Max Gaebler, a long-time, now-retired Unitarian Clergyman. Another minister in the same denomination, Reverend Richard Allen, echoed his sentiments:

As for the world, my real concern is population explosion. All the problems we have come down to that. We're cutting down forests, not because corporations are so greedy and they like to grind them up; it's because there are more people and they need houses. The environmental problem is a crucial one we are facing and we're not going to solve it by the direct approach as long as we are making more people on the earth.

I think there is an awareness of this among Unitarians but I'm not sure it's strong enough. Population is the problem which is the aggravant in every other problem we have.[3]

Ordinary folks, not just the one-issue zealots, are slowly becoming interested, despite the traditional enthusiasm for growth of all kinds in America. People interested in population control tend to coalesce into groups such as Zero Population Growth (ZPG), the Environmental Defense Fund, the Population Institute, Negative Population Growth, and dozens of others. Their message:

Failure to curb the rate of world population growth will magnify the deterioration of the environment and undermine economic and social progress.[4]

Zero Population Growth cites these frightening statistics:

In the seconds it takes you to read this sentence, 24 people will be added to the Earth's population. Before you go to bed two nights from now, the net growth in human numbers will be enough to fill a city the size of San Francisco.

- *It took four million years for humanity to reach the*

2 billion mark. Only 30 years to add a third billion. And now we're increasing by 95 million every single year.

- *Globally, over one billion people suffer from malnutrition*—with 14 million children under the age of five dying each year.
- *Hunger and overpopulation are inextricably linked in places like Africa, where devastating drought—combined with the fastest population growth in all of human history—has led to widespread famine. In Mexico City, now the world's most populous city, 40 percent of its 22 million inhabitants are forced to live in slums.*
- *Both Mexico and Central America, already facing unemployment rates as high as 50 percent, can expect tripling of their labor force in less than 50 years.*

ZPG says that other, equally ominous danger signals of overpopulation exist right here in America's backyard:

- *In Los Angeles and Phoenix, air pollution abounds and water supplies are dangerously scarce; in the Florida Everglades, human competition for water and habitat has evicted or destroyed a disturbing number of native wildlife species, including the endangered Florida panther and the peregrine falcon; and on Chesapeake Bay, overdevelopment contaminates water quality and degrades Shoreline ecology.*

Other early warning signs cited by ZPG are:

- *Drinking water poisoned by excessive and poorly processed toxic wastes.*
- *Vital topsoil and farmland lost to development of shopping centers, highways and subdivisions at the alarming pace of one million acres per year.*
- *Rapid dwindling of American wildlife, including the grizzly bear, California condor, sea otter. If population demands necessitate continued cutting of the planet's tropical forests, at least a quarter of all wildlife species could disappear within the next fifty years.*

- *With an annual growth rate over 1 percent, the United States is adding well over 2 million people yearly—making us the fourth most populous nation.*[5]

The National Academy of Sciences calls population growth "the biggest single driver of atmospheric pollution."

The population of the world, now 5.5 billion, is growing by 95 million per year, and, if current trends continue, could triple to 14 billion by the latter half of the 21st Century. While the industrial nations' population will grow about 60 percent to almost 1.35 billion by 2025, their share of the world's population will shrink from 33 to 16 percent, as third-world numbers explode to 7.15 billion.

Half of the world's population depends on wood to heat their homes and cook their food. Scarcity of wood already affects 1.3 billion people and that number could more than double during this decade."[6]

Animal experiments as well as observation of human groups have proven that as the protein level in the diet increases, the fertility rate decreases. Apparently, Mother Nature increases fertility in direct proportion to the threat of starvation. This is not unlike the harsh winter in Canada which decimated the elk population so the remaining elk would have enough to eat and the species would survive.

The developed countries should assist overpopulated countries to feed themselves by expanding their own agricultural production, thus contributing to the natural decline in the birth rate. This would also be a defensive measure for developed countries. Many people in less developed countries see immigration into one of the industrial nations as a quick solution to their economic problems.

Of course, as the first Unitarian clergyman suggested, perhaps natural events—starvation and war in Africa and elsewhere around the world and the AIDS epidemic everywhere will dampen the rate of population increase. Thus far, however, these occurrences have failed to slow the current population trend. Besides, depending on these inhumane forces is neither a compassionate nor a scientific approach to the problem. Even before such hardly benign neglect could mitigate the population problem it appears the momentum for growth could make our planetary environment uninhabitable.

So, what to do?

Lindsey Grant says we must "reconcile Texas and Berkeley," meaning addressing population growth and arriving at the concept of optimum population. Grant uses Texas as "the spiritual home of the viewpoint that 'I am entitled to a great big air-conditioned car, and I have the right to drive it as fast as I want.'" He uses Berkeley (California) as proxy for "believers in alternative life styles, bicycles for transport, and a vegetarian diet so as to feed corn to hungry foreigners rather than American beef cattle. The more we incline toward the 'Texas' view of consumption, the smaller the population the environment can bear."[7]

And how small is that? Negative Population Growth believes that a substantial reduction in U.S. and world population size is the essential precondition to the creation of an economy that will be sustainable indefinitely, in a sound and healthy environment, with an adequate standard of living for all. NPG believes that the optimum (best) population for the United States (now 256 million) is in the range of 100–150 million. That's slimming down to the level when Will Rogers was a popular actor and political commentator or no more than the 150 million folks in the U.S. just after World War II.

How? Through appropriate education, NPG would lower worldwide birth rates voluntarily to the one-child family or the two-child maximum family depending on the circumstances of a particular country. In 1990, the U.S. total fertility rate (1.8 live births per woman) was already slightly below the long-term replacement rate. Since then, NPG reported that American women's fertility had moved back up from 1.8 to 2.0 children. The trend is toward increasing longevity, something no one disagrees with. Thus, immigration is the only practical factor which can be adjusted downward to effect a slow decline in the population of the U.S. Unfortunately, new legislation will sharply increase immigration in the foreseeable future. Taken together, these rates would lead to a population in 2080 between 409 million and 558 million in the United States.

In December, 1992, the Census bureau revised its view of America's future. In the next 58 years, the nation's population is expected to increase by a stunning 50 percent from the current 256 million to 383 million in the year 2050. The Census bureau estimates the average woman will have 2.12 children by the middle of the 21st century. Also it overestimated the ability of the

Immigration and Reform Act of 1986 to restrict illegal immigration. In addition, the 1990 Immigration Act now allows 25 percent more people into the U.S. legally, up to 675,000 a year. Because life expectancy has increased, there is still more pressure on population growth. The report predicts that the average person born in the year 2050 will live 82.1 years. For those born last year, that figure is 76 years.[8]

NPG believes legal immigration should be reduced to an overall ceiling of 150,000 per year, *including all relatives and refugees*. Such a ceiling would bring immigration into rough balance with emigration or out-migration.[9]

No one quite knows how many illegal immigrants slip into the U.S. every year. Paul Harvey estimates this number at 3 million! NPG believes there is no possible reason for allowing illegal immigration to continue and the number of illegal aliens living here (which NPG estimates to be between two and six million) should be reduced to as near zero as possible. As Paul Harvey points out:

> *Our nation is trying to absorb millions of illegal immigrants while increasing numbers of Americans are unemployed. Our nation is suffering an overwhelming negative economic, ecological and social impact.*
>
> *Agents in the front lines see our nation's failure to enforce the Immigration Nationality Act as an open invitation to an influx of the least desirable illegals, many of whom are criminals, convicted felons in their homeland.*
>
> *Further encouraging the invasion are the generous health, education and welfare services that are claimed by illegals—for which you pay. Nationwide 70 percent of refugees are on welfare. If our nation were invaded even by a handful of hostile outsiders with guns, we'd man the ramparts and drive them back into the sea. Instead 3 million outsiders—many of them hostile and armed with fake documents—are intruding on our country every year.*
>
> *The United States is now receiving for permanent resettlement more immigrants and refugees than all of the rest of the world combined.*[10]

Even so, as the Haitian boat-people were turned back from Florida by the Coast Guard, some Americans complained we were violating the spirit of America as a haven for all the distressed and economically deprived people of the world.

To try to hold the population line in the United States, let alone try to reverse the trend and cut the population in half, will be dismissed out-of-hand as totally impossible by many people. But thoughtful people should stop and consider this as a rational goal.

Leon F. Bouvier, in the second of a series of *NPG FORUM* papers, plots the demographic route to optimal population size—how to get there from here. Citing a built-in bias for growth, he said we have been convinced that "Growth is Good."

The fertility rate in America dropped from its baby-boom peak of 3.7 children per family in 1957 to 1.8 in 1972, pointing up the fact that educated, middle class Americans have fewer children. Nevertheless, there is a built-in momentum for growth in any relatively young population. The children of America's baby boomers are now having their children and the population of America continues to grow. A continuation of those demographic trends (that is, fertility of 1.8 and net immigration of 800,000) would yield a population of 346 million in the U.S. by 2050 and 360 million by 2080. And the U.S. population would still be growing at the rate of a million a year. Obviously, this is not an "optimal population." Now, those revised population estimates by the Census bureau show even this high rate of growth to be unrealistically low.

One hundred twenty-eight million more people in a mere 58 years is far too many for the nation to handle, if its quality of life and its infrastructure are to remain at least at current levels, much less improve! Negative Population Growth proposes two scenarios:

The Practical Scenario envisions a maximum of 300 million in the U.S. in 2040, declining to 289 million by 2080. Beyond that year, the population would decline slowly, reaching 'stationarity' at about 120 million some three centuries later. This assumes 1.8 fertility and net migration of 300,000.

The Hard Scenario appeals to people less patient with population growth. Indeed, even 50 million additional people would be hard for our country to absorb. This involves lowering the fertility rate to 1.5 live births per woman, now the rate in Austria, West Germany, Italy and among affluent Americans. Bouvier believes reduction in the U.S. fertility rate could be achieved if government policy encouraged such change. With net migration at 300,000, the nation's population would still grow to 278 million in 2020 before falling to 218 million in 2080.[11]

Certainly, government attention better focused on improving the economy and the educational system in America would go a long way toward preventing the negative environmental effects of over-population. Most importantly, the words on the Statue of Liberty about sending the huddled masses of the world to America no longer apply in these modern times. There are millions of people out there who would like to come to the United States but we can't employ or house the people already in America. The unemployment rate exceeds 6 percent and caring for the homeless is a growing problem.

Recent changes in the immigration laws, long overdue, are finally limiting inflow partially to people who can make a contribution to the economy and quality of life in America, but the gross number of allowable legal immigrants, 675,000, is greatly excessive. We should no longer take in everyone who sees America as a refuge, such as the Cubans, Mexicans, Central Americans, Asians, and other refugees. To be sure, America is a melting pot, but there are too many people in the pot.

Immigration laws should be progressively tightened along the lines of these most recent changes, which emphasize what the immigrant can do for America, not what we can do for the immigrant. The Immigration Act of 1990 was the first comprehensive overhaul of measures governing legal immigration in 25 years. It gives preference to 140,000 workers with 'extraordinary ability' in sciences, arts, education, business or athletics, including managers transferred from overseas affiliates; to advanced degree holders, to skilled and unskilled professionals, to investor immigrants (individuals investing in a new business in the U.S.), and to special immigrants, i.e., church workers, U.S. government employees overseas and others. In addition, temporary visas are available for another 90,000 professionals with bachelor's degrees and internationally known athletes and entertainers.[12]

One problem is that the U.S. is running out of space—witness our national parks, and particularly our cities like New York and Los Angeles. Urban sprawl is everywhere. It is well known that smaller cities tend to have more living space, stable neighborhoods, lower housing prices and lower taxes. Despite its climate, Pittsburgh was a recent winner. Its population is down and its steel industry is gone; it should be a basket case because the common wisdom is that a city must have growth for job opportunities.

Indianapolis, which paid dearly to acquire the United Airlines new maintenance facility still believes that. But Pittsburgh, in May, 1989, had unemployment of only 4.3 percent. Zero Population Growth, Inc. (ZPG) has found that smaller cities tend to have better environmental and living conditions than larger ones, a rather obvious conclusion.[13]

As the economy improves, raising the general standard of living, the birth rate will decline as a built-in effect, but this trend should not be offset by opening wide the portals for immigrants the taxpayers must support.

Slowly, the idea of constraining immigration seems to be gathering some credence in Washington. Doris Meissner, a former immigration official says, "Our refugee policy is totally a creature of the Cold War, and now with that gone the basic moorings of the policy are adrift. We need to take a more comprehensive look at how to protect people where they are and then help provide for their repatriation." Still, the U.S. accepted as many as 142,000 people in 1992 for permanent resettlement as refugees.

Robert DeVecchi, director of the International Resuce Committee, says that in California, where huge numbers of refugees settle, the combination of recession and a general inclination to turn inward now that the Cold War is over makes refugees more of a burden. After a 12-year period during which nearly one million refugees arrived in the U.S., "there is some increasing sentiment in Congress and the administration that it's a bottomless pit and costly."[14]

With the current conflict between Pro-Life and Pro-choice forces raging in the streets around abortion clinics and the action on abortion rights by the Supreme Court plus the prospect of further action on Roe vs. Wade, this subject has become an even greater emotional issue. Religious fundamentalists believe that abortion is wrong; feminists believe that women should have control over their own bodies. Most thinking people understand that bringing an unwanted child into the world is a tragedy.

Hazel T. Baker of Norman, Oklahoma, in a January 11, 1992, letter to the editor of *The Daily Oklahoman*, cited some interesting statistics about the impact of abortion on population growth. Since the mid-1970s, approximately 1.5 million abortions have been obtained each year in this country. Had these women not had abortions, the U.S. would have added 22.5 million babies to its population, more people than in the state of New York.

Using 200 children as an average size school, America would have had to build and supply 112,500 new schools for those additional children. Ms. Baker observed that most states are having great difficulty funding the schools they now have.

In the 1980s, the United States grew by 10.4 percent. Forty percent of that growth came through immigration. Meanwhile, the world's population grew only 2 percent. In contrast, some nations, like China and Thailand are working hard to curb their population. Strangely, in a country known for the love of children, the Italian birthrate has halved in less than 30 years. It is the only Western industrialized nation that is showing an actual drop in population, of about one percent annually. Experts account for this phenomenon as the result of Italy's rapid increase in living standards, the growing emancipation of women, and the waning influence of Catholic doctrine.

An estimated 28 million abortions are performed each year in Third World nations, 26 million in industrial nations. Without these curbs on population growth, the planet's inhabitants would increase by 134 million a year or a billion every 74 years.[15, 16]

In December, 1992, the Food and Drug Administration said that the abortion pill RU-486 could be approved for sale in the United States without further testing if a company steps forward to license and distribute the drug. Clinical trials have already been conducted in Europe. Representative Ron Wyden, (D-Ore.), said this represents a significant change in the government's position on the controversial drug and signals a more receptive political climate since the election.[17]

But prevention of pregnancy may be a more appropriate measure. A New York-based organization called the Association for Voluntary Surgical Contraception claims that half of the women in Developing countries who already have children don't want any more. The AVSC promotes voluntary sterilization as a one-time procedure which is the most economical and effective form of birth control; simple and safe.

The Association informs and educates people, trains physicians and medical personnel, offers technical expertise and sends surgical equipment to family planning clinics in Developing countries. It also researches better and safer medical procedures. Perhaps efforts such as these will mitigate the world-wide population explosion.[18]

Population Communications International, based at the United

Nations Plaza in New York, works with national broadcast systems in Asia, Africa, and Latin-America to motivate viewers/ listeners to small family size by presenting family planning soap operas.[19]

Thus, various volunteer groups are taking imaginative steps to get population growth under better control.

In the 1992 World Summit in Rio de Janeiro, Brazil, agreements were signed to protect endangered species, to save the rain forests, reduce air pollution and to counteract global warming, but strangely the problem of population growth, the root cause of our environmental problems, wasn't even on the agenda!

There is a World Population Conference planned for Cairo, Egypt in 1994. Perhaps this time, delegates will treat the cause instead of the mere symptoms of the over-population crisis, facing squarely the harsh realities about the people-carrying capacity of the planet we share.[20]

As far as the United States's problem is concerned, Daniel James had this observation, "The Battle of the Deficit goes on, with no sign of a letup. But part of the solution lies under our very noses. All Congress need do to cut spending is cut immigration."

Writing in *The Wall Street Journal*, James quoted a new study by Donald L. Huddle, professor emeritus of economics at Rice University, which says immigrants residing in the U.S. cost taxpayers more than $45 billion annually. Huddle also projects that in the 1993–2002 period the "net cost to taxpayers of all immigrants [in the U.S.] will total over $450 billion"—nearly the total of President Clinton's five-year deficit reduction goal. The major costs involve education, Aid to Families with Dependent Children, food stamps, Medicaid, but include 18 other government programs.

In addition there are the costs of high rates of labor displacement. The study estimates that more than two million American workers were displaced by 1992 by the 18 million legal, illegal and amnestied immigrants in this country.

Mr. James recommended that President Clinton call both houses of Congress into special session to freeze all immigration forthwith.[21]

Chapter Eleven

Export American Know-how to Developing countries

When Will Rogers died in 1935, America was in the midst of the Great Depression, so there was not a lot of concern here for the plight of people in foreign countries. The term "Third-World Country" had yet to be coined; President Roosevelt was desperately trying to spend the country out of the Great Depression. The Peace Corps was still decades in the future.

Then, people were flooding into America as the land of opportunity, coming here to search for a better way of life, for a chance at economic freedom. That hasn't changed. America is not only the place for a better economic life, America is the principal haven for the politically oppressed of the world. Now, 59 years after Will Rogers died, America's end of the boat we call Planet Earth is getting overloaded and is in danger of destroying the very way of life which has been created here. It is in danger of being swamped by too many people searching for the good life.

While this may sound like an "us four and no more" attitude, it is obvious that America cannot absorb all of the people from other countries who would like to immigrate. Countries around the world, in all stages of development, must become self-sufficient insofar as possible if they are to become partners in the worldwide trading system. Every country must be able to feed itself and produce something of value which they can trade for something they need or want.

Greece, for example, is a member of the emerging European Common Market, yet it is probably the poorest country in the group. It has almost nothing it can trade. More than half the people are employed by the government; the country's greatest source of income is tourism—people from other countries spending their money to experience this historic land and sail to the Greek Islands of the Aegean. When terrorism depressed the travel business several years ago, Greece was in real trouble because it had little else to trade.

Rather than sending foreign aid in the form of dollars which we do not have, America should send help in the form of agricultural, manufacturing, engineering and business expertise aimed toward the development of free enterprise—ways to produce a broad range of valuable goods attractive in the world marketplace. Countries as ancient and as culturally advanced as Greece might consider this kind of help insulting, but less developed countries, such as Bangladesh, Mali, Haiti and Somalia might welcome the idea. Certainly, in its shift from communism to a free market system, the Commonwealth of Independent States, the former Soviet Union, needs all the help it can get.

Such an organized service would be a practical expansion of the Peace Corps idea, and could be sponsored by private companies and organizations which, in cooperation with both governments, could help these countries meet the goal of self-sufficiency.

Many of the experts coming out of the armed forces who have technical skills could become the teachers the less developed countries need. For example, Army Medical Corps people could teach the people of these countries basic sanitary methods and preventive health care. As Benjamin Disraeli, the Earl of Beaconsfield, said in 1877:

> *The health of the people is really the foundation upon which all their happiness and all their powers as a State depend.*

Experienced armed forces personnel are well schooled in their specialties, have traveled extensively, are adaptable and are less likely to be unsympathetic with the plight of people in other, less developed countries. Retired military officers could afford to provide such services because their entitlements would support them during the process.

Of the 250,000 men and women scheduled to leave the Army by 1995, 20 percent are officers, of whom 99 percent have baccalaureate degrees. At the rank of major and above, 80 percent have either master's degrees or doctorates. Many have taught full time at one of the military academies or served on the faculty of the U.S. Army Command and General Staff College, the National War College, or one of the Army Branch Schools. This does not mean that all they can teach is military science. The Army often exists under primitive conditions not unlike those in underdeveloped countries and must have skills in sanitation, transportation, food service, water supplies, housing, administration; skills which may be lacking in less developed areas of the world.

The concept of utilizing Army veterans as teachers in the nation's schools was advanced by Patricia Hines, a deputy assistant secretary for training and education, Department of the Army. She said the Army is "strongly encouraging these men and women to consider teaching as their new career." With half a million men and women moving from the armed forces into civilian life over the next five years, the pool of talent should be ample also to provide needed know-how to less developed countries.[1]

This expanded effort would be more effective than sending dollars to be mismanaged by the governments or lost in the political systems of the recipient countries. Also, Americans are currently less interested in helping people of other countries than in easing the plight of the unemployed and the under-educated in America. Yet official U.S. policy permits hundreds of thousands of immigrants to add to this domestic problem.

It seems patently obvious that exporting American know-how would be better than trying to solve the economic and political problems of refugees by allowing them entry into the United States. Our overly generous policy of providing a political haven for any immigrant who knows the magic word "asylum" and the cumbersome system of determining whether or not they were actually persecuted in their country of origin, has led to a great increase of illegals who never show up for the court hearing on their immigration status. A 1993 example of this growing problem was the tide of boat people from China, who are smuggled in by criminals charging $25,000 to $40,000 for their passage. The U.S. Immigration and Naturalization Service intercepted and turned back boats carrying 4,300 in the past two years. There is no way of telling how many Chinese illegals slipped into the country.[2]

Also, promoting trade between countries of similar economic and social development levels would be more practical than trying to bring third-world countries into the world-wide trading system all at once. With our help, people in third-world countries can gradually improve their lives *where they live*.

America has been a leader for a long time and should continue to set the example for the world. Lately, however, we are increasingly less able to handle our own problems. In the "New World Order," America must be solvent, prosperous, and capable before it can expect other countries to emulate our democratic, free-enterprise practices.

These American ideas are becoming more theoretical than actual. Voting privileges are so taken for granted that many Americans don't bother to register their opinion in the voting booth. More and more, we have government by lobby and special interest group. "Free" enterprise is increasingly hamstrung by excessive government regulation. Our changing, complicated tax code is only one example. OSHA and EPA requirements are often excessive and expensive.

Ironically, as the former Soviet Union pulls away from communism, America trends more and more toward socialism, depending on and expecting ever increasing services from a government which is less and less able to deliver.

We Americans should demand less of our government and more of ourselves.

Chapter Twelve

Reevaluate Environmental Protection Agency Programs: Balance Short and Long Term Benefits with People and Animal Concerns

> *You know, we're always talking about pioneers and what great folks the pioneers were. Well, I think if we stopped and looked history in the face, the pioneer wasn't a thing in the world but a guy that wanted something for nothing. He was a guy that wanted to live off everything nature had done. He wanted to cut a tree down that didn't cost him anything, but he never did plant one. He wanted to plow up the land that should have been left to grass. We are just now learning that we can rob from nature the same way we can rob from an individual. That pioneer thought he was living off nature, but it was really future generations he was living off of.*
>
> —*Will Rogers*[1]

As Max Gaebler, the retired Unitarian minister, pointed out in Chapter Ten, "The environment is the first and most obvious casualty of the population explosion." In this view, too many people is the root cause of environmental deterioration and until the current trend of population growth can be turned around, perhaps by the middle of the 21st century, America must reach some practical compromises. We must do the best we can to accommodate more people without causing America to become a vast, continuous wasteland. Somehow, as the song says, we've got to quit "paving the world and making a parking lot."

It's hard to know *what* to believe these days. According to Columnist Paul Harvey, in 1991, Carl Sagan, the astronomer, predicted that Kuwait's burning oil fields would trigger a "petroleum autumn," cooling the Earth, but this did not happen. We have been warned about acid rain, loss of the ozone layer, global warming, and other dire events over which the individual has little control and must depend on scientists to measure and governments to act. In order to get their point across to a sometimes indifferent public, single issue zealots often tend to exaggerate the danger we face.[2]

What we do know is that vast sums of our tax money have been spent to postpone the demise of endangered species of animals. In 1975, the construction of the Tellico Dam on the TVA system was halted after $50 million had been spent because it endangered the snail darter, a three-inch, snail-eating fish. This finny fellow was first observed in 1973, six years after Tellico construction had begun.

After a suit to halt dam construction went all the way up to the Supreme Court, which ruled for the snail darter, an exception was made for the completion of the half-finished dam, the snail darter was found to exist in other rivers, its status was downgraded to "threatened," and after completion, the $100 million Tellico Dam turned out not to be the expected economic dynamo predicted by its supporters.[3]

The lesson here seems to be that both the environmentalists and the developers can be far off the mark, wasting a lot of money in trying to accomplish dubious ends. This is the reason *practical* compromises are a must.

Species come and species go; it has been ever thus. Apparently, environmentalists spend more government (read: taxpayer) money to save the higher species, such as the northern spotted owl ($9.7 million), the grizzly bear ($5.9 million), and the Least Bell's vireo ($9.2 million). When it came to saving the lowly eastern beach tiger beetle, they could come up with only $500.[4]

After listing a species, the Fish and Wildlife Service develops a "recovery plan." It has approved 364 such plans at a cost of $4.6 billion, compared with its annual budget for such activities of $10.6 million. All state and federal budgets for the preservation of all endangered species add up to only $102 million, so the effort is either totally overly-ambitious or desperately under-funded.[5]

As Susanne Winckler points out, there's a better way to get more ecological bang for the buck. She says, "If our goal is to preserve as many kinds of plants and animals as possible, it makes little sense to spend limited funds on heroic steps to rescue a handful of near-extinct species. A more effective strategy would focus on protecting ecosystems that support maximum biological diversity."[6]

Thomas Palmer, a naturalist, argues the case for human beings. He believes apprehension about the disappearance of animal or plant species may be misplaced, and may arise out of a mistaken and Shortsighted view of the evolutionary process. Students of evolution have shown that species death, or extinction, is going on all the time, and that it is an essential feature of life history. But what alarms so many life historians is extinctions are occurring at a greater rate than they have at all but a few times in the past, raising the specter of the sort of wholesale die-offs that ended the reign of the dinosaurs. This raises such questions as: Exactly how much of our planet's resources do we mean to funnel into people-making?

Palmer says that if we believe that all life shares a quality of sensitivity, or self-awareness, then *Homo Sapiens* was an astonishing leap forward in this respect, because human beings manifested an idea of personhood never before achieved. He is concerned that the image of our species as a vast, featureless mob of yahoos mindlessly trampling this planet's most ancient and delicate harmonies portrays the human presence as a sort of monolithic disaster, when in fact *Homo Sapiens* is the crown of creation. "To say that the changes we have brought, and will continue to bring, are somehow alien to the world, and are within half an inch of making its 'natural' continuance impossible, displays some contempt, I think, for the forces at work, along with a large dose of inverted pride."[7] It is thus apparent there are two sides to the ecological story, sides which need to be examined with care. The fight over the fate of the endangered northern spotted owl is typical of the war between environmentalists and those who feel the land is here equally for the benefit of its human inhabitants. The environmentalists, supported by the Endangered Species Act, have "convinced the courts and the federal government to limit logging on millions of acres of land to help save these reclusive birds, which nest in old trees."

Obviously, this effort doesn't set well with the loggers who see their way of life threatened and who feel they themselves are an endangered species. The decline of logging towns has been greatly accelerated by political decisions and court rulings, to the extent that Forks, Washington, area loggers cut a third less timber in 1991 than they did previously. As a result, unemployment is 20 percent and rising, up from 7 percent in 1989 and 10 percent in 1990. Logging began in this area in 1860 and Forks people think of it as "just a big old tree farm. We cut down trees, they grow back. What's the problem?"

The environmentalists look at it differently, probably because of the practice of clear-cutting, which leaves charred areas the size of a dozen football fields stretching across the 300-year-old stand of trees near Hunger Mountain in the Olympic Peninsula rainforest. This practice allows mudslides, which fill trout streams and cause the trout to disappear and also obliterates salmon spawning grounds. About 95 percent of the old growth of trees is now gone.[8]

Is any compromise possible? Scientists are embarking on a $4.6 million study in southern Oregon to see if foresters can cut timber without destroying the habitat of the northern spotted owl. Researchers for the Bureau of Land Management will take detailed measurements of existing stands to determine what makes them attractive to owls, develop logging methods to reproduce those characteristics and develop computer models that can estimate timber yields. All of this will require ten years. Scientists have said the owl needs the protection from predators provided by a forest with various levels of canopy, large trees with cavities for nesting, and downed logs that provide habitat for the rodents the owls feed on. These features are generally found in old-growth forests. The habitat in Northern California, Oregon and Washington supports 450 pairs of spotted owls.[9]

Clear-cutting seems to be the method of logging which devastates the spotted owl habitat and causes other environmental damage such as erosion, mudslides, and muddied streams, to say nothing of the ugly appearance of the cut-over areas. The U.S. Forest Service, organized to protect the national forests for public use, has become the chief agent for the timber industry. According to Perri Knize, there are three parts to what he calls the Great Federal Timber Mythology:

Myth No. 1—Federal timber is needed to meet an ever-escalating demand for wood fiber.

Myth No. 2—Timber sales overall make a profit for the federal treasury.

Myth No. 3—Federal timber, even if sold at a loss, aids timber-dependent communities.

The national forests supply only about 15 percent of the nation's wood, and Forest Service research shows that if that timber were removed from the market, half of the loss would be replaced by wood from private industrial tree farms and half by wood substitutes already on the market. While the Forest Service continues to predict the demand for national forest timber will rise, it has actually declined. "Crop forests are where our timber supply really comes from," a former logging manager at Weyerhauser Corporation said. He explained that the industry wants the old timber in the national forests because with minimal processing these logs bring a premium price overseas.

More than a quarter of the money the Forest Service spends comes from selling timber—whether the sales make money or not. A little known law enacted in 1930 allows the Forest Service to retain virtually all its gross timber receipts in order to fund projects like tree planting. Thus the Service has a perfect *incentive* to over-estimate demand and promote the sale of timber from the national forests. In 1990, this source of funds added $475 million to the Forest Service budget, often the only resource on which the Service can depend to finance many of its non-timber activities such as erosion control, campground improvements, and plant and animal inventory.

It is ironic that the revenue from clear-cutting the forest, causing erosion, is used to control erosion. There is something amiss in this kind of reasoning. But then, as Will Rogers recognized years ago: "The Government has never been accused of being a businessman."[10]

As Knize concludes, "The greatest threat represented by our current national-forest policy is that it will destroy biological diversity on public lands." Knize observed that our old growth forests encompass everything from bacteria, fungi and insects to grizzly bears, wolves and ancient sequoias. "They constitute a complex, interdependent plant and animal kingdom upon which we humans eat and breath. If the Forest Service gets funds for its programs by selling timber, and timber management is destroying the forest for other uses, then we must find a means other than timber to fund the programs."[11]

When candidate Clinton selected Senator Albert Gore to be his running mate during the 1992 campaign, he sent a signal that the environment would be an important consideration during his administration. He also inferred that his vice president would do more than stand in the wings in case the president became incapacitated. It will be interesting to see how Vice President Gore influences the tug-of-war between development and environmental proponents. The country's environmental problems certainly do not stand still nor does the plight of the unemployed.

The least we can do is change Forest Service and EPA directions to stop funding the Forest Service with revenues from timber sales from national forests, cease clear-cutting on these lands, and reorient endangered species activities toward preserving habitat rather than making heroic and expensive efforts to rescue plants and animals which are on the brink of extinction.

The difficult questions of containing industrial pollution, where to spread New York sludge now that it may no longer be poured into the Atlantic Ocean, whether or not to hunt for oil in the Alaska wildlife refuge, how to require better gas mileage to reduce automobile air pollution, what substitutes for fossil fuels can be developed, how to improve the supply of clean water desperately needed by over-crowded, desert areas like California, how to expand the use of clean fuels like natural gas to reduce pollution and dependence on foreign oil, and other sticky environmental problems must be confronted by a Congress which is not beholding to particular interests—either environmental or developmental—so America can get through the next difficult decades.

The key word is *balance*. But balance between environmental and economic interests is difficult to achieve. For example, government wildlife scientists protested a decision by the National Marine Fisheries Service not to require big changes in the way dams on the Snake and Columbia Rivers are operated. The objections of the agency's own biologists were overcome by heavy politicking by pro-dam economic interests. The biologists charged that the dams were the main culprits in the steep drop in salmon populations along the two rivers. It seems the way the dams now operate minces millions of salmon.

environmentalists—and some federal biologists—are highly disturbed. "We think good science had gotten rolled again by powerful political interests, says Charles Ray, head of Idaho Rivers United.[12]

And so the differences of opinion continue. Question: Where was Vice President Al Gore, the environmentalist?

Chapter Thirteen

Reduce Credit Abuses and Bankruptcies

We don't have to worry about anything. No nation in the history of the world was ever sitting as pretty. If we want anything, all we have to do is go and buy it on credit.

—*Will Rogers*[1]

Because in America it's so easy to buy things now and pay for them later, the savings rate has not provided sufficient capital to permit low interest rates for stimulation of business expansion. Another reason interest rates remained relatively high until now is that the United States government, deeply in debt, must live off other people's money so interest rates must be high enough to attract a steady flow of funds. Although in 1992 we saw interest rates come down markedly in order to jump-start the economy out of a recession, this probably won't last as the economy improves and assuming the Congress continues to pile on deficit after deficit. President Bush's budget for fiscal year 1993 proposed to spend $400 billion more than the government receives in taxes. A record deficit of $290 billion was piled up during fiscal year 1992. A record deficit of $290 billion was piled up during fiscal year 1992, falling to $225 billion in 1993. A November, 1993, projection indicates the 1996 deficit may climb to a record $292.5 billion. As Will Rogers once noted:

A debt is just as hard for the government to pay as an individual. No debt ever came due at a good time. Borrowing is the only thing that is handy all the time.[2]

A lot of people get into trouble because they have no reserves, nothing put away for the inevitable rainy day. When it does begin to rain, they go belly up and "take bankruptcy." And since the 1978 revision of the bankruptcy law made it easier to wipe out debts in court, bankruptcies have exploded. In 1992, bankruptcy filings totaled 971,517, of which 900,874 were personal. The remaining 70,643, or 7.3 percent, were corporate bankruptcies.[3]

In November, 1991, when unemployment was rising, people were hanging on to their money and credit counselors were urging people to control their spending, President Bush suggested that issuers of credit cards should lower their interest rates so people would be encouraged to buy more. This was suggested in order to jump-start the economy out of its cyclical stall.[4]

The Senate voted to restrict the 18 to 19 percent credit card rates to 14 percent. This made the stock market nervous because of the possible effect on the banking system and there was a one-day, 120-point plunge in the Dow-Jones Industrial Average. The Congress quickly set that idea aside, vowing to study it for nine months.[5] A few days later, economists declared it wouldn't have stimulated further buying anyhow. While consumers were not buying as much as before, outstanding card balances were rising.[6]

People need two kinds of credit cards. The first one, a special convenience card, which *requires* full payment every month, should be available for current expenses such as meals, gifts, gasoline, etc. Such cards could have a limited credit ceiling reflecting the holder's previous record of purchases and payment. The first time the card-holder missed a full payment, however, the card should be canceled and that fact added to the credit record of its former holder. This would weed out credit card addicts who have no impulse control, tend to buy beyond their means, and are at risk for bankruptcy.

The second card would provide credit extended beyond a month and be available for items which are essential for the card holder's work. It should be for the exclusive purpose of helping an employee hold his or her job, or, if an independent entrepreneur, hang on to his or her business. If an employee needed a better car or a set of tires to get to work, this card could be used or long-term credit could be supplied by a bank. Employed persons who need a washer and dryer so they could be presentable at work would be eligible for extended credit, but could not use that credit to buy a recreational vehicle, a set of golf clubs or a cruise to the Bahamas.

Credit is too easy to get and people seem unable to handle it. There are more credit cards in use (283 million) than there are Americans (256 million). The typical American owes $1,644 in credit card debt, and the average borrower pays about $300 in loan interest each year. Only about 113 million credit card holders pay the entire balance when the monthly bill comes in, thus avoiding any interest.[7]

Not only do credit card issuers want the high interest profits but hard-pressed retailers use credit to lure people into their stores. Sears offers to defer payment for six months to their credit card holders; the only catch is that the interest meter keeps running all that time.

Saks Fifth Avenue enticed shoppers during the 1991 Christmas season with offers of "holiday gift checks" for spending at least $750 on their charge card between November 15 and December 15. These checks provided discounts on subsequent purchases made during February through April, 1992.

The General Electric Company combines credit-limit increases with discount coupons and other deals.[8]

At Christmas in 1992, credit card issuers again bombarded consumers with *incentives* to use their cards for holiday shopping. Mastercard International offered discounts of 10 to 50 percent on items or services purchased through December 31 from 43 merchants. Sears, Roebuck and Company raised credit limits on their store cards by several hundred dollars. Dayton-Hudson sent two certificates that could be used for 10 percent discounts at Marshall Field's, Dayton's or Hudson's stores in the three days after Thanksgiving. The result was that consumers charged holiday gifts at a record rate during November and December, 1992. Mastercard use surged 20 percent and Visa cardholders purchases went up more than 16 percent

To be sure, application of a government-mandated, two card system would strain the economy until people got caught up and saved enough money to purchase those items not essential to their livelihood. On the other hand, relieved of the usurious credit card rates charged by the banks and the threat of bankruptcy, they would have more money to spend and could spend it with a sense of peace and security. What's more, they would avoid the situation Will Rogers talked about:

> *Us middle class...never have to worry about having old furniture to point out to our friends. We buy it on*

payments and before it's paid for it's plenty antique.[9]

In 1991, the national average credit-card interest rate rose to 18.94 percent a year, while banks paid their customers and average of 5.81 percent on one-year certificates of deposit. With this spread of 13.13 percent, the banks made enough so they could sustain losses from those who defaulted and still make a handsome profit, paid for by the honest people who pay their debts.

During the following two years, home mortgage rates, auto loan rates and the prime rate have declined to the lowest level in a decade. As these interest rates declined, interest on credit card debt went down to the 13 to 15 percent range, even down to 9.3 percent for card holders who ordinarily paid off the balance every month, but the rate the banks paid their depositors declined as well, so the bank's profits held up well. It seems that people who use their credit cards for groceries and clothes—the necessities—have the attitude that as long as they can make the minimum payment, they don't care about the interest they are charged. Money-wise people, usually the more affluent, use their credit card as a convenience, pay the bill promptly and in full each month, thus avoiding any interest payment.

It is too easy to go bankrupt and let someone else worry about your debt. This became possible when the Federal Bankruptcy Act of 1978 was passed in the name of consumer rights. Of course, it is clearly unethical for a person who can pay his just debts to declare bankruptcy, because this cheats his creditors.

Chapter 7 of the act permits debtors to wipe out their obligations by turning over their assets, but also specifically exempts certain ones, such as $4,000 in accrued dividends, $7,500 equity in a home, $1,200 in a car, $500 in jewelry and $200 in household items. Chapter 13 of the act requires that debtors show only a regular income to handle a reasonable, three-year payback plan. The court allows a "reasonable" level as low as 1 percent and 10 percent.

The law does not require the debtor to show he has no alternative to bankruptcy and the court even takes away the stigma of taking this drastic step by forbidding the use of the term bankrupt when legally defining a debtor. The debtor does have to pay a lawyer, usually up front, to file the papers, and the bankruptcy goes on his credit record for up to ten years.

Whatever happened to those people who work a lifetime to

pay off a just debt? The values of America have been eroded as a result of easy bankruptcy, courtesy of the federal government. Some people no longer seem to care whether their creditors are paid. For example: a business professor earning $50,000 dollars at Western Maryland College filed for bankruptcy after borrowing $191,000 on credit cards to "support his lifestyle," according to a Visa deposition. Asked in a deposition about the debt buildup, the professor explained, "Hey, it was the Eighties."[10]

No, it is no longer *caveat emptor*. It's the creditor who must watch out. The law should be changed so that debts cannot be sloughed off just by declaring bankruptcy. A debt should be a debt until it's finally paid, or the debtor dies, whichever comes first.

As previously noted, these credit control measures would slow the economy, but if they were gradually instituted during the four year period that the income tax was being eliminated (see Chapter Four), the two measures would offset each other. At the end of the period, the economy would be purged of careless spenders, bankruptcies would decline and savings should increase, providing more capital for investment purposes. When companies suffer losses because people who owe them money have gone bankrupt, these costs are passed on to hard-working people who do pay their bills promptly. Which is hardly the American way of fairness!

James Davidson was not impressed by the improvement in the economy in early 1993. He believes the prior three years were a depression, not a recession, and thinks the economy will decline into a "triple dip" followed by yet a deeper stage. Citing historical evidence, he says "we are now experiencing the end of the ninth great credit cycle since the middle of the 16th Century...The current depression was set in motion by the OPEC shock...Looking across the globe, there is little sign that sustainable recovery is at hand...Debt levels have reached the saturation point in all the leading countries.

"History shows that once nominal growth slows in a heavily indebted economy," Davidson pointed out, "there can be no recovery until the excess debt is eliminated. Political efforts to expand debt do nothing to lift the burden of debt service, which is the cause of slow growth and falling incomes in the first place.

If this is a depression, as I believe, the worst is yet to come.[11]

Columnist Paul Harvey observed that for politicians to encourage "credit card junkies" to spend more money is like urging a drowning man to drink water.[12] Will Rogers had this advice:

> *Don't make the first payment on anything. First payments is what make us think we were prosperous, and the other nineteen is what showed us we were broke.*[13]

Chapter Fourteen

Revitalize the Deteriorating Centers of Our Cities

> *There is just three towns in the whole of America that are different and distinct, New Orleans, San Francisco and San Antonio. They each got something that even the most persistent Chamber of Commerce can't standardize.*
>
> —*Will Rogers*[1]

It would appear that city standardization, with or without the efforts and blessings of the Chamber of Commerce, includes a central business district which is deserted at night and on the weekends and which is surrounded like a dirty moat by a ring of urban deterioration. Almost all of the people have escaped to the suburbs.

Will Rogers did not worry about the livability of cities because he lived before the population exceeded 125 million, when many people still worked the farms and made their home there and in small towns; when cities like New York, Washington, Chicago and Los Angeles were pleasant places to visit, even to live in. The Oklahoma humorist died before America became a mobile society during World War II, before the post-war baby boom and the rush to the suburbs, before the government started Urban Renewal in the mid-Sixties and the building bust of the Nineties.

Over the 59 years since Will Rogers and Wiley Post crashed 15 miles from Point Barrow, Alaska, in 1935, it has been the habit of Americans to move out when an area becomes too old, too crowded, too run down or no longer provides employment opportunity. The people moved West in such droves that there is no

"West" left. When a city's housing stock deteriorates, people, particularly young people just starting out, leave the city's decaying nucleus to the poor and move to a different city or to the suburbs. Of course, the poor do not have the money to improve property so without effort and planning, things go from bad to worse.

America can no longer afford to spoil the nest and fly away. Richmond, Virginia, is a typical example of this process. "The threat of the death of downtown has really frightened a lot of people," says Alan Gayle, chief economist of Crestar Bank and longtime Richmond native. Thalhimers, the city's venerable, pre-Civil War department store closed in February, 1992 the last department store downtown. Two years previously, the Miller and Rhoades store closed.

In an effort to revitalize the downtown area, Richmond built the Sixth Street Marketplace in 1985 by spanning a covered bridge across two city blocks with stores on either side. With Thalhimers gone, the cornerstone of the Marketplace had disappeared. The problem is that the people also are disappearing from the central city. Richmond's population is now 203,000, down 10,000 in the past ten years.

While Richmond is not about to become a ghost town, improvements such as an expanding convention center and a new state office building are expected to bring 300 jobs to the city. But these are jobs, not residents, so the business leaders are now trying to attract tourists to the shopping district.[2]

Richmond is just one more city which proves the point that to have a vibrant, thriving downtown there must be people living close in. Manhattan, San Francisco, New Orleans, Chicago, and Santa Fe are prominent among the very few which haven't lost the bustling, 24 hour ambiance of an alive and prospering center, although New Orleans is changing, becoming more and more dependent on tourism.

Oklahoma City is another case in point. After 18,000 people who still work downtown take off for the suburbs, you could aim a shotgun in the middle of any downtown street and never hit a soul or a moving automobile. One visitor from Manhattan had a 7 A.M. meeting at an attorney's office in December, 1990, and as she walked from her downtown hotel to the attorney's office building through the still-dark, deserted streets, she had the feeling she was moving through the "Twilight Zone."

Urban Renewal began in Oklahoma City's central business district in 1965 with an elaborate plan dreamed up by I.M. Pei, the famous architect. This plan included a new convention center called the Myriad and an adjacent, four block park called the Myriad Gardens, fashioned after the Tivoli Gardens in Copenhagen. These were built, along with a theater for live performances, two skyscraper banks, the 19-story McGee Tower in the square-block Kerr-McGee Center, and four large office buildings. A huge shopping galleria was also planned, but it never happened. Meanwhile, the major department stores and specialty shops moved to the suburbs to join the five major shopping malls ringing the city. In 1991, more than a third of the downtown Oklahoma City commercial and office space was vacant. By the first quarter of 1993, the vacancy rate, still 32.2 percent, was the highest in the nation. Close behind were Dallas at 30.2 percent, Tampa at 20.5 percent, Tuscon at 27.6 percent. The national average was 17.2 percent.[3]

Perhaps *not* building a shopping mall in downtown Oklahoma City was a blessing in disguise. Many urban malls, developed to reinvigorate downtowns, proved to be disappointments. Atlanta and San Jose are examples of the couple of dozen malls which sprouted up in the 1980s. Sales have stagnated and many retailers have moved out. It's a tough sell to get people to drive in from cozy suburbs, pay for parking and venture into urban areas with tough reputations. "Most of them would be considered a financial disappointment," says Carl Steidtmann, a Columbus, Ohio, retail consultant.[4]

The critical mistake in the rehabilitation of Oklahoma City's downtown was that only one, 114 unit apartment/condominium complex, Sycamore Square, was built to add to the 273 unit Regency Tower, the only existing modern apartment building.

The planners left the people out!

This does not mean that people do not come downtown for special events such as the annual spring and fall arts festivals, the Fourth of July celebration, the monthly philharmonic and pops concert presentations, traveling stage shows at the Civic Center, Christmas and New Year's Eve festivities, but that is not enough to sustain year-round restaurants and entertainment establishments. With the one exception of Bricktown, a newly refurbished warehouse area, similar to Larimer Square in Denver, just east of the Santa Fe railroad tracks next to downtown, restaurants and nightclubs are on the outer fringes, primarily on the northwest side of the city or in Edmond, a separate town to the north. Currently, Bricktown is expanding as an entertainment center because it fits the description of an "attraction" as described by Thomas J. Black., vice president for research at the Urban Land Institute. "There's definitely a demand in large areas for nighttime entertainment focused around food, drink and music."[5]

In the meantime, the academic, tertiary health campus known as the Oklahoma Health Center was expanding on the near northeast side from a 24-acre area into a 200-acre campus; from three institutions to eleven, from eight buildings to 35, from a group of 920 students in medicine, basic science and nursing to more than 2,500 in the health sciences, adding dentistry, public health, pharmacy and allied health.

In Oklahoma City, the near northeast side has traditionally been the black community, and while many upwardly mobile African Americans were moving out, no white people were moving in. There was an attempt in 1984 to integrate the new, 140-unit apartment complex, Chaparral, just two blocks from the Oklahoma Health Center, but that effort failed. The tradition of separation of the black and white neighborhoods was too strong to expect change. Urban Renewal cleaned out many acres for the health center expansion and tore down hundreds of substandard dwellings in this part of town but few new houses sprouted where the old ones were leveled. Five hundred vacant lots, owned by the Urban Renewal Authority—i.e. the taxpayers—are currently available for residential redevelopement.

An expressway was cut in the corridor between the health center and downtown, know as Harrison-Walnut, and a state science and math high school established there, plus an architect's office in a remodeled and expanded church building, a blood bank, a money bank, and a building for the University credit union. Plans for a research park in Harrison-Walnut may yet materialize, but no one talks about building more houses or apartments in this area, despite the fact that more than 12,500 people work at the health campus and more that 4,000 at the state capitol complex, less than a mile to the north. Tradition dies slowly.[6]

Meanwhile, developers sought large chunks of cheap, accessible land in the direction of affluent growth: northwest. In addition, Edmond, a separate college town about 20 mile north of the city, experienced a residential boom as a result of the flight to the suburbs. Developers eagerly provided the new housing that the people demanded.

While developers in Oklahoma City have to pay back the city for extending water and sewer lines to their projects, there are no real incentives for them to rehabilitate old, worn-out neighborhoods no matter how convenient they may be located to the center of the city. As the residential development has occurred, office and commercial development has followed the people.

So what to do?

A systematic gentrification of our central cities is needed to reclaim the land we have ruined and from which we have retreated. Half a century ago, this happened in Georgetown when the proximity of that old residential area to central Washington, D.C., became too valuable to allow it to deteriorate further. This occurred spontaneously, obeying the law of economics.

Now however, there must be further incentive in addition to historic preservation and like programs. This is the "growth management" concept described by Peter Navarro, who ran for mayor of San Diego in 1992 and lost by a 52 to 48 percent margin. He says growth management involves three steps:

1. Define where development shall not occur, to protect environmentally sensitive lands, provide open space and direct development to areas where it can be most efficiently served by mass transit.
2. Ensure that police, schools and other facilities are built at the same time as the subdivisions, office buildings and industrial parks.
3. Require developers to pay for facilities.

Because San Diego growth was not managed, its tourist industry stagnates, the downtown withers—sucked dry by suburban sprawl and overwhelmed by crime. Businesses flee the area, and traffic, water and other growth-related problems are ignored. In Navarro's opinion, unmanaged growth is a welfare program for land speculators and developers that creates sprawl, fosters an anti-business climate, and enriches a few at the expense of many.[7]

Cities could reverse this trend of suburban flight by requiring that developers rehabilitate as many square feet of land and/or as many residences in the decayed rings just outside of the city-center as they propose to build on the outskirts. Otherwise, no building permits would be granted. This would fully utilize the infrastructure—streets, traffic controls, street lights, fire station, et cetera—already in place. Old water and sewerage systems usually have to be replaced, however.

Could this idea work in Oklahoma City? It hasn't been tried, but it worked in San Francisco, although for a different purpose. A builder who wanted to construct a high-rise office building in the downtown area was required by the city to invest a certain amount in the purchase of land for housing. The new offices would accommodate new jobs and the people who filled those jobs would need a place to live. San Francisco already had a critical mass of people in the center city area.

If the 34,500 people employed in downtown Oklahoma City, at the health center and in the capitol complex had attractive living spaces in the area, the critical mass of humanity required for a thriving city center could be established and the ring of urban decay eventually could be erased.

New housing on already cleared land could be built. The City is proposing to dam the North Canadian River which trickles to the east a few blocks south of the central business district. There is ample land on both banks of what will then be a scenic waterway to establish high rise apartments overlooking both the river and city skyline, just a whipstitch away from the center of downtown. This land is already in the hands of a trust whose objective is to develop the river-front when the dam is built. The plan is to create a "string of pearls" along the river for both residential and recreational purposes.

Between I-40, which bounds the central business district on the south, and the river, there are now old commercial and scattered residential areas where rehabilitation is past due. It is a center devoted primarily to the automobile after-market and loaded with junk cars, acres of parts and other unattractive and deteriorating accumulations. It is an area that has excellent location and could be developed into a highly attractive and convenient residential area, enhancing the periphery of downtown.

In addition, there are other whole neighborhoods which could be re-established close to the city core. There is land east and south of the health center which is clear now or could be cleared inexpensively for new residential neighborhoods. There are neighborhoods crying for attention south and north of the state capitol complex. This sprawling city, now reaching farther and farther out, should implode for the number of years it takes to clean out the decay and bring the people back to the central city. Otherwise, the central business district of Oklahoma City will indeed become a failing heart surrounded by advancing decay.

Moreover, the cost of suburban construction should include all the cost of extending city services, like fire stations, traffic lights, and expanded sewage treatment plants serving the area, placing the burden on the developer and ultimately on the owner or occupant of new, suburban facilities.

Before this title and honor (?) was assumed by Jacksonville, Florida, Oklahoma City was the largest city in the nation by virtue of its 638 square miles within the city limits. The original reason for expanding the city limits so dramatically was to protect the tax base and prevent adjacent small towns from expanding into territory the city wished to claim. The disadvantage, of course, is that providing city services to this sprawling, lightly-populated metropolis continues to be extremely expensive.

Such a rechanneling of costs from the taxpayer to the user would tilt development values toward the center city and accelerate the gentrification process. The marketplace would then work to the advantage rather than to the detriment of the central city.

Some people fear that the density of highly-developed downtowns spawns crime. But Marcia Lowe, senior researcher at the World-Watch Institute, says that population density alone is not in itself a cause of crime or blight, citing Hong Kong, the most densely populated of the world's 100 largest cities, which has the 12th lowest murder rate. Other cities such as Vienna and Stockholm are compactly developed yet have healthful environments and high living standards. Lowe goes on to say the "communities can use further development to their advantage, to fill in under-used space and to free themselves from dependence on cars." Her report suggests cities could accommodate growth needs more effectively by using the huge quantities of under-developed, abandoned or tax-delinquent properties already existing within their boundaries—and not have to bulldoze another square foot of undisturbed land.[8]

A new building in downtown Oklahoma City has just been completed, so located because the Internal Revenue Service is expanding (again) and will lease space to centralize its 700 tax workers. The reason the downtown area was the low bidder for the site is because 700 workers would have required six-and-a-half additional acres for parking space in the suburbs, a requirement not applicable to the center city. But because there is no conveniently available and acceptable living space, these workers still have to commute.

Oklahoma has not had to worry too much about air pollution because, as the song "Oklahoma" sings, "the wind blows freely down the plain." Although the wind still blows, pollution is becoming a problem, recognized by the Environmental Protection Agency if not by the average citizen.

The expressways serving the north and northwest are clogged with bumper-to bumper traffic during the twice-daily rush hours, wasting time and gasoline, as well as contaminating the air we breathe. Oklahoma City is just beginning to face the problem Los Angeles has had for years. It could be mitigated by reducing the miles people must commute each day. What's more, the vacant office space in downtown buildings could be used before more offices are constructed 15 miles from the center of the city.

On December 14, 1993, Oklahoma City voters approved a five-year, one-cent improvements program called Metropolitan Area Projects (MAPS). Included in this $276 million program are: renovation of the Civic Center Music Hall; a new library and learning center; a light rail transit system connecting downtown with a hotel cluster on I-40 five miles to the west; a new, triple A baseball park; a new arena calculated to attract National Basketball Association and National Hockey League teams; and other improvements. In addition, the North Canadian river will be dammed, creating seven miles of pooled water and a downtown canal, similar to San Antonio's, that will run from the new arena through Bricktown to the river, creating a river-walk with restaurants and shops.

The purpose of these improvements is to attract tourist dollars, not to revitalize the center city for Oklahomans who work downtown and might choose to live in if attractive apartments and town housed were available. Perhaps modern housing will be added if the MAPS tourist attractions succeed. But once again, the local people have been left out, perpetuation a deserted central core every evening some special event is not occurring, which is most of the time. Oklahoma City appears to be taking the dubious Richmond route.

Don't we ever learn?

Chapter Fifteen

Control Costs and Expand the Accessibility of Health care Services

> *All Doctors should make enough out of those who are well able to pay to be able to do all work for the poor free. That is one thing that a poor person should never be expected to pay for is medical attention, and not from an organized Charity, but from our best Doctors. But your Doctor bill should be paid like your Income tax, according to what you have. There is nothing that keeps poor people poor as much as paying Doctor bills.*
>
> —*Will Rogers*[1]

During the 1992 presidential campaign, Bill Clinton said that health care costs were out of control and deficits could not be reduced until the system was reformed. He also repeatedly stated that to get the health care system under control and provide health coverage for the 37 million uninsured Americans would cost no additional money because it would all be paid for with the millions of dollars saved by reforming the system. In the economic summit held in Little Rock in December, 1992, the President-elect kept emphasizing this perception. He promised to present a health-care reform plan to the Congress during his first 100 days in office.[2]

He had read the sentiments of the voters accurately because a Harris Survey for *Prevention* magazine indicated three of every four people interviewed favored universal health insurance funded by tax dollars. The voters want their government to do something about the problem and Clinton put health care reform high on his list, right behind job creation and deficit reduction.[3]

After months of closed-door sessions of a 400-person health care reform task force, chaired by Hillary Rodham Clinton, there were rumors that the Clinton "managed competition" plan would not be self-financed by reducing the cost of the health care system, as the Democratic candidate had so strongly declared, but would cost between $30 billion and $150 billion additional dollars. Before the middle of June, 1993, the Congressional Budget Office announced the Clinton plan will cost $270 billion over five years.[4]

A few days later, a top administration health adviser said most of President Clinton's health plan is "pretty much done" and only awaits some decisions by the President.[5] His first announced decision was to wait to disclose his health care plan until the Congress had completed deliberations and passed their version of the Clinton economic plan, a process which took the rest of the summer. If, when and how the health plan can be passed and financed remains a major problem.

American health care today is a curious hybrid of private enterprise and government programs. But it doesn't work for everybody. It costs so much that more than 37 million Americans can't afford to use the system as they should to prevent illness and get early treatment when they do get sick. This is because they lack even basic health insurance. And if they had insurance or the money to pay, medical services aren't available where a lot of Americans live—in ghettos, small towns and rural areas.

In 1990, spending on health care grew 10.5 percent and then consumed 12.2 percent of the GNP, according to the Department of Health and Human Services. Forty-two percent of the $666.2 billion spent was paid by government for Medicare and Medicaid care of the elderly and the poor.[6] In 1992, the health care bill rose to $830 billion.[2] Both inflation and the volume and intensity of services were elements in these increased costs.

According to a study released in December, 1991, by Families USA, the average family would spend 11.7 percent of its income on health care in 1991, a figure that's expected to grow to 16 percent by the end of the decade. This non-profit organization is pushing for health-care reform. Between 1980 and 1991, it said, average family income grew 88 percent but health-care costs rose 147 percent. Overall, the average family paid $4,296 for health care in 1991, up from $1,742 in 1980.

Families in the Northeast pay the most for health care; ranging between $5,321 in Massachusetts and $5,585 in New York state.

But health care is claiming the biggest chunk of the family income in North Dakota—14.1 percent, in Alabama—14 percent, and New York—13.9 percent.[7]

The American health care non-system sort of grew like Topsy. Efforts to develop a national health plan were made long before the Murray-Wagner-Dingell Bill was introduced during the Truman administration. Prepayment in the form of Blue Cross-Blue Shield hospital and medical insurance began in the 1930s, the Hill-Burton Hospital Construction Program started in the late forties and the Medicare/Medicaid programs came about in the mid-1960s. About that same time, the Health Professions Educational Assistance Program began providing federal funds to build colleges to expand the supply of physicians, dentists, nurses, pharmacists and other health manpower.

Now there's no acute Shortage of professional health services. In fact, some believe we have a surplus of doctors, particularly specialists, a major factor in the rise of medical costs. Hillary Clinton is urging that medical schools turn out more family doctors and fewer specialists. Today, the problem is how to pay for health care and how to have those services close to where people live. In addition, so many people lack adequate insurance protection that the problem of access to the system has, in the opinion of the Clinton Administration, reached crisis proportions.

So what should be done? Should the system swing toward more government control and management or should the invisible hand of the marketplace be given free rein to govern the system? There are enthusiastic advocates of each alternative who claim their program is the only logical way to go. Examples:

Some people believe the Canadian health care system, which is controlled by the government, financed by provincial and national taxes as well as individual monthly premiums, and provides "free" services for all Canadians, could also work in the United States. But critics of this system, although it costs only 9 percent of the Canadian GNP, cite long waits for surgical procedures and limits on the total number of procedures as a result of funding constraints and hospital bottlenecks.

There is one positive feature of the Canadian system which deserves mentioning. Canada controls where its physicians practice. For example, if a neurosurgeon wants to practice in Winnipeg and there are already enough neurosurgeons in that city, he is not authorized to set up his practice there. The number and location of doctors are related to the medical needs of the citizens.[8]

In the United States, doctors are no longer in Short supply but they are often not located close to the people who would like convenient medical services. Rural areas and small towns most frequently are so affected. A 1973 survey of Oklahoma physicians and the population they served showed that even then the state had enough doctors; they just weren't located in the small towns and rural areas where a lot of Oklahomans live. The problem was distribution, not numbers. Also, the study revealed that as the supply of physicians in an area increased, the fees they charged went up, which is not the way the free enterprise system is supposed to work. This fact alone leads to the suspicion that health care is not an open market.[9]

The Canadian system would redistribute doctors but, of course, American physicians, operating in what they like to think is a free market, don't want to be told where they may practice.

Despite the lack of frills and some delays in the Canadian system, Canada seems satisfied with it. A couple who moved to Montreal from San Diego said, "I'm surprised how personal the care is. Here you have the feeling you get the same quality care as everybody else. In the U.S., doctors have this look—'pay my fee, and then I'll look after you.'" Canadians are almost universally devoted to universal health insurance. One pollster said, "Canadians' secret nightmare is that their health-care system will change and come to resemble the U.S. system." Canada's system is the second most expensive in the world but in 1990 they spent only $1,991 per capita compared with $2,566 in the U.S. At the Royal Victoria Hospital in Montreal, a quadruple coronary artery bypass costs an average $12,236, including physician fees, compared with and average of $25,439 in a comparable Boston teaching hospital. The chief operating officer at the Royal Vic says, "I don't think the system is perfect. But the system works."[8]

In December, 1992, a survey by *Medical Post*, a trade magazine, showed that few Canadian doctors now "seriously" consider leaving Canada. Sixty-four percent believe that Canada's government-run health system offers a better working climate than the U.S. and 87 percent think that patients get better care in Canada.[10]

In the U.S., despite continuing through fewer nurse Shortages and little improvement in the maldistribution of doctors, medical and hospital services are readily available for those who can pay out of their pocket, those who have government or private insurance and indigents who are eligible for service in charity clinics. The uninsured and the near poor, as well as those with catastrophic or chronic illness, are in real financial trouble. However, people are not dying in the streets for lack of acute medical help, available at urban hospital emergency rooms.

Regina E. Herzlinger, a professor at the Harvard Business School, strongly insists that private enterprise can best improve the American health care system. She says that "the national-health insurance prescription could be deadly, saddling the economy with billions of dollars more in taxes while endangering the world-class research, free choice, and abundance of top-quality providers that are the hallmarks of our system." She suggests that "Competition had never been attempted in the health care industry. A competitive market requires many buyers and sellers, who freely interact to reach an equilibrium level of prices, costs and quality. The hospital market has none of these characteristics." She claims that hospitals are at the root of the problem, in 1988 accounting for 39 percent of all health expenditures—more than doctors, nursing homes, drugs and home healthcare combined. Two years later, in 1990, hospitals were absorbing 46 percent of the health care dollar.[11]

Since the mid-1980s hospitals have mounted vigorous advertising campaigns, characteristic of a free market, but this apparent competition certainly has not caused a slowing of hospital costs. One reason is that many procedures are now being done on an out-patient or day-surgery basis, reducing the demand for hospital care, as Herzlinger observes, so only the very sickest patients are admitted, those who absolutely have to be there for the intensive care they need. This kind of service takes more people per patient and lifts the cost of hospital care. For example, recovery from cataract surgery once required the patient to be immobilized in a hospital bed for ten days. Now cataracts are removed and intra-ocular lenses are inserted in a single day-surgery procedure.

Herzlinger believes "the gap between consumers and cost could be bridged if employees bought their own health insurance and other health services. Every year employers would transfer the money they now spend on health insurance to their employees, who would use it to buy their own policies. With this change employees would come to treat health-care funds as their own, and would exercise the vigilance which transformed the American car market." When Quaker Oats gave employees some freedom in allocating "their" health-benefit dollars, they experienced a compound annual increase of only 6 percent from 1983 to 1990. The employees reduced hospital usage by 46 percent and kept increases in their health-care costs 27 to 64 percent lower than the national average, according to Ms. Herzlinger.

Herzlinger claims her cure would cause employees to "exercise the vigilance that transformed the American car market." She said that while median U.S. family incomes nearly quintupled from 1965 to 1988, new-car prices increased only 2.4 times.[12]

A closer look at the history of automobile prices shows that in 1968, you could still buy a new Chrysler for $2,249, a Plymouth for $2,049 and a Toyota for $1,666. Had car prices actually increased only 2.4 times, those cars could have been bought in 1988 for $5,398, $4,908 and $3,998.

Actual new car prices for the 1988 model were not that low. The Chrysler LeBaron cost $10,000—up 4.4 times, the least expensive Plymouth $9,500—up 4.6 times, and the Toyota was priced at $8,695—up 5.2 times. In 1991, the least expensive models were: Chrysler, $15,600 to $16,500, Plymouth $10,500 to $11,300 and Toyota $10,000. And current prices are well beyond these levels.

Apparently, people buy well-equipped cars and want modern, state-of-the-art health care. Nevertheless, Ms. Herzlinger has a valid point about de-linking employers and the purchase of health care. Why should employers be responsible for providing health insurance as a fringe benefit for their employees? They no longer offer company housing and a company store as they once did in West Virginia mining towns.

Years ago, when health costs were reasonable, such insurance wasn't a big item in the budget. Now, for example, employee health care adds $1,000 to the cost of every new automobile, more than the cost of the steel in it.

All employers except hospitals and other health care providers have totally different goals and should not have to fight rising medical costs and submit to proposed government requirements to furnish their employees health insurance to stay in business. The National Association of Social Workers has advanced a health care plan, now being considered by Congress, which is no longer employer-based.[13]

To bring about this de-linkage, employers could raise their employees salaries or wages by the amount they now spend for health insurance coverage. This would take the employer out of the loop once and for all. Then the employee could shop for health insurance, a health maintenance organization (HMO) or other health care as needed, according to Hertzlinger's competitive market theory.

This idea of eliminating employers from the financing loop would not be acceptable to the Clinton Administration which, in June, 1993, was talking about "financing health care coverage for all through a payroll tax—called a 'wage-based premium'—on employers and workers. The administration was also considering a requirement that all employers pay a flat premium for health plans for each of their workers, or it could be some combination of the two.[5]

A high-deductible, catastrophic insurance plan was proposed in 1971 by Martin Feldstein, a Harvard economist, but it involved universal major-risk insurance [MRI] provided by the federal government, eliminating private, competitive health insurance. Financed by general tax revenues, this coverage would be universal and automatic. The deductible, paid by the MRI credit card holder before the catastrophic coverage kicks in, would be related to his income. Also before the payor reaches the ceiling for his income, he would have to pay a percentage of any medical bill he or his family incurred. The example given by Laurence Seidman, a professor of economics at the University of Delaware, in a *Wall Street Journal* article was:

> *...A household with $60,000 of income might pay 30 percent (its cost-sharing rate) of any medical bill until its annual burden reached 8 percent of its income, $4,800 (its out-of-pocket ceiling). Note that this would occur when its annual medical bill reached $16,000. MRI would then pay 100 percent of any additional medical bill. The lower a household's income, the lower would be its cost-sharing rate and out-of-pocket ceiling.*

The household would use the MRI credit card from the government to buy medical care. The government would pay the doctor or the hospital and then bill the household for its share. The objectives of this plan are to give the household an *incentive* to look at the right side of the menu before ordering, i.e., become cost-conscious, and to reduce the risk from a medical problem.

Theoretically, the system becomes self-regulating rather than rule-bound and micro-managed by government bureaucrats. Mr. Seidman concludes:

> *The only way to cure this worsening regulatory disease is to restore consumer cost-sharing; the only way to make cost-sharing acceptable to the public is to relate it to incomes; and the only way to have income-related cost-sharing is to enact government MRI.*[14]

Several years ago, the elderly protested so vigorously when the Congress passed a catastrophic health care addition to Medicare that the law was rescinded. It was not a well-thought-out measure because it was greatly overpriced for the protection it offered, the apparent reason the elderly protested. This incident demonstrated how difficult it will be to devise a health care system that will satisfy all Americans.

One of the problems with current, essentially free government health programs is the *lack of financial incentive* for the patient to concern himself with the cost. If he must share a major portion of that cost, he is more likely to be careful how much expensive health service he uses. True, Medicare patients have to put up 20 percent of the cost of their professional care and a portion of their hospital bill, but the amount of deductible the patient must pay is based on the size of the professional fee or the fact of hospital admission, not on his ability to pay.

All well and good. But how are the rising fees for doctor services and the inefficiencies of full-service hospital operation to be reduced? Despite "Certificate of Need" programs operated by state governments to approve capital expansion of hospitals, these institutions frequently duplicate expensive equipment in order to attract and keep medical staff, although there may not be sufficient demand for full utilization of this equipment. While this makes modern health services convenient, with no standing in line as critics of the Canadian system report, the community, and particularly the patient, pay for this expensive redundancy, one of the reasons the American health care system costs so much. Community health facility planning, active in the mid-1960s, has essentially disappeared in the current competitive climate. Some people argue that Hospitals are more like public utilities than McDonald's and Wendy's. Advocates of competition to the contrary, Hospitals and doctors do not operate in a free market and should not be viewed that way. Like utilities and other monopolies, some regulation is indicated.

Another example: I had a hip replacement in December, 1990; the total out-of-pocket cost to me was $1,537.73, excluding pre-operative diagnosis and post-op follow-up care. Fortunately, my surgeon accepted Medicare assignment which reduced his fee from $3,500 to $2,100, a 40 percent reduction in the "going rate." But the anesthesiologist did not accept assignment so I had to pay $288.16 of the full $525.24 he charged. Here are the details of my out-of-pocket expenses:

Surgeon and assistant surgeon	$517.97
Anesthesiologist	288.16
Hospital deductible	592.00
Pathology lab	40.44
Radiology	6.32
Walker	17.84
Elevated toilet seat	75.00
Total	$1,537.73

Had all doctor and hospital charges been rendered at full rate, the total cost would have been $21,948.72. Under a standard reimbursement system known as diagnosis-related groups (DRGs), Medicare pays the hospital a specific sum based on the medical problem for which the patient was admitted, regardless of the length of stay or possible complications. For a total hip replacement, this is about $7,900, including the $592 deductible I paid, so the hospital received less than half of the amount it billed. Said another way, the hospital wrote off more money than it collected for my nine days of inpatient care. Either hospitals are charging all patients significantly more than it cost to render the service they provide so what they lose on the elderly can be shifted to private, paying patients or they are rapidly going bankrupt. I doubt the latter is happening.

Actually, there are few private, paying-out-of-their-pocket patients left to whom costs can be shifted, maybe one percent of the typical urban hospital's in-patients. The remaining private patients have insurance coverage so the insurance company gets the total bill, since there is no mandatory DRG deduction for non-Medicare patients. Understandably, insurance carriers don't think that's fair because it raises the premiums they must charge. But this is the way the hospital makes any "profit" or surplus it accumulates to expand services, build additions, buy new equipment, absorb the cost of indigent patients and, in the case of nvestor-owned hospitals, like Hospital Corporation of America facilities, pay dividends. How much surplus any hospital should accumulate is a judgment call.

Because my income is about the same as cited in the MRI example above, I would have paid $4,800 out of my pocket instead of $1,538 for this operation. How much I should have paid is a matter for discussion, but certainly some reasonable ceiling on charges for physician and hospital services is essential.

As the supply of physicians increases, there is a tendency for them to see half as many patients and charge each one twice as much, thus maintaining the income to which they feel entitled. But how much is that? As my secretary once asked, "Who told all these doctors they were entitled to be millionaires?"

Hospitals now compete in open-market fashion, spending thousands of dollars on advertising, dollars which are included in the patients' bills. This does not include the want-ads to attract professional personnel, nurses, pharmacists, etc. In Oklahoma City, just the Help Wanted ads in *The Sunday Oklahoman* each week cost hospital patients half a million dollars a year.

But all of the hospitals' PR efforts rarely influence patients in their choice of hospital. Ordinarily, patients select their doctor and the doctor then admits them to the hospital in which he or she practices. Of course, it doesn't always work this way, but when was the last time you selected which hospital to use? Was it different from the one your physician ordinarily uses?

On January 22, 1992, a *Wall Street Journal* article referred to health care as a "Closed market," stating that the laws of economics often don't apply in the health-care field. Prices and quality vary widely but patients and insurers rarely "comparison shop." The article cited a case in which a retired telephone installer, suffering badly clogged coronary arteries, said, "There really wasn't any question as to where we would be going. Our family physician is associated with Harrisburg Hospital." But government figures showed the death rate for bypass surgery was substantially higher at Harrisburg than at Lancaster General Hospital, just 38 miles away. What's more, Harrisburg Hospital charges 50 percent more than Lancaster. Patients do not have adequate information to comparison shop nor are they inclined to do so. As the article said:

> *In a conventional market, a high cost, low-quality producer would be doomed, or, at the very least, worried. But the laws of economics have been repealed in the health business...many Hospitals compete to buy the latest technology rather than provide the lowest-cost quality service. And providers resist outsiders' attempts to gauge quality. The result: a seemingly unstoppable increase in the cost of health care.*[15]

Milton Friedman, the Nobel Prize-winning economist previously of the University of Chicago, cited "Gammon's Law," otherwise known as "the theory of bureaucratic replacement," as applicable to the health care system in America. Max Gammon, a British physician who researches medical care, observed that "in a bureaucratic system...increase in expenditure will be matched by fall in production." He found that in the British socialized hospital system, while the number of employees (input) increased sharply, the number of hospital beds (output) actually fell. Friedman added that such systems "will act rather like 'black holes' in the economic universe, simultaneously sucking in resources, and shrinking in terms of 'emitted' production."

Friedman investigated Hospitals in the U.S. and found that Gammon's Law has been operative here since the end of World War II, and especially since the enactment of Medicare and Medicaid in 1965. At that point, "a mild rise in input was turned into a meteoric rise; a mild fall in output, into a rapid decline."

Personnel per occupied bed, which doubled from 1946 to 1965, more than tripled from that level after 1965. Cost per patient day, which had more than tripled from 1946 to 1965, multiplied a further eight-fold after 1965.

Of course, changes in medical technology and payment systems have pushed treatment procedures out of the hospital as well as reduced the length of stay of those who had to be admitted, so counting occupied beds is no longer the best way to measure hospital efficiency, as Dr. Friedman recognized. While life expectancy is a better yardstick to measure the effectiveness of health care, so many other things affect this bottom line that "it will take a far more detailed and informed analysis to reach any clear conclusions about what is happening to the output of the medical care industry, whether in terms of length of life, and even more, the quality of life. Nonetheless, for total medical care, as for

Hospitals, it is hard to avoid the conclusion that Gammon's Law is at work."

Friedman claims we should not be surprised because "evidence covering a much broader range of activities documents that bureaucratic structures produce high cost, low quality and inequitable distribution of output. The U.S. medical system has become in large part a socialist enterprise." He observed that despite this evidence, nearly all the suggestions for improving our medical system involve *expanding* the role of government!

Friedman believes we must go in the opposite direction, toward re-privatizing medical care, but he recognizes "this would be violently opposed by the bureaucracy that plans, controls and administers today's structure of medical care." Friedman's solution has two major steps:

1. End both Medicare and Medicaid and replace them with a requirement that every U.S. family unit have a major medical insurance policy with a high deductible, say $20,000 a year or 30 percent of the unit's income during the prior two years, whichever is lower.
2. End the tax exemption of employer-provided medical care; it should be regarded as a fully taxable fringe benefit to the employee—deductible for the employer but taxable to the employee.

The cost of the major medical insurance should be tax-deductible. The government would help low-income families pay for the necessary major medical insurance. These policies would be chosen by each individual or family from competitive private insurers who would administer these private coverages.

According to Friedman, these two reforms would completely solve the problem of the currently medically uninsured, eliminate most of the bureaucratic structure, free medical practitioners from an incredible burden of paper work and regulation, and lead many employers and employees to convert employer-provided medical care into a higher cash wage. The taxpayer would save money, since total government costs would plummet.

The family unit would be relieved of one of its major concerns—the possibility of being impoverished by a major medical catastrophe—and most could readily finance the remaining medical costs, which, Friedman speculates, would return to something like 5 percent of total consumer spending that it was before the federal government got into the act. Families would once again have an incentive to monitor the providers of medical care and to establish the kind of personal relations with them that once were customary. The demonstrated efficiency of private enterprise would have a chance to operate to improve the quality and lower the cost of medical care.

But Friedman is not optimistic that this simple plan can ever be put in operation. "It would displace and displease the large number of people who are now engaged in administering, studying and daily revising the present socialized system. They are sufficiently potent politically to kill any such reform before it could ever get a real following, just as the educational bureaucracy has repeatedly killed even modest programs for privatizing the educational system, even though poll after poll shows that the public supports privatization through parental choice."[16]

Other ideas have been advanced for coping with the rising cost of health care, as it has now become a major issue faced by the Clinton administration. In fact, as early as mid-February, 1992, there were 43 bills involving health care before the Congress.[17] Some of the major ones were:

1. Former President Bush's $100 Billion Plan: This plan would broaden access to medical care, make its delivery more efficient, and build on the current system. It involves tax vouchers and deductions to help the 37 million people without health insurance as well as the underinsured to buy private medical coverage. But the former president didn't say how his plan would be funded nor did it include a scheme to control health care costs, two rather critical points. But then, it was an election year. In 1992, health care costs consumed 14 percent of the GNP, twice the cost when Richard Nixon was president two decades before.[18]
2. "play or pay" plan: This plan, backed by many leading Democrats in Congress, would still connect health benefits with the employer, who could choose either to provide at least a minimum specified package of health insurance benefits to all their employees and their families, or pay roughly 7 percent of payroll into a government fund that would provide coverage to the uninsured.[19]

3. Health Access America: This is the American Medical Association approach, which is composed of 16 recommendations to achieve "expanded access" to health care for all Americans. It builds on the present employment-based health insurance system by requiring all employers to provide basic health insurance to employees. It would also extend coverage to the uninsured, low-income families, the elderly and people with pre-existing health problems, through various partially or fully government-financed programs. It would establish state risk pools, where medically uninsurable people could buy health insurance at group prices.
4. Medical IRA: This plan, proposed by J. Patrick Rooney, chairman of the Golden Rule Insurance Company, would have employers give each employee an annual allowance of, say, $3,000 for routine health care for him and his family. If the employee spent less than his allowance in a year, he could keep the balance. To protect the employee against bills exceeding the allowance, the employer would continue to buy insurance. This plan amounts to a medical care savings account, which, with a simple modification of the law could accumulate tax-free in this medical IRA. This plan would provide an incentive for the employee to shop around, compare costs and be careful about over-using the health care system.[20]

So what *is* President Clinton's health care reform plan? Early on, it was purposely vague. His objective was to reduce spending for medical services. He believed this is the key to carrying out his other economic proposals, such as creating jobs with federal money should that be necessary to stimulate the economy, and to reduce the federal deficit, which he vowed to cut in half over his four year term of office. But at the same time, he proposed covering 37 million people who couldn't afford health care insurance and said it could be done with the savings his plan would achieve.

The president proposed a "global budgeting" method that would establish an annual health budget for the nation, limiting both private and public expenditures. It would be a mixture of the "play or pay" idea and something he calls "managed competition." All employers would be required to provide health insurance to their full-time workers or pay a portion of the cost of obtaining coverage for workers and dependents through newly created "health insurance purchasing pools." These pools would consist of small businesses and other groups of similar purchasers in order to obtain lower insurance rates. Networks of insurers and health care providers would be required to offer at least a standard benefits package and compete on the basis of the prices they charged for it, similar to Herzlinger's idea. Apparently, budgetary decision-making would be pushed down to the states which are in the best position to know the needs and costs in their region. Then these results would have to be hammered to fit into the overall national budget. This plan would build on current elements of private health insurance and the privately-operated institutions, such as Hospitals, clinics, HMOs, and other centers for health services now in place.

With Hillary Rodham Clinton having managed the competition of ideas within the health care task force and developed the Clinton health care reform plan, it will be interesting to see how it is restructured by the Congress and how it is received by the American people.

Will Rogers would undoubtedly be amazed at the way Hospitals have changed since his gall bladder operation on June 17, 1927. He almost died and it was a month before he could again write his Weekly Article. When he came home from the "COAX 'EM IN AND CARRY 'EM OUT FOUNDRY" (California Hospital, Los Angeles) he reported:

> *"Yes, I am out of the hospital and the old 'stomacker' is percolating along on all four. If it wasn't for argueing with the nurse over what you can do, and what you ought not to do, why I would have a lot more time than I have now. You can't look cross-eyed but what you hear, 'Now you look out! You know what the doctor said!'*
>
> *"Say, the doctor don't have to keep warning me. I'm not looking to be spread out and inhaling ether as a steady diet. It didn't take much to put me insensible, but I hope I have heard my last 'lay perfectly quiet now, you will feel better in a little while. It's the ether wearing off.'"*[21]

Is President Clinton feeling better now that the campaign rhetorical ether has worn off and he has revealed the cost of his plan? Any changes in the current system of health care face the cold reality that the doctors are lined up against any reduction in their average $163,000 a year income (1990). Another reality is the $265 billion hospital industry which wants more patients but no more controls. Hospitals don't want to be told how much they can spend; they want to do everything they know how for the patient and then pass along the cost to government, insurers, or paying patients, whoever will stand still long enough to pay the bill. A third reality consists of the providers who use reams of paper creating fees for their services and the insurance people who shuffle those same papers paying part of the hospital and doctor bills, who spend *$130 billion a year* just in this paper chase.[22]

Because there is no practical constraint on the professional lobbyists from the "medical-industrial complex" who hang around Washington and pass out reelection money to congressmen, both Clinton and the Congress will need all of the courage they can muster to roll back the high cost of the entrenched health care system.

Despite (or perhaps because of) forty years in the health business, I do not have the solution to this knotty problem, but there are certain basic principles which should be seriously considered:

1. If the United States government actually *operates* the reformed health care system, as it does in the military and in Veterans Administration Medical Centers, costs would continue their upward spiral. Government workers have the *incentive* to protect and expand their power, not to reduce the cost of their services.
2. Significant, out-of-pocket copayment by patients as a part of any health insurance is essential to hold down over-use of the health care system.
3. Because Hospitals and doctors do not operate in a free market, cost controls are absolutely necessary. If you are sick and need to be in a hospital, you have no choice but to use the system. Thus, your options are the same as buying water, or natural gas or electricity from utility monopolies—none. That's the reason Oklahoma has a Corporation Commission which governs the operation of public utilities within the state. The same type of governance is needed for the health care system.

4. Medicare insurance is a good model for the control of charges except that, unlike the Hospitals, physicians are not required to accept Medicare assignment. Under the current system, total Medicare expenditures will rise steadily as the population ages, people live longer, medical technology expands, and physicians continue to increase fees. The fees paid all physicians should be controlled as under Medicare so they are kept within reasonable bounds. Why should these fees exceed the rate of inflation?

Better still, the fee-for-service system should be traded in for a simpler way of paying doctors. If physicians were paid an annual salary based on their preparation, qualifications, skills and experience, on a "relative value" scale, and perhaps a bonus based on the number of patients they take responsibility for, they could perform their professional services and enjoy reasonable compensation without becoming business entrepreneurs. Just as the professional fees for each service now paid to physicians come from insurance premiums, these annual salaries could be derived from pooled monies set aside for the purpose by insurance carriers.

After all, the physician's education is highly subsidized by taxpayer money, so the taxpayers should have control over how much they have to pay the doctors they put through school.

5. The current system of payment to Hospitals for Medicare patients should be expanded to all hospital patients. This system based on diagnosis-related groups, DRGs, pays the hospital a flat rate for each patient admitted. If that rate is, say, $3,000 for an appendectomy and allows three days stay, that's all the hospital can collect. Of this, the patient is responsible for an established deductible and the government pays the rest.

If the hospital can treat the patient for $3,000, it breaks even. If it can, through cost-saving efficiency, render the needed care for $2,500, the hospital makes a $500 profit. If there are complications, such as a hospital-acquired infection, and the cost rises to $5,000 because the patient uses more drugs and has to stay longer than average, the hospital loses $2,000.

Thus, there is an *incentive* for the hospital to operate effectively at reasonable cost. This kind of cost control is essential in a closed market. Hospitals advertise like Wendy's and McDonald's, but operate like the city water department or the power and light company.

6. Encourage Hospitals in urban areas to plan together to take advantage of non-duplication of services and sharing of expensive equipment. Because each hospital wishes to be a "full-service" institution to attract as many doctors as possible to its staff, they often duplicate services and equipment well beyond the need of the community they serve. This race to be the biggest and the best in town increases rather than reduces hospital charges, demonstrating once again that health services are not an open market.

In the late 1960s, the federal government funded the establishment of state and area-wide health planning agencies, but now, in this 1990s era of competition and advertising, the Justice Department treats Hospitals as though they were airlines, controlling them under anti-trust laws. The federal government does not understand that health care is not an open market.

But the government is not totally to blame. When the Oklahoma Health Center, a multi-institutional, academic health campus in Oklahoma City, was planned in the mid-1960s, there was a list of some twenty facilities and services which would be centralized and shared. But almost all of the planning we laboriously accomplished promptly went down the tubes! There was to be a central emergency suite or trauma center to serve all patients who came to the campus in urgent need of treatment. The idea was to transfer them to one of the five Hospitals after they had been stabilized in the emergency room. Instead of one emergency center, the campus now has a suite at the V.A. Hospital, HCA Presbyterian Hospital, Oklahoma Memorial Hospital and Oklahoma Children's Memorial Hospital: count 'em—FOUR emergency suites operating around the clock. Only the O'Donoghue Rehabilitation Hospital doesn't have an emergency room!

The central steam and chilled water plant, built and operated by the University of Oklahoma was the single, centralization success and even that wasn't total. The V.A. Hospital insisted on operating its own heating and air-conditioning plant, making the central system less efficient than it could have been.

It took a while for me to understand why this non-duplication and sharing idea didn't work. It finally dawned on me that Hospitals and medical people want to control their own facilities and services, no matter what it costs, and they also want to be able to point with pride that they have the best in town. So why did the steam and chilled water plant work for all but one of the Oklahoma Health Center institutions? Nobody can see the chilled water pipes that run under the campus in a maze of tunnels and nobody cares where the heat or the cool air comes from. Besides, advertising that your hospital has the best heating and air-conditioning in town doesn't attract doctors or patients![23]

The problem of expensive duplication was recognized recently (December 24, 1992) by Richard Wright, director of the biomedical ethics program at the University of Oklahoma Health Sciences Center, the academic nucleus of the Oklahoma Health Center. He said, "Everybody is trying to be everything to everybody. That doesn't make sense. And it doesn't make business sense." That's precisely what the Oklahoma Health Sciences Foundation which coordinated the planning for the Oklahoma Health Center was saying a quarter of a century ago.

Mr. Wright did not have a solution to the problem he cited and neither do I, but non-duplication and sharing is a principle that should be considered in the Clinton plan for health care reform.[24]

7. The expenditure of taxpayer money should be directed toward the greatest good for the greatest number. The heroic and expensive efforts to save two-pound premature babies in the neonatal intensive care unit would often be unnecessary if appropriate prenatal care had been provided. Such preventive care costs a fraction of the expense of prematurity. In addition, many damaged premature babies need continuing costly services after they are sent home with their mother and often wind up as wards of the state.

At the other end of the life span, costly organ transplants, bypass surgery and heroic efforts to sustain the life of superannuated patients may not add significantly to the quality of their life. Nobody wants medical care to be rationed, but the reality is it has always been rationed, and that neither the available public money nor the available services are infinite. Both should be used as effectively as possible for the greatest good.

8. An ounce of prevention is still the best way to reduce the explosive cost of health care. According to the American Medical Association, 35 percent of hospitalized patients are there because of alcohol and drug abuse problems. What's more, 390,000 Americans die from tobacco-related illness, costing $22 billion each year, reports the Centers for Disease Control. Many lives and injuries could be saved if motorists would use their seat belts. health insurance policies should build in dollar incentives for policy holders to choose and pursue a healthy life-style.

Regarding the control of physician income, the former editor of *The New England Journal of Medicine* fears his profession has lost its ethical way. In an article entitled "What Market Forces Are Doing To Medicine," in the March, 1992 issue of *The Atlantic Monthly*, Arnold S. Relman, M.D. argues that doctors are not, and should not be, businessmen, and yet financial and technological pressures are forcing more and more of them to act like businessmen, with deleterious consequences for patients and society as a whole.

The Hippocratic Oath encourages doctors to serve only "for the benefit of the sick." A twelfth century physician, Mose Maimonides, asked God not to allow "thirst for profit" or "ambition for renown" to interfere with the physician's practice of his profession. George Bernard Shaw, in his preface to *The Doctor's Dilemma*, written in the early 20th century, said:

> *It is not the fault of our doctors that the medical service of the community, as at present provided for, is a murderous absurdity. That any sane nation, having observed that you could provide for the supply of bread by giving bakers a pecuniary interest in baking for you, should go on to give a surgeon a pecuniary interest in cutting off your leg, is enough to make one despair of political humanity. But that is precisely what we have done. And the more appalling the mutilation, the more the mutilator is paid...*
>
> *Scandalized voices murmur that...operations are necessary. They may be. It may also be necessary to hang a man or pull down a house. But we take good care not to*

make the hangman and the housebreaker the judges of that. If we did, no man's neck would be safe and no man's house stable.

As late as 1957, the American Medical Association declared that "the principal objective of the medical profession is to render service to humanity," and admonished the physician to limit the source of his income to medical services actually rendered by him, or under his supervision, to his patients.

(In China, physicians were paid as long as their patient was healthy; when the patient became sick, the payment stopped. This is motivation—*incentive*—in the right direction.)

As Dr. Relman pointed out, the situation is now rapidly changing. Health care has been commercialized and professionalism in medicine seems to be giving way to entrepreneurialism. Now, there is an "unprecedented degree of competition for paying patients." With insurance available to pay the bills, physicians have powerful economic *incentives* to recruit patients and provide expensive services. A multitude of tests and procedures provide lucrative opportunities for extra income, encouraging an entrepreneurial approach to medical practice and overuse of services, he observed.

Dr. Relman went on to talk about the "medical-industrial complex," citing nvestor-owned hospitals, nursing homes, clinics, and diagnostic laboratories and their effect on voluntary, nonprofit institutions, whose "altruistic concerns are being distorted by a concern for the bottom line." Physicians now struggle to maintain their income in an increasingly competitive economic climate, engaging in advertising, marketing and public relations in order to attract more patients. This self-promotion is no longer considered unethical. A recent study in Florida revealed that approximately 40 percent of all physicians in the state had financial interests in facilities to which they referred patients. Nationwide, the AMA estimates this figure is about 10 percent.

The result of these changes, according to Dr. Relman, will be that paying patients will get more care than they need and poor patients will get less. In a commercialized system the cost of health care will continue to escalate and yet we will not be assured of getting the kind of care we really need. In such a system we will no longer be able to trust our physicians, because the bond of fiduciary responsibility will have been broken. To control costs, government will be driven to adopt increasingly stringent regulations. Ultimately health care will have to be regulated like a public utility, and much greater constraints will be placed on physicians and Hospitals than now are in place or even contemplated, Dr. Relman concluded.[25]

It is this writer's opinion that the medical profession has already gone too far to return to its ethical base and the governmental controls Dr. Relman fears are long past due. That is the reason for the suggested change in Principle 4 (above). Dr. Relman recognizes that "the medical profession is not likely to change its direction without help," and says "the *incentives* that now encourage—indeed, in many cases require—physicians to act primarily as businessmen will have to be changed...In my opinion, a greater reliance on group practice and more emphasis on medical insurance that prepays providers at a fixed annual rate offer the best chance of solving the economic problems of health care, because these arrangements put physicians in the most favorable position to act as prudent advocates for their patients, rather than entrepreneurial vendors of services."

Dr. Relman's recommendation is the basis on which some health maintenance organizations (HMOs) work, emphasizing the need as well as the *economic incentive* to keep the patient healthy and out of the hospital. Dr. Relman believes that physicians hold the key to "reaffirming the medical profession's ethical contract with society."[26]

I am not as confident as he that this return to the Hippocratic Oath can be achieved without irresistible governmental intervention, inspired and abetted by strong pressure from the public. Currently, the American doctor makes about seven times the average wage of U.S. workers and has no *incentive* voluntarily to reduce his standard of living. In addition, the fee-for-service system has been in effect so long in America that it will be difficult for the profession to change without substantial legal pressure.

We need to reorganize the health care system, with the government building in positive and negative incentives, for both patients and health-care providers, so patients will not over-use the system and doctors and Hospitals will be motivated to do what they know they ought to be doing. Deductibles, DRGs and possibly MRI are a good start for getting a handle on this important problem of health care costs. If we could control governmental bureaucracy, perhaps Dr. Friedman's simple plan could be implemented.

Fortunately, the politicians are at long last recognizing the gravity of the situation. During the 1992 campaign, presidential hopeful Bill Clinton contended that a better health care system, lowering costs and improving accessibility, could be designed without spending more of the GNP to pay for it. Of course, since becoming President, he and Hillary are scrambling to invent new labels for the taxes which will be required to pay for their plan.

And what do some of the people want? A 1992 survey by Congressman Glenn English (D-OK), conducted in his 6th Oklahoma District, found that:

66 percent think the American health care system needs major changes.
55 percent wouldn't want changes to cause longer waiting periods.
53 percent would favor spending less for high-tech medical equipment.
90 percent would swap fewer options to sue their physician for lower health care costs.
73 percent think a system which provided basic care to all Americans with the option to purchase additional services on their own would be an improvement over the current system.
59 percent said they'd take the chance that pending health care programs, while providing less expensive care for most Americans, would require others to pay more.
60 percent would be willing to pay a fee to the government if their total health care costs were reduced.
55 percent feel the overall amount of money the nation spends on health care should be reduced.
68 percent think their health insurance should be administered through a private company.
56 percent would not support a national health care plan that provided funds to the states which would then be responsible for developing their own health plans.[26]

At least, this review of the health care situation in 1993 can provide a check list against which to measure the final Clinton health care plan, assuming it survives the lobbyists, the Congress and public reaction. Remember, its antecedent, the Murray-

Wagner-Dingell national health insurance bill, was proposed more than forty years ago!

Since the 237 page working draft of the Clinton HealthBill was released in mid-September 1993, efforts to understand it and ways to oppose it or devise simpler, less expensive plans have been pursued by numerous interest groups, including the American Medical Association, the drug manufacturers, Hospitals, small businesses and the health insurance industry. Merger of rural and urban Hospitals into multi-unit systems, have accelerated and cost containment has become a major concern of these institutions.

By October 28, Clinton's working draft ballooned into a 1,336 page health care reform bill, which faces rigorous competition by a half-dozen rival plans created by congressmen of both parties. The president vowed he would not sign any bill which did not include universal coverage, insuring the estimated 37 million Americans without health coverage.

The Democratic and Republican parties both appear eager to resolve the health care reform problem in 1994 prior to the fall election, which could change the balance of power in the senate and alter the political momentum in the house.

Chapter Sixteen

Promote Free Trade: Stimulate American Technological innovation: Recognize the Reality of Multinational companies

An English capitalist...he was telling me about the Japanese manufacturing so many different things. He seemed to think that there was nothing that they wasn't doing, and doing pretty good. And always underselling anyone else.

—Will Rogers[1]

In 1991, Americans were more than a little miffed at the Japanese because they were "doing things so good," selling shiploads of cars in the U.S., building up a huge trade surplus and getting more market share. Although we now sell more American goods to Japan than to any other country except Canada, a lot of people, especially the auto workers, still feel the Japanese are eating our lunch. The impression is that Japan just won't open up its market so we can sell more stuff over there.

All of this causes Americans to think about retaliation, limiting what Japan can sell over here, the whole issue of trade tariffs. Protectionism is in the air once more.

What a lot of people forget is that the Smoot-Hawley Tariff Law and other anti-trade barriers in the 1930s contributed to the worldwide reduction of employment and output, a factor which deepened the Great Depression.[2]

More recently, in the 1980s, we tried restricting the importation of Japanese cars. This protection did not make the U.S. automakers get on the ball and produce better, less expensive cars. When the Japanese cars became more expensive because of the quota, GM raised its prices, too. It is interesting the way U.S. carmakers try to repeal the law of supply and demand. When supply exceeded demand, as during the 1991–92 recession, did they cut their prices? No, they raised them, causing even more acute sticker shock and buyer resistance. Then they wonder why they lose so much money. Is that the way to sell more cars?[3]

The American automakers have improved the quality of their products so they are now on a par with Japanese cars. Now, the American car buyer is once more buying Detroit-built automobiles, as increased sales during the first two quarters of 1993 showed. But not before General Motors had lost billions of dollars, put in new management, drastically down-sized their operations, and planned to close even more of their plants during the next few years. Chrysler now leads the minivan market and Ford is making a profit, so a turnaround is occurring.

Because President Bush's trip to Asia, including Japan, in January, 1992, was less than successful as a trade mission, members of Congress were looking to get back at the Japanese. Of course, when the Aussies complained we were subsidizing our farmers and creating problems for Australian wheat exports, Bush declared he would continue to support our farmers the way the Europeans support theirs. In addition, the United States has over 8,000 taxes on imports, so we are hardly a free market ourselves.

While President Bush proclaimed his trade talks with Japan a success, a few days after he returned to the United States, the Japanese said the deal Bush thought he had to sell more cars and auto parts turned out to be only "targets" the Japanese negotiators would aim for. Later they decided it was a deal after all, agreeing to stick to the "managed trade" agreement they originally made. It called for doubling the purchase of auto parts from U.S. suppliers by Japanese factories in the U.S. from $7 billion in 1990 to $15 billion in 1994, and going up from $2 billion to $4 billion in auto parts imports by Japanese auto makers in Japan.[4]

Because President Bush was an advocate of free trade, he had an aversion to managed trade, but this is not the only principle he violated in the election year of 1992. Columnist Alan Murray says, "If the auto-parts agreement leads Japanese multinationals to become more open to the rest of the world, then the end result of this flirtation with managed trade could be a freer world trading system."[5]

"Fair trade" has been described by James Bovaird this way:

"Fair trade consists largely of the U.S. government devising new ways to protect American consumers against the scourge of low prices." Columnist Mona Sharen says that protectionism always winds up benefiting one American industry at the expense of another. For example, the recent tariff on semiconductors did wonders for American semiconductor companies, but hurt American computer makers.[6]

Perhaps we should look at what we Yankees are doing wrong and try to get our own house in order. Columnist Don Feder asked some penetrating questions like: Why is it the Germans can sell cars in Japan and we can't? (One answer is that they make them with the steering wheel on the right because the Japanese drive on the left hand side of the road.) How come Japanese plants in the United States have an output 30 to 50 percent higher—per worker, per day—than Detroit?

There seems to be plenty of blame to go around. United Auto Workers union rules stifle creative use of manpower. GM, Ford and Chrysler have 60 job classifications; Japanese-owned American plants only three to five. American firms are forced to pay laid-off workers 85 percent of their take-home pay for up to three years.

Lee Iacocca, CEO at Chrysler before he retired in 1992, raked in $4.65 million a year and the company paid out $12 million in Christmas bonuses to corporate executives; all the while, Chrysler was going in the red by $1 billion. The boss at Honda gets just $400,000 a year.

The Oriental schools produce whiz kids while ours graduate functional illiterates. (No doubt the 240 days a year Japanese students spend in school, compared to 180 days in the U.S., is one reason.) Our high school graduates are putting American cars together, which may be why Americans wouldn't buy them until the quality improved.

According to Feder, the Japanese have the work ethic, which we've lost. They have family values, pride in workmanship and a sense of duty to their employer and society. Americans seem to have a "the-boss-is-mine-enemy" attitude, a "don't-ask-me-I-just-work-here" mentality and a TGIF (Thank God it's Friday) ethos.[7]

Despite the Japanese claim that American workers are lazy, illiterate and overpaid, U.S. manufacturers have pulled off a stunning turnaround during 1985–1990, showing a decline in unit costs while most other countries experienced double-digit increases. In dollar terms, the annual percentage changes in manufaturing unit costs during that five year period were:

United States	-0.1 percent
Canada	+7.9
Japan	+10.3
Britain	+10.8
France	+11.0
South Korea	+11.3
Italy	+14.3
Germany	+15.6

This is the exact opposite of what happened in the preceding six years, 1979–85. Then the unit costs in U.S. factories rose 3.9 percent a year, while they fell in 11 of 13 other countries surveyed. More recent figures are not available but the Bureau of Labor Statistics, the source of this information, suspects that the U.S. has continued to excel.

All of this recent progress reflects gains in U.S. productivity. Also, the annual gains in U.S. pay slowed from 6.8 percent to 3.5 percent in the 1985–90 period. Wages went up faster elsewhere, so that the 1990 U.S. hourly rate of $14.77 is now exceeded in 14 other countries.

These improvements are reflected in the balance of merchandise payments. Since 1987, the trade deficit has declined from $152.1 billion a year to $66.2 billion in 1991, but bounced back up to $96 billion in 1992. As Alfred L. Malabre, Jr., writing in *The Wall Street Journal*, points out, "Recent calls in Washington, Detroit and elsewhere for stricter protective measures for U.S. industry seem, to say the least, unwarranted. Indeed, if such steps are taken, they may come just when U.S. manufacturers are at last regaining much of their former competitive vigor and would stand to reap benefits if trade flows freely.[8]

An almost unnoticed trend is the recent increase in American service exports. U.S. companies that don't make a thing are turning America into an export powerhouse. Everyone talks about the U.S. merchandise deficit because that's what the Commerce Department reports. Indeed, that deficit was $96 billion in 1992 and topped $100 billion in seven of the past nine years, a situation which provokes repeated outbursts against America's trading partners.

But companies which sell services, rather than raw materials or manufactured goods, racked up a $59 billion trade surplus in 1992, almost fivefold increase from 1986. While these service companies create fewer U.S. jobs, the ones they do add are high-paying. Well-known examples are American Express Company, McDonald's Corporation and the Walt Disney Company, and there are numerous smaller consulting companies exporting information, know-how, creativity and technology. Some experts believe the $167 billion in service exports for 1992 may be underestimated by 20 percent.[9]

Multinational companies are here to stay. They move manufacturing plants to third-world countries where labor is cheap and not sufficiently organized to demand higher wages. The goods they produce are manufactured for export to developed countries and can be sold at lower prices than the same item produced in a first-world country.

Also, multinationals put together products using materials, parts and expertise from a number of countries, which makes it very difficult to say that a product is purely American or Japanese or British or German. Parts in many European automobiles are manufactured by American companies in the U.S.

In considering trade or merchandise deficits, it is easy to forget the equation: trade deficit = investment surplus. While the U.S. runs a $40 billion trade deficit with Japan, this money flows back into the United States as investment. As *The Wall Street Journal* pointed out, nations that provide good investment opportunities run trade deficits. A zero trade deficit is not necessarily a good thing—a sign of economic health. The U.S. ran a trade deficit in nearly every year of its first century, as Europeans sent investment money and goods to develop the continent.

A committee of eminent economists said in 1976 that the words "surplus" and "deficit" should be avoided because they are frequently taken to mean that the developments are good or bad. While we concentrate on the "merchandise deficit," we tend to ignore the export of services, stocks, bonds, and deeds to surplus Houston office buildings, i.e., the investment that flows back into the U.S. The idea of Japan, the country we defeated in World War II, "buying up America" is repugnant to many patriotic Americans, but the Japanese are smart enough to know America is probably the safest place in the world to invest their profits.[10]

As *Wall Street Journal* editor Robert L. Bartley pointed out, "Given the investment-trade seesaw, a zero trade balance is not normal or even desirable. The United States ran a trade deficit for nearly all of its first 100 years, and generated trade surpluses under Smoot-Hawley (tariff laws) in the midst of the Great Depression."[11]

To stay ahead in the world of production, U.S. manufacturers must not only continue to up productivity and hold down costs, but America needs to concentrate on the innovation and production of high tech goods with high-value-added, and generate new services which cannot easily be duplicated in other countries.

U.S. high-tech firms recently have staged a little-noticed comeback, particularly in the semiconductor business, where Intel, the American chip maker, has taken back market leadership from Japanese producers. This was accomplished with help from government financing, which may be one way President Clinton will recommend investing tax money to create jobs.[12]

Obviously, it takes people accomplished in math and science to take advantage of opportunities in high-tech industries. Taking its cue from Triangle Research Park associated with Duke University and the University of North Carolina at Chapel Hill, Oklahoma has opened a special high school for outstanding juniors and seniors interested in a scientific career. These students have mentors in the adjacent University of Oklahoma Health Sciences Center where they become acquainted with the methods of laboratory science and research activities. As pointed out in Chapter Seven, education is a critical key to America's future economic health.

We have recognized the need to nurture the potential geniuses of the next generation. What distinguishes a genius? They can be any age, but are most often found in the 18 to 35-year-old category. Few of them are one-hit wonders; most great minds will have more than one great idea. They are hard-working risk takers, original thinkers who can simplify and communicate their insights to others. They are also stubborn and lucky!

When *The Wall Street Journal* asked nearly three dozen leaders in the high-technology industry to talk about geniuses in their business, they responded this way:

What three words capture the definition of genius?
Insight, creativity, vision.
How many geniuses are there right now in your industry?
Fewer than 200.

What proportion of these people are technical visionaries?

More than 50 percent.

Who are the rest?

Marketing, sales, business.

What year would we be in, technologically, without these people and their predecessors?

1965.

How old is a genius?

Any age.[13]

Of course, every student in a special math and science high school will not turn out to be a genius, but encouragement and nurturing of the gifted teenager will help assure the future development of American technology and industrial progress in the information age.

In December, 1992, President Bush signed the North American Free Trade Agreement (NAFTA), subject to ratification by the U.S. Congress, the Canadian Parliament and the Mexican government. Bill Clinton went along with NAFTA, although he recommended a lot more attention by Mexico to environmental and labor concerns. A coalition of activists, known as the Citizen Trade Campaign, opposed this treaty; activists including Rev. Jesse Jackson, the Sierra Club, the AFL-CIO and Ralph Nader. And Ross Perot spoke vehemently against the proposed treaty with Mexico during the 1992 presidential campaign and again in 1993. However, Clinton vowed he would negotiate side deals with Mexico that would stiffen enforcement of environmental and labor laws.[14]

On June 15, 1993, when President Clinton was questioned about NAFTA, he said, "Look what's happened in the last five years. There have been any number of plants that have moved into Mexico. They cannot continue to do that now under the present law. The *maquiladora* line has been extended well beyond the Rio Grande River. There are lots of plants down there.

"But just a few years ago we had a $5 billion trade deficit with Mexico; now we have a $6 billion trade surplus. Last month they replaced Japan as the second biggest purchaser of our manufactured products. There are over 80 million Mexicans. As their incomes go up, they will buy more from us.

"If we can work out an agreement with them, we will then be

able to move to similar agreements with countries even farther from us but in our region—in Latin America—like Argentina and Venezuela and other countries. And I believe that will create far more jobs than it will cost. There will be some changes, but I believe NAFTA will help us create jobs."[15]

After weeks of intensive campaigning and deal-making by the president to gain democratic votes, the House passed the North American Free Trade Agreement by a margin of 234 to 200 votes on November 19, 1993. Republican congressmen furnished 132 votes while Clinton's own party could muster only 102. Bowing to the traditional influence of organized labor, the great majority of Democrats cast 156 votes against free trade.

The Senate approved NAFTA Shortly thereafter and President Clinton signed the measure into law by in early December.

Chapter Seventeen

Change Government regulation Procedures to Reduce Paperwork for Businesses and the Cost to Consumers Who Ultimately Pay the Bill

> *The more men have anything to do with trying to right a thing, why, the worse off it is. The government has not only hundreds, but literally thousands in Washington to see that no man can personally tend to his own business.*
>
> —*Will Rogers*[1]

Government regulation has been more pervasive and more costly than it is today, hard as that may be to believe. In 1977, federal regulations cost each household in the United States $5,800. Just to list all of the rulings and regulations established in 1976 required 57,027 pages of fine print in the *Federal Register*. William E. Simon, who was then the outspoken Secretary of the Treasury, said "this is a disease of government; it is not government." He added that most existing regulation is so irrational that it should be wiped out by law, along with the bureaucracies that have spawned it.[2]

Since then, regulatory costs dropped to $4,100 per household in 1988 but under President Bush were climbing again, up to $4,300 (in 1988 dollars) and are expected to hit $4,500 in 1996.[3]

How does this happen? The Congress devises the basic regulatory policies and passes the laws creating agencies to enforce them. Boards, commissions and agency heads are appointed by the administration to run the Occupational Safety and Health Administration (OSHA), the Environmental Protection Agency (EPA), the Federal Trade Commission (FTC), the Justice Department antitrust division, the Securities Exchange Commission (SEC), the Federal Communications Commission, and of course, the Food and Drug Administration (FDA). Then there is the Federal Trade Commission (FTC), the Consumer Product Safety Commission (CPSC), the Commodity Futures Trading Commission, and on and on.

All of the agency heads and commissioners have the incentive to carry out the intent of the law as they interpret it. They have the job of making up the rules and regulations and are quite diligent in the pursuit of their charge. They don't have to worry about how much it is going to cost because that is borne initially by the affected business which passes along the cost to the end user of the product or the service. That's where that "cost per household" figure comes from, a cost of living item of which most taxpayers are blissfully unaware.

This is not to say some of the regulations are not valuable. They are. To mention only one industry, we need air traffic controllers, FAA aircraft inspectors, airline pilot medical examiners and many others to keep public airline travel safe. As another but negative example, if the Congress had not increased the FSLIC depositor guarantee to $100,000 and relaxed the rules about what Savings and Loan associations could do, the taxpayers would not have been saddled with the massive bailout expense which the S and L scandal has created.

In January of 1992, President Bush, viewing with alarm the rising cost of regulation and the depressing effect it has on the economy, declared a 90-day moratorium on new regulations. During those three months, the regulating agencies were expected to review all their regulations, particularly the new ones, with an eye toward scrapping rules that unduly burden business or slashing the cost of such regulations. He said, "That rule imposing the largest unnecessary burden should be the first to be revised or eliminated."[4]

Presidential indifference to domestic matters has been blamed for reregulation. While Bush invited regulators to the White House for cocktails in 1990 to talk about his days as deregulatory chief for President Reagan, that was the last such meeting. The administration failed to appoint a senior regulatory person at the budget office and did not nominate anyone for that post. What appears to have been benign neglect may turn out to have had a malignant effect on the health of the American economy. Michael Boskin, chairman of President Bush's Council of Economic

Advisers, says that "over-regulation is one of the major impediments to a growing economy."[5]

It has been estimated that environmental regulations eat up two to three percent of the Gross National Product. A typical, medium-size energy company, with $3 to $5 billion in annual sales and up to 10,000 employees, must employ several hundred people working full time to comply with regulations stemming from federal and state laws. It will expend upward from $50 million a year to meet these requirements.

The compliance process in such an energy company involves corporate staff, perhaps half a dozen people in the legal department, as well as the technology division which evaluates and develops ways to control product manufacture, guards against improper disposal of toxic waste, devises clean-up processes such as scrubbing out caustic elements from ground water, etc. It is an absorbing process, starting with the highest executives who meet quarterly in management environmental and safety committees, down to the operators scattered in far-flung sites around the world. Everyone in the company is in some way involved. Unless the company follows federal regulations meticulously and consistently, it can find itself out of business in Short order.

A current problem is the 1990 clean Air Act passed by the Congress which stipulates the amount of sulfur which may be contained in gasoline. One such company now must figure out if it can still operate one of its smaller refineries and pay the $5 million to $10 million cost of complying with these stiffer rules. Because the company cannot control the market price of gasoline, the refinery may well be squeezed into extinction between the increased cost of production and the return it can get for its product. In fact, Chevron has already decided to shut down its Port Arthur, Texas, 300,000 barrels-a-day refinery, in part because of these new clean air standards.

During the 1980s, Congress spent $500 million studying the effects of acid rain on lakes and forests in the Northeast. These effects were found to be less than feared. Evidence of damage to plants and trees is non-existent and emissions from power plants, which were earlier forced by the government to convert from coal to natural gas, can't be established as a cause. Despite this lack of evidence, the Clean Air Act forces industry into costly, continued cleanup of sulfur dioxide emissions. A study by Robert Crandall, senior fellow at the Brookings Institute, shows that compliance with environmental regulations has reduced economic growth by $150 billion since 1974, not including the immeasurable effects of investments not made.[6]

All businesses have the chance to review proposed environmental legislation which may affect them because this information is published in the *Federal Register*. They can submit their comments to their congressional representatives. Furthermore, when the legislation becomes law and is turned over to the regulatory agency, companies may assist in crafting the rules and regulations by which the intent of Congress will be carried out.

However, at this point, regulatory agency bureaucrats who write the rules often get carried away in their interpretation of the intent of Congress and tend to create regulations which are overly stringent and costly. What's more, they have the power to override any suggested changes submitted from the business world. For example, EPA for years has threatened and may yet classify as hazardous the saltwater which is a by-product of drilling for oil. This implies more rigid and more costly disposal procedures.

There is only one commercial hazardous waste site in the Oklahoma, which eager environmentalists want to shut down. The state generates minimal hazardous waste so this site also accommodates waste from adjoining states. But if this dump is closed, Oklahoma will have to ship its waste out of state, assuming any other state would take it. Each state should take care of its own waste because other states don't want it dumped in their back yard.

In 1992, New York tried to ship its sludge to Oklahoma and spread it on farmland as free fertilizer, but there was so much resistance to the idea that local contractors could find no community which would accept it. Besides, it was highly doubtful the state health department would have allowed the sludge to cross the Oklahoma state line.

Many professionals believe that regulatory efforts will accelerate and become even more costly. There is certainly no slackening in federal regulations currently. Because some environmental laws are always up for congressional reauthorization, they tend to become more "prescriptive," that is, more detailed in telling business or industry precisely what they must do.

Some also believe the attitude of regulatory agencies constitutes a major problem. In their zeal to "do a better job" of enforcing the law, they assume all businesses are crooked; taking for granted that businessmen are guilty until they prove they are innocent of violating the rules, the exact opposite of traditional legal philosophy in America. Criminal as well as civil charges can be levied. A high level officer of the company must certify that the data submitted are accurate. Federal and state programs overlap, making it more difficult to be sure the requirements of each level of government are met. It may be exaggerating to call the process a "witch hunt," but that's the way it feels to people who have to see that the government's demands are satisfied.

It is apparent that the government is not utilizing its resources to attack the most prevalent problems, to benefit the most people, and thus to save the most lives. Instead, EPA concerns itself with such things as mine tailings containing thorium and uranium, substances which could cause cancer. But the danger which radon from these tailings theoretically presents is significantly lower than the risks of smoking, alcohol abuse, illegal drug use, high cholesterol levels, automobile accidents and the other hazards of living we experience daily and know a lot more about.

The cost-effectiveness of governmental regulations should be examined carefully. Science should be used to evaluate risks and the data should govern. And it should be recognized that most manufacturing businesses have the built-in cost of waste management.

But it doesn't appear that common-sense changes will be coming about soon. President Clinton and Democratic congressmen apparently favor a government "far more willing than Mr. Bush's to use regulation, the tax code, government dollars and the presidential podium to get what it wants—from more recycling to better training for assembly-line workers."

Vice President Gore will surely press for tougher enforcement of environmental regulations. President Clinton says business isn't bad, but many executives are—and they make too much money. He also complains that employers spend 70 percent of the money they devote to training of the top 10 percent of their work forces. He may force employers to spread that money more evenly, demanding that even the smallest businesses spend at least $300 a year on training every worker to enhance productivity. It is clear the government under Clinton will further micromanage American business.[7]

In the first two years of the Bush Administration, federal agencies churned out 17 percent more rules than in the 1980s. Federal regulatory staffing climbed above its 1980 records and costs to job-creating businesses multiplied. EPA spending jumped 31 percent and its staffing grew 23 percent in the four years of the previous administration. If this trend continues in the Clinton years, the cost to the economy will be significant.[8]

The U.S. budget in FY 1992 financed the largest number of federal regulators ever—122,400, even more people than employed by the Internal Revenue Service. In March, 1992, the president of General Motors said that costs associated with the Clean Air Act would consume 25 percent to 28 percent of his capital budget. GM had lost $4.5 billion during the previous year.

Small businesses fare even worse. To get a set of clean air permits, a small manufacturing company must spend $10,000 to $15,000 to collect the data and do the paper work. The monitoring devices to track emission rates will cost an additional $10,000 to $50,000.[9]

Federal regulations now cost the U.S. economy $400 billion a year, according to studies reported in the *Journal of Regulation and Social Costs*. By contrast, the Reagan administration cut nearly 35,000 pages from the *Federal Register*. Business responded by creating 18 million new jobs.

Regulations written in Washington, and to a lesser extent in various state capitals, make it difficult for American business to beat foreign competitors. Instead of concentrating on more efficient, productive operations, being innovative, and making long-term investments, U.S. firms must deal with reams of regulation.[10]

In fact, taxes and regulation make it difficult for small operators to *stay* in business. Just ask Herb Kelleher, the chairman and CEO of Southwest Airlines, the low-fare, Short-haul operator that is the only profitable U.S. carrier of size. He cites the 25 percent increase in the ticket tax that is fattening the treasury in the 1990s. "There's no more logic in choosing airline passengers than there is in choosing podiatrists, or hardware-store owners or barbers. Tax hikes on passengers and freight accounted for half the loss of the airline industry last year [1992]." Requirements for mass random drug testing cost Southwest about $120,000 a year for scant safety gain, Kelleher says. That is just one of a dozen new regulations the industry has been fighting.[11]

Government has no money. All it can do is take money away from one group and give it to another. Only people in business and industry can create products and services of value, thus adding to the wealth of the nation. For this reason, irresistible *incentives* should be applied to Congress; a *negative incentive* to spend less and a *positive* incentive to look after the people and organizations that assure the economic health of the nation, as suggested in Chapter Four.

Chapter Eighteen

Increase the Retirement Age: Take Advantage of the Production of Older Americans; "work Harder, Save More and Pay the preacher"

Our problem is not what is the dollar worth in London, Rome or Paris, or what even is it worth at home. It's how to get hold of it, whatever it is worth.

—*Will Rogers*[1]

When the Social Security System idea was put forth by Franklin D. Roosevelt in the mid-1930s, it was supposed to provide a supplement for people in their old age, something to add to the money they'd saved for a rainy day and their retirement.

Over the years, though, as Congress has increased the benefits of the system, along with the taxes necessary to pay for them, Social Security has become less secure for two reasons:

First, the number of retirees is growing rapidly, while the number of workers paying taxes to support the system is shrinking. Between 1980 and 1990, the number of Americans age 65 and older shot up 22 percent while the remainder of the population grew only 8 percent. Nationally, older people numbered 31.2 million in 1990, representing 12.6 percent of the population, 89 percent of seniors were white, 8 percent were black and the remainder of other races. The percentage of Americans over 65 has tripled since 1900, from 4.1 percent. By the year 2030, there will be about 66 million older people in America.[2]

Second, and probably more important, the Social Security taxes collected have not been kept in a capital fund earning interest, but have been drained off by the Congress to pay for the current expenses of the government. Thus, all the Social Security

Administration has is a stack of I.O.U.s signed by the government.

Unless things change, Social Security benefits will continue to be paid from current income, an increasingly difficult problem as more people retire, as retirees live longer and if budget deficits continue to balloon. The trend today is toward retirement as early as possible, whenever there seems to be enough pension built up to make quitting work safe. Because people are healthier and their life expectancy is increasing, sticking with the arbitrary retirement age of 65 years no longer seems to make sense. You can retire at 63 under Social Security if you are willing to take less income.

If the fertility rate again goes down to 1.8 live births per woman, immigration can be significantly restricted and the population of the United States trends downward, a Shortage of skilled labor looms which may not be made up by automation and computer-controlled production processes. The retirement age at which Social Security benefits begin should be increased to 70 and applied to all persons now 55 years old or younger. This would give everyone at least 15 years to adjust to the idea of later retirement. By adding five years to the average 40 year working life of each American, the labor input eventually would be increased by 12.5 percent and the strain on the Social Security System would be eased commensurately.

Would people think this was a good idea? Maybe, maybe not. Those who want to quit as early as possible wouldn't like it, but even now, many retirees either get bored with doing nothing and start looking for a job or they say, "I'm busier now than I ever was when I was working." So the necessary energy and the desire to do something worthwhile are not significant problems. If people did work an extra five years, they would earn that much more money to finance their retirement.

Nobel Prize-winning economist James Buchanan maintains that the harder people work, the better off everybody in the economy is. He presented his thesis, "work Harder, Save More and Pay the preacher," in three lectures at the University of Oklahoma, Norman on October 7–9, 1991 as part of the W. R. Howell, Sr. Second-Century Lecture Series. His lectures in ethics and economics pointed up what we're doing wrong and how we ought to change our habits in order to improve the economy and thus our standard of living.

Dr. Buchanan was awarded the 1986 Nobel Prize in Economic

Science for his work applying economic principles to political decision-making. He said, "The deficit of economic thinking among our political leaders has no doubt contributed to the burgeoning federal deficits.

"Ethical principles affect the well-being of people because the way people behave toward one another influences the economy. And some ethical principles are 'better' than others." Buchanan boiled down his presentations to the "economics of Puritanism."

In Short, Professor Buchanan maintains that everyone of us should work harder because by so doing we inject more effort into the economy which causes it to grow and diversify. As a result every person in that economy benefits from better products at lower prices—as he says, every person gets "more bang for the buck."

Buchanan says that everyone should save more because the money saved is then available for investment in the machinery of production which permits the economy to grow. Thus everybody, including the saver, benefits from the greater array of products and the lower prices which this investment ultimately produces.

Professor Buchanan's third idea is that we should all "pay the preacher," that is, contribute to the support of the people who espouse the first two ideas and other principles he places under the general label of the "Puritan Ethic." Below, the Nobel Prize-winning economist explains these ideas is detail. All of the following information, whether or not shown in quotation Marks, are Dr. Buchanan's words or an abstraction of his message.

Why We Should All work Harder

"Because it's good for all of us," claims Dr. Buchanan.

On New Year's Day six years ago, he had the opportunity to watch four football games on television. But the prospect of sitting on the couch watching football for 15 hours seemed to him a horrible waste of valuable time, even though he dearly loved the game. To assuage his guilt, he spent the time cracking black walnuts he had gathered on his farm, and storing the nutmeats in jars while viewing the games. This initiated his economic inquiry into the work ethic.

Buchanan wanted to discover if his Tennessee/Presbyterian heritage which he retained had anything to do with 20th century economics. This was the question.

While working harder involves quality of work and its results, the professor concentrated on the hours worked—hours per week, weeks per years, years per career. He also assumed that people who worked more hours got more pay and thus had more money to spend. In other words, people who work more time supply more labor to the market, an input of value. He stated the question a different way. "Why should I be concerned about how hard *you* work and why should you care how hard *I* work?"

Adam Smith, in his great book, *The Wealth of Nations*, (1776), located and identified the primary source of a nation's productivity as the effective exploitation of the *division* or *specialization* of labor. Much more value can be generated in an economy where different persons produce different things, and then exchange these goods among themselves. Buchanan asked his audience to imagine what it would be like to try to produce everything we needed on our own, even something as simple as a pencil, without interaction with others. In the frontier West, an isolated homestead was *forced* to be self-sufficient in many of its activities. This independence was purchased at the price of a very low standard of comfort. As other families moved closer and a town took shape, specialization increased and production was tremendously enhanced as people devoted themselves to a single activity.

As the town grew larger, the economic nexus expanded, and as *communication* and *transportation* improved, productivity again increased dramatically. The whole technology of production and specialization proceeds as the numbers of suppliers and demanders increase. And people began to accept this as a worldwide phenomenon.

Today, people pay almost no attention to their dependence on all the others participating in the market. A person expects to be able to sell his own resources (his labor) for a salary or wage or other type of payment. And further, he expects to purchase a "bundle of goods" that he desires from the local supermarket or discount store.

As Adam Smith advanced as a general principle, the division of labor depends on the size of the market network. If we acknowledge the non-exhaustibility of the advantage of specialization, then the question is, "What happens when we work harder, when we supply more hours of work per week in exchange for more wages, which we turn around and spend for an increased quantity of goods and services?" The answer is obvious; we increase the size of the market.

A larger market means that specialization can be expanded further, with generalized increases of productivity of the whole economy. Dr. Buchanan then asked, "Suppose you were in a spaceship, circling above two planets, thinking about landing on one of them. They are similar in population and other respects but there is one major difference. On Planet A, persons work 40 hours per week. On Planet B, you notice that persons work an average of only 20 hours per week. Which would you land on?

"If you consider nothing but your own economic advantage, it is clear you would choose to land on Planet A, because no matter how much you decided to work, the value of output to purchase compared with the value of input would be higher because of specialization, possible because the economy is twice as large.

"Technology on Planet A would not even have been developed on Planet B. That pencil I mentioned might take only a minute to produce on Planet A where it might take 3 minutes to produce on Planet B. An economy in which all persons allow their naked preferences to dictate their choices between work and loafing will not be productive. Harder work on the part of everybody involved provides spillover benefits to everybody. Loafing involves spillover damages to everybody.

"New technologies of production are possible only through enhanced specialization which the increase of market size makes possible."

Dr. Buchanan continued to emphasize that an ethic of work is a psychological state that tells us internally that work is good and loafing is bad—that makes us feel guilty when we loaf too much. The long process of cultural development may have generated within us an ethical norm which benefits us economically. That is to say, we are better off with the work ethic than we would be without it. (As noted in a previous chapter, in the collective culture of the former Soviet Union, where people "pretended to work" because there was no *incentive* or commensurate reward if they did or didn't, the economy failed.)

"Our economic well-being is enhanced by our ethical restraints on our behavior that prevent our expedient response to the temptation offered by the example of the 'beach boys' and the 'flower children.' When you listen to the advice, 'go off and smell the flowers,' recognize that you are doing some economic harm to everybody else when you do so," Dr. Buchanan reminded his audience.

He summed up this way: "work, that is, the supply of labor to the market, is the means through which we can change the size of the whole economy—the market. In a larger market, the division of labor, or specialization, can be exploited more fully than in a smaller market. Each of us, as a user or consumer of the final goods, would rather live in an economy where there is more economic value than where there is less. We'd rather have more available for any amount of labor (input) that we personally supply. That is to say, we all want 'more bang for the buck.'"[3]

In January of 1992, the Japanese Prime Minister Kiichi Miyazawa accused American workers of having lost the work ethic, implying they are lazy. Perhaps that is because Japanese men spend about 56 hours a week working. During World War II, everybody in America worked six days a week (48 hours); it was a matter of survival. Shortly thereafter, the work week went down to five-and-a-half days, and declined to an official five days, or forty hours, sometime in the mid-1950s.

Some offices and industries now require no more than 37.5 hours a week. Few workers today stack up to their parents in the number of hours they work. In addition, holidays such as Martin Luther King's birthday and extra days at Thanksgiving and Christmas have been added to the leisure time schedule.

But there is a shift within the Shorter work week. Americans work just as many hours as they have for several decades, absenteeism is down, and families as a whole work more because more women have jobs outside the home. Since the 1960s, two-earner families have increased and prices as well as expectations have gone up, so people have been working more in order to have the things they now consider essential. In fact, according to two economists with the Washington-based Economic Policy Institute, a liberal research group that draws its funding from labor unions, foundations and corporations, U.S. workers are putting in longer hours than they did in the 1960s. Full-time workers put in 138 hours a year more in 1989 than they did in 1969. The study said that figuring in the rise in work hours, commuting time and the decline in days off, Americans are working the equivalent of an extra month each year. Juliet B. Schor, who authored *The Overworked American*, says, "There will be more leisure time only when people become convinced that they must have it." How much the funding from labor unions may have colored the researcher's conclusions remains unknown.[4] Will Rogers said,

"Samuel Gompers has spent his life trying to keep labor from working too hard and he has succeeded beyond his own dreams."[5]

But just because Americans show up for work doesn't mean their heart is in it, the work ethic being more a psychological state than an economic one. An article in *The Wall Street Journal* about "Employee Ennui," pointed out that workers seem now to be disenchanted, feeling abused by their employers and society at large. Alienation, not laziness, seems to be the reason people don't work as hard as they once did.

The recent recession has taken its toll. People felt compelled to stay in jobs they didn't like because it wasn't easy to find another one. Because a lot of long-time workers were laid off, they felt they could no longer trust their employer. People say, "Gee, if the company doesn't care about me, why should I care about them."

In 1904, Max Weber, the German sociologist, identified the "Protestant Ethic" as the driving force behind capitalism. He argued that capitalists and workers imbued their work with religious fervor, which made them want to accumulate wealth as an outward sign of their piety. Heaven was the ultimate reward for hard work.

The percentage of Americans in the work force has risen steadily since 1948, according to the Bureau of Labor Statistics, and jumped 77 percent for women. A record 6.2 percent of Americans are holding down two jobs.

When given a chance, responsibility and the incentive to participate in the workplace, Americans often respond and work-ethic complaints disappear. But some say these opportunities are rare.

During the Great Depression, there was no safety net for the unemployed, so people were more fearful of losing their job. Now, with unemployment insurance and other benefits, workers have more options, which perhaps explains what some observers see as a dwindling sense of duty.

Alienation of women workers and minorities occurs because of pregnancy, race and sex discrimination, and sexual harassment. The attitude today seems to be, "Why should I put in 110 percent when the employer puts in 10 percent?" No doubt the earnings gap between the CEO and the average worker has something to do with this point of view.

But some workers just don't have the sober habits of their

parents. A Pittsburgh store owner had to try out six or seven applicants before she found one to hire. "They wouldn't take any initiative. You have to tell them the same 10 things every day."

Also, tough union work rules can block attempts to improve the work habits of people. Absenteeism at General Motors hovers around 8 percent, about twice the national average, but before GM can fire a malingerer, the union contract requires the company to show that a worker has been absent 16 days in one year, over and above normal sick leave. Then GM can issue a warning, and it takes another three warnings before the worker can be fired.[6]

The "don't work so hard" attitude is even being encouraged now in Japan, theoretically so that workers will be under less stress and perhaps be more productive. And the worker attitude seems to be softening, too. Unfortunately for Japan's high level of production, this change comes at a time of worker Shortages. Despite the government's encouragement to young Japanese women to have more babies, the liberated female there is more apt to emulate her sisters in America. So it could be that Japan's period of economic leadership as a result of the Puritan values is coming to an end. The Rising Sun may have passed the zenith and may be moving toward the evening of its day of economic dominance.

Why We Should All Save More

> *If there ever was a time to save, it's now. When a dog gets a bone, he don't go out and make the first payment on a bigger bone. He buries the one he's got.*
>
> —*Will Rogers*[7]

At the beginning of his second lecture, Dr. Buchanan said, "There are important differences between the supply of labor and the supply of savings in the sense of general acceptability, that is, public opinion. My decision to work more is different from my decision to save more out of current income, both in the agility and satisfaction in making that change and in the ultimate economic effects on others than myself."

Savings rates are too low and should be increased. We should all save more, not for our children's or grandchildren's sake, but in our economic interest.

It is not necessary to say how much should be saved. Aggregate savings in the United States are relatively low by comparison with savings in other developed countries and savings in earlier periods in our own history. Net national saving in the U.S. out of current income, as a share of total value product, lies somewhere in the range of 2.5 to 5 percent. In Japan, the ratio is three to four times this large and in other developed countries it's roughly between the Japanese and the United States.

Historically, the savings rate in the U.S. has been falling, with the exception of 1991 during which there has been a slight turnaround. Countries that exhibit low rates of savings don't grow very rapidly and rates of growth are widely accepted as criteria for national success or national failure.

One could argue that in the U.S., the savings rate is only too low because of governmental policy that discriminates against saving behavior of individuals and institutions. The inference is that the aggregate savings rate would increase, perhaps substantially, if policies didn't intervene in the working of the economy. That charge is clearly on target to the extent that the net dissaving of the federal government in the form of its large, persistent and increasing budgetary deficits makes up a large, negative item in the calculation of the nations net savings rate. Also, the tax structure at all levels of government could be noted as discriminating against savings.

In any case, Dr. Buchanan said, it is not necessary that I examine these familiar arguments. My central proposition that we should save more is quite different.

In the 1930s, during the Great Depression, Lord Keynes advanced the proposition that if people saved too much it could depress the economy even further; it would backfire. This was the "paradox of saving." Then, almost one fourth of the people were unemployed and this was interpreted as a breakdown of the capitalist economy, and specifically a failure of the economy to generate enough demand to take supplies off the market. Thus, the diagnosis was underconsumption; the remedy, spending—public or private.

But the fundamental problem was the failure of the
, which allowed the supply of money to fall dramatically. We now know that proper action should have been just the opposite. If that had happened, there would have been no Great Depression at all.

The result of the Keynesian delusion was that consumption, or spending, was given praiseworthy social status and a social stigma was placed on savings.

Simply put, Dr. Buchanan said, the act of saving allows for a release of resources into the production of capital, rather than consumer goods, and that this increase of capital into the market operates in essentially the same fashion that an increase of the supply of labor into the market. Increase in capital expands the economy and this expansion allows for an increase in exploitation of the specialization of resources. Economic value of output per unit of input expands and this result insures that all persons in the economic nexus, whether they be workers, savers or consumers, are made better off on their own terms.

To save is not to spend. The flow of income received by an individual allows voluntary disposition in two categories. The individual may purchase bundles of goods for consumption or may save that income. In a real sense, savings are the residual, the amount left over after spending on goods and services.

What form does this saving take? Savings are allowed to return to the circular income flow of the economy by being made available to persons and institutions for the purchase of capital goods.

Dr. Buchanan gave this illustration. We can think of the same person acting in both the saving and investing roles. Robinson Crusoe, alone on his island, saved by forgoing his gathering of coconuts long enough to build himself a fishing net, which is capital goods. Usually, however, the people who save are different from those who invest the capital. In the macro-economy, an act of saving will find its accompaniment in an act of purchase of capital goods. A dollar of new saving, i.e., a dollar not spent on final goods, is available and allows for a dollar purchase of capital goods. Capital goods are instruments or tools that are used in the *production* of final goods, inputs in the production process. Loosely speaking, any input that is transformed into valued output is productive. More accurately, to say that capital is productive is to say that the value produced by the employment of capital is greater than the value given up or sacrificed in the acquisition of capital. Capital goods produce surplus over and beyond their cost of production.

This productive surplus is produced only in time. Productivity through time, and only through time, has caused many economists to attribute the net productivity of capital to time itself, rather than to the attributes of capital, with a great deal of intellectual confusion in the process.

The investment of a dollar today yields an investment return of, say, five percent over a year's time for a gross return of $1.05. The economy one year hence is larger by five cents than the economy today when the decision is made to save and invest an additional dollar. When the economy next year increases in size, there are increased prospects for specialization and resource use.

The person who chooses to save a dollar today does so in the full expectation he will receive $1.05 a year from today. This is his motivation *(incentive)* for saving. How does his decision benefit others in the economy?

As with the work input analogy, a spillover benefit exists from the saving decision. The next year the saver is able to spend $1.05 rather than a dollar and the economy grows to that extent, increasing specialization and the use of resources. When this process is multiplied by many savers, a technology which was just on the margin of economic viability may now be pushed beyond the threshold of survivability.

Dr. Buchanan went on to explain that capital, once created, is permanent in an economic value sense. A dollar invested in capital goods will not only produce a nickel in goods the first year but in all future years. If the capital instrument or tool of production operates for twenty years, it becomes equal to a dollar received from additional labor and spent for consumer goods. Both expand the market.

Thus, both an ethic of work and an ethic of saving, which we label the "Puritan Ethic," retain economic content even in the last decade of this century. To the extent these ethical constraints exist and continue to influence our behavior, we are better off with them than we would be in their absence.

The strengths of these ethical constraints, of course, vary from one person to another, will vary in different social environments, and will not be constant over time. Buchanan said, "I do sense some erosion in the strength of the work ethic, with predictable consequences. My concern with the erosion in the saving ethic is even more acute. The consequences for our own well-being ought to be clear. We must become poorer in our own terms as we save less, as our economy fails to grow as fast."

It's easy to identify several sources of this erosion in the saving ethic. In addition to the stigma against saving and the treatment by politicians of *incentives* to save, financial innovations have made it much easier to spend, especially from income not yet earned (the availability of easy credit through the use of credit cards), allowing persons to *dissave* much more readily than before. The emergence of the welfare transfer state during this century (is another source of erosion).

Politicized schemes for social insurance against income loss during retirement are the institutional embodiments of these changes. As experience suggests, governments have been willing to promise retirement support but have been unwilling to levy taxes sufficient to cover future costs. In effect, the Social Security System has been financed with current income, rather than from productive capital investment. Thus, individuals have been motivated to reduce those savings which might otherwise have been set aside to secure income flow during retirement. The failure of democratically-elected legislatures to accumulate fund balances sufficient to meet pension obligations has been characteristic of the American system. Dr. Buchanan pointed out, "The dramatic increase in the transfer sector of the economy has undermined the *incentive* to save. The cradle-to-grave security promised in the idealized slogan of the welfare state stands as an open invitation to the individual to live 'hand to mouth.'"

Inflation, especially in the 1970s, has made real savings very difficult. Monetary instruments carry no assurance of the maintenance of real value through time (creating) a clear bias toward items of consumption.

The family has become less important in our whole scheme of social interaction. Even the limited ethical constraint that sometime instructed wealthy families not to eat up their capital has now lost much of its *incentive*.

It should be clear, Dr. Buchanan emphasized, that the force of any such ethical norm must continue to erode further in the face of continuing and possibly accelerated shifts in *incentive* structure. "The State will take care of you," is the decisive mark of socialism and there is little sign of that changing. Why should we expect individuals to save very much at all?

However, there does seem to be a developing recognition of the effect of our low savings on economic growth. Also, there is acknowledgment that the incentive structure of the tax transfer system along with the huge budget deficit plays a role (in the low savings rate.)[8]

On January 16, the editorial writer for *The Daily Oklahoman* agreed with Dr. Buchanan's thesis. In a piece entitled, "Encouraging Nest Eggs," the message was: The lack of *incentives* to save and invest continues to cause the American economy to stagnate. While other industrialized nations encourage investments and nest eggs, Congress has methodically taken away *incentives* over the years.

The editorial pointed out that "Two simple measures, reduction of the capital gains tax and reinstatement of full deductibility for Individual Retirement Accounts (IRAs), would do more for the economy than all of the welfare expansion being talked about."[9]

Why We Should All Pay the preacher

> *Preaching is one of the few things that folks have never been able to dope out exactly what its worth anyhow. Some preachers ought to pay admission to get into the church themselves, but as a rule preachers do a mighty good job and are underpaid. Will Rogers*[10]

Dr. Buchanan completed his lecture series by explaining the reasons to invest in the institutions that advocate practice of the "Puritan Ethic," that is, "pay the preacher," because it is in everyone's economic interest to do so. The following is an abstract of his lecture.

"We may start from the premise that human behavior is morally or ethically constrained," Dr. Buchanan began. He said we know we don't behave opportunistically in each and every encounter we experience. Many of us do not and would not steal even if we should be absolutely certain there would be no possibility of discovery and punishment. We may recognize that moral constraints that guide our behavior have evolved in a long process of cultural evolution and we really can't expect to understand either their origins or their logic.

My primary focus, the professor emphasized, is on the individual's evaluation of constraints on others than himself. But first it is helpful to look at self-imposed constraints. Generally, we impose constraints on our own choice behavior when we don't trust our own situational responses to the choice options. We go on diets, try to stop smoking, to prevent ourselves from being in situations where temptation arises.

Economists are perhaps more comfortable with models in which persons impose constraints on their behavior but only in a quasi-contractual exchange-like process. In such a setting, the individual need not impose constraints on his behavior in an isolated calculus of long-term benefits. Instead, constraints are accepted as the price that must be paid—the bad that must be suffered—in order to secure the good that is represented by the reciprocal constraints accepted by others in the exchange. Each party seeks to modify the behavior of the other, but only on the supposition that behavioral change can be secured at some price.

Dr. Buchanan then presented a simple illustration. Suppose you have an apple and I have a quarter. I want you to give me the apple and you'd like me to give you the quarter. That is, I want you to modify your behavior by giving me the apple and you want me to modify my behavior by giving you the quarter. Your action is strictly dependent on my response.

My "bliss situation," or the ideal situation for me would be for you to give me the apple while I *keep* the quarter. Similarly, your ideal program is just the opposite, whereas I give you the quarter and you keep the apple.

If you were to give me the apple without expecting the quarter from me, you would have to be constrained by some ethical reason. Clearly, it's to my interest to instill in your psyche some kind of ethical constraint that will make you do that, and I'll be willing to invest resources in order to get that result. Such an investment would have to be less than a quarter since I know you'll give up the apple for a quarter. If, through an investment of ten cents in changing your psyche or your preferences, I can persuade you to give me the apple without entering into the exchange, I can improve my position by fifteen cents.

If we look at social interaction in that way, we get a different interpretation of the origins of ethical constraints. Such constraints do not emerge from a rational choice calculus on the part of the person whose behavior is constraining, as in the case of self-control and the contractarian model, but instead emerges from the rational choice calculus of others with whom the person to be constrained is expected to interact in a social relationship. In that sense, this model locates the origins of ethical constraints in the rational self-interest calculus of others than the acting individual, and at once is simpler and more strictly economic than the alternative.

This model incorporates what we might label as the standard ethical stance for the individual actor who expects to be confronted with choice situations that involve other persons. The actor, or chooser, will prefer that he retain the option of choosing opportunistically, while the other partners are somehow programmed to behave both predictably and non-opportunistically, so as to benefit the actor.

The professor went on to explain: In the example I gave, my generalized ranking of the four possibilities would be as follows:

1. The most preferred of all possible situations would be for you to give me the apple while I keep the option open as to whether or not I give you the quarter.
2. My second most preferred situation would be for you to give me the apple and I give you the quarter in exchange.
3. You simply keep the apple and I keep the quarter—the status quo remains.
4. The bottom situation for me would be that I give you the quarter where you retain the option of giving me or not giving me the apple—where your behavior remains independent of what I do.

As a mental experiment, the professor suggested, let's suppose that trade or exchange simply doesn't exist, so the second option is not available. In that case, no alternative to the status quo could be better for both parties despite the fact there could be a final position that would be mutually preferred. In that setting, it is clear that if by some investment in mutual persuasion, each could change the ordering of the other so that you would genuinely prefer to give me the apple and I would genuinely prefer to give you the quarter, independently of the response of the other party, we could attain the position described as exchange, which we would both prefer to the status quo, but without resort to the explicit trading reciprocity.

"How might that mutually beneficial outcome be secured?" Dr. Buchanan asked. If the preference orderings are amenable to change at all, each party will find it advantageous to invest resources in modifying the preferences of others so as to produce the desired behavioral change. If the institutions of moral and ethical persuasion, which I here call "the preacher," are even marginally effective, each party to a potential interaction will have an *incentive* to "pay the preacher," that is, invest in bringing the orderings of others around in the direction that will bring spillover benefits to us.

This simple illustration shows that exchange or trade does minimize the necessary role for ethical constraints in facilitating the achievement of mutually-desired outcomes of social interactions. When exchange is not possible, individual behavior that involves ethical constraints may be required to generate mutually-desired results. Contrariwise, when trade *is* possible, individuals may not be nearly so concerned about the preference orderings of others in the social nexus.

It is appropriate for the economist to concentrate on the trading process and on institutional design that opens up further opportunities for trade. As Sir Dennis Robertson, the famous British economist in the middle years of this century, asserted, "The role of the economist is to issue warning barks when he sees proposals being advanced that depend on love for efficacious outcome." On the other hand, neither the economist nor anyone else should ignore or neglect the potential economic usefulness of ethical norms, and especially in settings where explicit exchange arrangements cannot readily and practicably be implemented.

Of particular relevance here are those interactions that involve the simultaneous interdependence of large numbers of persons, where any complex exchange contract, or trading scheme, would be highly complex and difficult to enforce. For such cases, it is as if trading is not a choice option for the participants.

In this context, Buchanan said, think of the specific ethical norms I discussed in the first two lectures, the work ethic and the saving ethic. As the analysis shows, all of the participants in the economy secure benefits from the extension of the work or saving ethic of any individual. All of the participants gain if any person works harder or saves more than his own naked preferences dictate.

If these earlier arguments are accepted, there are mutual gains to a trade of sorts that might be worked out among all participants. Think how difficult it would be to organize a formal contract in such a setting. Each participant would be required to work harder or save more if all the others in the economy agreed to do the same; which is surely a contract that is unimaginably complex and impossible to enforce.

Now, the welfare economists of the mid-century would have

turned their attention then to the prospects of politicized action in the presence of the potential failure of ordinary market arrangements. But the whole enterprise of welfare economics foundered on the selfsame grounds that rule out the exchange or contractual alternative. In any broadly democratic politics, individuals must choose among the alternatives confronted, even if they are aware they are choosing publicly rather than individually. But any politicized contract that might emerge from the interplay of interest in a democracy would surely be far too simple to secure more than a tiny share of the potential gains that effective internalization of economic interdependence might offer. Politicized correction for the failure of market arrangements to capture economic value that might be possible or behavioral shifts along appropriately-defined margins of adjustment, they suffer from implied universality of application.

So we are left, almost as if by default, with ethics as the only viable means of capturing the potential economic value that lies over and beyond that which is secured by the workings of ordinary politics. A major advantage of ethical internalization of the externalities involved that cause persons to work and save lies in the elementary fact that ethics are not explicitly contractual—there is no *quid pro quo* as in political or economic exchange. Any participant in an economy is made better off economically if others work harder or save more and the same applies to all participants. But there is no requirement that if others do work harder and save more, any referenced person must necessarily follow suit.

Dr. Buchanan pointed out that recognition of economic interdependence does, however, present each participant with an *incentive* to change, if possible, the behavior of others. And if the contractual processes of both economic and political exchange are precluded, the natural outlet for such *incentive* is investment in those institutions that embody attempts to modify behavior non-contractually. Each participant has, in this sense, an *incentive* to "pay the preacher," even though free ridership may emerge here as in all public relationships.

"What I've tried to do here is to derive a logical essence from the rational choice calculus of participants in an economy, each one of whom recognizes his own economic well-being depends on the behavior of others and this interdependence extends beyond the limits of ordinary market institutions."

The origins of ethical constraints, the ones I'm talking about, are strictly economic. Persons have economic interest in the behavior of others with whom they socially interact, and they will act to further these economic interests through investments in institutions of socialization and culturalization. We can look at the behavior, both actual and potential, of a person whose preferences are assumed to be exogenously determined. As noted, all that is required is that a person exhibit a preference ordering for the preferences of others than himself.

Each of us is concerned about preferences, or the utility functions of others than ourselves. Still, I can remain totally indifferent about your preference ordering among alternatives so long as your choices among these do not affect my economic well-being, but I cannot remain rationally indifferent if your choices do, in fact, affect my well-being.

If I am indeed interested in your preference ordering among potential choice alternatives, you will be equally interested in my preference order. Whereas it seems straightforward to postulate that my preference orders are exogenously determined and not subject to my higher level choices, we cannot extend this exogeneity to imply that my choices are totally immune to influences by you and others. If we generalize the model to that extent and say that preferences are all fixed and any attempt in changing choices in others must fail; in that case the productivity of investment in paying the preacher would be zero by presupposition.

Economists become uncomfortable, of course, when analysis goes beyond the fixed preference posture. Most economists' research programs do embody either explicit or implicit acceptance of this posture of preference. Normally, economists leave the domain of preference inquiry to their peers in the other social sciences. Persons have biologically-determined needs that are not socially endogenous. But even here, the translation of these needs into preferences among alternatives that might be presented for choice must allow for widely divergent parents. Once we move beyond strict biological limits, the range over which preferences may vary among persons and within the life cycle of the same person covers a whole spectrum.

We acknowledge that preferences may be modified in processes of socialization that describe the operation of the whole social environment in which a person is born, grows and continues to live. In sum, it becomes rational to pay the preacher only in settings that depart from the strict economist's model of fixity in preference ordering. But the productivity of investment in preference modification may fall well below that implied in some of the communitarian alternative discussion.

So let us acknowledge, Dr. Buchanan went on to say, we have a rational interest in the preferences of others with whom we interact if their choices affect our economic well being; and let it also be acknowledged that, within limits, we can change preferences by investment in the institutions of socialization. The logic of the economic argument for paying the preacher seems unassailable.

However, when we move beyond the general analytical argument and attempt to relate the result to the institutions we might actually observe, we face new difficulties. Not all of the preference modifications the preachers might induce are directionally consistent with our economic interest. We should indeed all pay the preacher but only if he preaches what upholds and furthers our economic interest.

It is observationally evident that not all of the ethical, moral teachings that describe the pronouncements of our preachers qualify for our support under this logic. (But) we should be willing to invest something in support of all those preachers who shout out these virtues (of working hard and saving more) from their pulpits.

By much the same logic, we could extend this to apply to those familiar precepts that call for honesty in dealings, for promise-keeping, for truth-telling, for respect for person and property, for sobriety, for tolerance. In Short, we could readily include the whole set of constraints summarized under the rubric of Puritan virtues. If we could but limit our preachers of all stripes, we should have no qualms at all about the social/economic productivity of their activities even if we should also recognize their preaching works some of its effect on us as well as on our neighbors.

But alack and alas! Our preachers and our moralists, whether they are institutionally licensed or self-proclaimed, don't restrict their preaching to old fashioned rules for prudence. These preachers also urge us to have compassion for and be charitable to the less fortunate, even to the extent of selling that we have accumulated and giving to the poor, to join the wretched of the earth in their claims against the productive, to cease the pursuit of economic values, to take time out to smell the flowers, to use the coercive powers of politics to protect the wilderness against exploitation, to assist the efforts of political majorities in the extraction of tribute from those members of the minority who do indeed practice the Puritan virtues. And of course, I could extend that list.

But, Dr. Buchanan said, it should be clear that successful preaching along these dimensions may be unproductive and may actually reduce value in the economy. This may make us worse off in our own terms if our preachers successfully cause our fellow participants in the economy to modify their behavior in accordance with that non-Puritan set of moral norms or constraints.

The upshot of all this is: Yes, there are good, hardheaded economic reasons why we should support the institutions that are designed to modify the norms that serve to constrain opportunistic behavior of participants in the economy. But it is essential that we be discriminatory in our investment. Here, as elsewhere, we should invest only where the returns are greatest, or at a minimum, where the returns are positive.

"My argument says only that the individual, any individual, will be better off in terms of economic well being if others work harder, save more, keep promises and so forth. It is the recognition of this sort of interdependence that makes it privately rational to pay the right sort of preacher."

Or does it? As a single participant in a large production/exchange economy, how can the effort of a single person affect the wider standards of behavior of the whole community other than in some minuscule way? Recognition of the vanishingly small relationship between individualized behavior and collectively-determined outcomes makes it difficult to bring cooperative behavior of many virtues within an explanatory model of rational choice. In a large number of electorates, individuals do not find it economically rational to vote, and if they do vote, they find it rational to remain ignorant.

In public good interactions, individual beneficiaries do not find it rational to contribute, despite the excess of aggregate benefits over aggregate costs. This logic would seem to apply here, that is, to possible individual investment in paying the preacher. The individual act of paying the preacher would in this argument remain irrational, and this in spite of the externalities that might be efficiently corrected. To an extent, however, we do find empirical evidence that individuals behave irrationally in some of the familiar interactions that present this cooperative dilemma. After all, individuals do vote, and some of those who vote do try to become informed about the alternatives. Individuals do contribute toward the cost of publicly-shared goods, even in situations where contributions are strictly voluntary.

It is important to recognize that there exists an active ethical discourse that encourages individuals to surmount those large numbers of cooperative dilemmas in such cases. There are campaigns urging you to vote, to get informed.

By contrast, to my knowledge there exists little or no ethically-directed, economically-motivated argument that encourages individuals to work harder, save more, and to generally hold the Puritan virtues, except in those pockets of our cultural heritage that have resisted the thrust of modernity.

Should we be surprised, therefore, when we observe the non-Puritan moral norms emerging as replacing the Puritan norms? Perhaps criteria of strict rationality do dictate that others ought to pay the right preacher. But criteria of understanding should inform us that in the cooperative solution, we should really *all* pay the right preacher.

The absence of such understanding must be laid squarely on the shoulders of the economists who have separated economics from its initial moorings as part of the moral philosophy. As noted earlier, orthodox economic analysis has no place for recognizing much of the ethical interdependence among participants in the economic nexus, no grounds for appreciating more than a minimal role that moral constraints on behavior can play in generating economic values. Unless and until economists bring their own science back into its proper relationship with ethics, we can expect little generalized encouragement for paying the right sort of preacher.

...[In the] rapidly developing Pacific Rim nations, most notably Japan, something akin to Puritan Ethics seems omnipresent in personal attitude and behavior patterns. My thesis is that regardless of its origins in theology or elsewhere, the set of attitudes that Max Weber in his widely acclaimed and controversial book, *The Protestant Ethic and the Spirit of Capitalism*, identified has been, is and can be important in generating and maintaining economic progress. A society whose members share the Puritan virtues, no matter what the source and for what reason, will be economically more successful than the society where these virtues are absent or less widely shared.

Dr. Buchanan summarized his lecture series this way:

Individual participants in an economy are ethically as well as economically interdependent, and the moral constraints that may inhibit strictly opportunistic responses to choice alternatives are important in determining the value potential of an economy. If someone works harder, earns more and spends more, the exchange network is expanded and the general relationship between the size of the network and the well-being of all of the participants may seem to follow as a natural course.

If a person works harder or saves more, he or she receives the full value of the additional product that the behavioral change generates. It follows as a matter of course that there are purely economic reasons for trying to instill this set of norms in all persons who may participate in the network of production, distribution and exchange.

In 1926, in the midst of the Roaring Twenties, Will Rogers sensed and understood what Dr. James Buchanan would be saying 65 years later. Returning from Russia, the Oklahoma humorist said:

I'm not going to pull the old gag about 'America looks pretty good to me.' It don't look good it looks 'Perfect.' We are better off that any Nation. Why? Why just because we work more. Prosperity is based on just what you produce and if you don't produce much you are just out of luck.[12]

Note: Dr. Buchanan's remarks are from *Ethics and Economic Progress,* by James M. Buchanan. Copyright by the University of Oklahoma Press; forthcoming in 1994.

Chapter Nineteen

Summary

Here is a quick review of the issues and possible answers presented in this book. It may help the reader recall or locate the suggested actions. More importantly, it can serve as a check list on progress by the president and the Congress during the four years of the Clinton Administration:

WHAT TO DO	HOW TO DO IT
Confront and solve the major problems of America	Build incentives into the nation's laws which will make people, including our political leaders and the voting public, want to do what benefits most Americans and enhances the future of the country.
1. Eliminate the annual federal deficit	Limit the U.S. senators and representatives to one, six-year term and do not allow them to run for a second term in either house. Do not permit staff members of any congressman to serve more than six years or more than one congressman. Encourage political parties to develop candidates who can bring a broad background of non-law-making experience to the Congress, particularly in business.

2. Free lawmakers from financial dependence on lobbyists and political action committees	Make it a felony for any lobbyist to give a lawmaker anything of value and apply the same constraint to any lawmaker who accepts anything of value from a professional lobbyist or other person seeking access or advantage.
3. Eliminate the income tax	Gradually abolish both the corporate and individual income tax by reducing these taxes two percent a month. Make the Federal Reserve the government's banker and restrict the government to no more than the percentage of Gross National Product it now spends. Allow this percentage to decline as the deficit is reduced by bringing expenditures into balance with FY 1993 federal income. Permit this percentage to increase only if approved by a vote of the people. Require the Federal Reserve to create the needed money (credit) for government operations in the same way it now expands and regulates the money supply to serve an expanding economy and control inflation.
4. Erase the national debt	As the economy improves and the GNP expands, dedicate a portion of the percentage the government is permitted to spend to the retirement of the national debt.
5. Reduce the cost of elections and the length of election campaigns	Have all national elections publicly financed, relieving candidates of fundraising responsibility and the resultant obligation to individuals and groups who contribute to their campaign. Limit campaigns for national office to two months or less and limit the funds which may be spent on them.

6. Improve the quality of public education; teach values to our children	Allow parents choice of public or private schools by providing a voucher which may be used in either, thus making schools compete for students. Lengthen the school year to 240 days. Include basic American cultural values in the school curricula grades K-12 and on to the college level.
7. Reduce drug abuse and crime	Working through the United Nations where possible, negotiate with illegal drug-producing countries to develop substitute agricultural crops which can be exported to the U.S. and elsewhere. Guarantee the market for these crops to support the farmers' efforts to produce alternative crops. Grant favored-nation status to cooperating countries. Pass Gun control laws to restrict the use of firearms, particularly hand guns and automatic weapons used in crime. Develop private security forces and citizen volunteers to augment the police force and protect law-abiding citizens in neighborhoods wracked by violence, gangs, drugs, and crime.
8. Expand employment opportunities; reduce dependence on welfare	While elimination of the income tax and cyclical improvement of the economy will provide jobs for educated workers, the under-educated face fewer job opportunities. Provide WPA and CCC-type public works projects for welfare recipients able to work and require that they work to receive government help. Also temporarily employ in these programs people unable to find work elsewhere until they can be trained and hired in the private sector.

9. Control immigration and promote Negative Population Growth	Recognize the hazards of over-population, develop a reasonable plan to reduce population over time and control immigration, both legal and illegal, the single factor which successfully can be limited by law. Promote population control in the U.S. and worldwide through educational programs.
10. Export American know-how to Developing countries	Develop more private and governmental Peace Corps-type groups to assist third-world countries to become self-sufficient, improving their standard of living to counterbalance immigration restrictions to the U.S. Assist these people where they live.
11. Reevaluate Environmental Protection Agency programs	Balance Short- and long-term benefits with people and animal concerns. Change Forest Service and EPA directions to provide more reasonable balance between environmental and developmental concerns. Encourage the Congress to face sticky environmental issues in a practical, cost-effective way which will best serve the American people.
12. Reduce credit abuses and bankruptcies	Create two kinds of credit cards, the first for current items which must be paid in full in 30 days or the card is revoked. The second card, which may be paid in installments, would be valid only for buying items necessary for productive work. Change bankruptcy laws to place more responsibility on the borrower.
13. Revitalize the deteriorating centers of our cities	Make development in the outer, suburban areas of cities dependent on assuming responsibility for a reasonable

	amount of rehabilitation of inner city areas for residential purposes, so people can once again live close to and rejuvenate the life of the downtown business districts of our cities.
14. Control costs and expand the accessibility of health care	Explore all of the proposed "solutions" to the cost and access crises in health care. Extend access to basic health service to people unable to afford it. Recognize that health services do not operate like a free market. Balance technological progress with the cost and benefits of its use. Emphasize preventive health care and healtheducation. Direct use of taxpayer money for health care toward the greatest good for the greatest number of people. Extend to all health services the tested cost control methods like DRGs in hospitals and Medicare assignment maximum fees for physician services.
15. Promote free trade; stimulate innovation in science and technology where Amer-ica excels; recognize the reality of multi-national companies	Support the free market concept and work to improve American industrial competitiveness. Improve educational system in the U.S. so young Americans can contribute to scientific and technical innovation.
16. Change government regulation procedures to reduce paperwork for businesses and the cost to consumers who ultimately pay the bill	Recognize that all governmental regulation costs are passed through to the buyers of products and services, a hidden tax. Strike a balance so that people will have essential protection but business will not be unduly burdened by over-eager regulators.
17. Increase the retirement age; take advantage of	Increase the retirement age for Social Security to 70 years. Change govern-

the production of older people; "work harder, save more, and pay the preacher."	mental cradle-to-grave security programs to promote self-reliance, hard work and increased savings.

Chapter Twenty

The Outlook

There's no other country with as much air, and not know where it's going as this country.

—*Will Rogers*[1]

In April, 1989, *The Atlantic* magazine published an introduction to the diaries of George F. Kennan under the title "THE LAST WISE MAN." A late September, 1988, note in his diary reflected Kennan's somewhat dismal view of the future of America. He wrote:

I am startled, as I look over these items, to note the bleakness of the impressions of my own country. A reader might think that I saw in it only ugliness, vulgarity and deterioration. I am sorry about this. Had I not had my own sort of love for the place, these imperfections on its surface would not have hit me so hard or found such abundant record in these scribblings.

I am not oblivious of the fact that the United States of 1988–1989 has its glorious sides. But these seem to me to lie primarily in two areas: the magnificence of those purely natural beauties that have not yet fallen to commercial development; and then the personalities of many fellow citizens I have been privileged to know. But natural beauty alone without the human element, much as it may offer for admiration and wonder, offers nothing for interpretation and makes poor subject matter for the traveling diarist, as it does for the artist. And as for the people: yes—many have engaged my admiration, along with a considerable number who have engaged the opposite. But to depict them individually is the task of the novelist, not of the traveler—particularly not of the traveler moving through regions where he has no personal acquaintances at all and where he sees, for the most part, only masses of anonymous figures with whom he has no possibility of interacting.

I view the United States of these last years of the twentieth century as essentially a tragic country, endowed with magnificent natural resources that it is rapidly wasting and exhausting, and with an intellectual and artistic intelligentsia of great talent and originality. For this intelligentsia the dominant political forces of the country have little understanding or regard. Its voice is normally silenced or outshouted by the commercial media. It is probably condemned to remain indefinitely, like the Russian intelligentsia of the nineteen century, a helpless spectator of the disturbing course of its nation's life. If love of country includes this sort of concern for its future, then I, too, love this particular country, and am a part of it.[2]

The two elements in Mr. Kennan's analysis stand out as root causes of the growing problems we face. The country cannot support our burgeoning population and retain the beauty which is the natural endowment we have inherited. With too many people, America is at risk of becoming a behavioral and environmental sink, of which Somalia is an advanced example. Unless we promptly get control of population growth in the United States, we shall remain on the slippery slope of further deterioration, particularly if the immigrants we admit have little ability to make a positive contribution to the improvement of the quality of life in America.

The second element is "the dominant political forces of the country which have little regard for the intelligentsia." These forces, well-meaning as they may have been when they achieved positions of power, quickly become dominated by their ambition to perpetuate themselves in office. More and more it seems there are two distinct groups in America: those with power who live off the government and the rest of us who pay taxes to support them.

George F. Kennan was right. If there is not radical change in America, we shall indeed become a tragic country as today's trends in crime, drug use, government mismanagement, inferior education, and the deterioration of basic human values continue.

And time is running out.

But it is by no means hopeless.

The changes suggested in this book are not utopian; they are quite practical if we citizens care enough to take control of our future and insist that our leaders build in the incentives needed to regain the American Dream.

It won't be easy and it will be messy, to be sure, because that's the way democracy is. But we can continue to reclaim our voting power and make sure we instill into the law those *incentives* needed to assure a strong, stable, prosperous country that can again be the model for the world. This is the kind of "New World Order" that begins at home and then expands outward as warranted, rather than expending our energy and resources off-Shore while America's problems continue to fester, becoming more intense, more complicated, and increasingly warped by selfish interest and neglect.

Fortunately, there is more than a glimmer of hope in the vigorous response of the voters during the 1992 presidential election. Perhaps the current administration will remind itself that it received only 43 percent of that vote, hardly an overwhelming mandate, and will be attentive to the needs and desires of the people who live outside the Beltway. Certainly Mr. Clinton and the Congress will be closely watched by the voters as the president faces the awesome challenges of the mid-1990s. There is no question the President has laudable goals—improving the economy, reducing the budget deficit, and making health care available and affordable for every American. The crucial question is whether his approach is an effective way to achieve these goals.

Recent American economic and political history suggests Mr. Clinton is determined to continue in the *wrong* direction.

Having backed off his campaign pledges of a middle-class tax cut, effective control of legislation by lobby, and reducing the budget deficit by $145 billion in four years, he is moving toward higher taxes, increased spending, and still more regulation of private enterprise, apparently based on the dubious theory that government can fix anything...and everything!

Do American taxpayers really believe that?

Back in Will Rogers' time, there wasn't much worry about health care because the family doctor took care of people whether they could pay or not and hospital care was not outrageously expensive. When I became administrator of the Memphis City Hospital in 1952, our cost for a day of care was less than 15 dollars, but neither did we have the benefit of the countless medical advances which have ensued in 42 years.

But the other issues—jobs and the economy, the cost of government, congressional behavior, politics and politicians—were ubiquitous and often the subject of Will Rogers' observations. Perhaps Mr. Clinton could benefit from the wit and wisdom of the Oklahoma humorist…

About jobs and the economy…

"Well, all I know is just what I read in the papers, and what I see as I prowl about. This is going to be a mighty noisy session of Congress for every man coming in will have a scheme to relieve the unemployed and it's going to take months just to read all the Bills that will be introduced. Of course they have to go to the Committee first, but it will take the entire Congress and Senate Members to make up enough Committees just to read them all."[3]

About the cost of government…

"I want to warn you of a few of the pitfalls into which our poorly paid (?) but highly costing politicians are driving us daily. We pay an awful lot of dough in the course of a year to try to get our country run in such shape that a certain percent of our citizens can stay out of the poorhouse. The shape we are in now, over and above all the taxes we pay, allows us to hang on to about 8 percent of our gross earnings."[4]

"Now here is what I can't savvy. Why is it that one of us, in fact all of us will work and save, and stint all our lives. For what? Why, to leave something to our children. When we die, we want everything to be left clear and unencumbered. We will break our necks to leave them without a single debt. In fact we won't die if we can help it till we get out of debt for their sake. Now that is what we will do as individuals, BUT when it comes to COLLECTIVELY, why it looks like we will break our neck to see HOW MUCH we can leave them owing."[5]

About working with Congress…

"Besides, nothing is so funny as something done in all seriousness. The material on which the Congressional Record is founded is done there every day in all seriousness. Each state elects the most serious man it has in the District, and he is impressed with the fact that he is leaving home with the expressed idea that he is to rescue his District from certain destruction, and to see that it receives its just amount of rivers and harbors, post offices, and pumpkin seeds. Naturally you have put a pretty big load on that man. I realize that it is no joking matter to be grabbed up bodily from the leading lawyer's office of Main Street and have the entire populace tell you what is depending on you when you get to Washington. The fellow may be all right personally and a good fellow, but that Big League Idea of Politics just kinder scares him.

"Now, they wouldn't be so serious and particular if they only had to vote on what was good for the majority of the people of the U.S. That would be a cinch. But what makes it hard for them is every time a bill comes up they have a million things to decide that have nothing to do with the merit of the bill. They first must consider is, or was, it introduced by a member of the opposite Political Party. If it is, why then something is wrong with it from the start, for everything the opposite side does has a catch in it. Then the principal thing is of course, 'what will this do for me personally back home?' If it is something that he thinks the folks back home may never read, or hear of, why then he can vote any way he wants to, but politics and self preservation must come first, never mind the majority of the people of the U.S."[6]

About politics and politicians…

"I explained to the audience why I was able to tell the truth. It is because I never mixed up in Politics… You know the more you read and observe about this Politics thing, you got to admit that each party is worse than the other. The one that's out always looks the best."[7]

"I tell you Folks, all Politics is Apple Sauce."[8]

NOTES

PREFACE

1. Will Rogers' original manuscript, *Tulsa Daily World*, January 10, 1926, Stillwater, Oklahoma, *Will Rogers' Weekly Articles*, James M. Smallwood, Editor, Oklahoma State University Press, 1980
2. Sterling, Bryan B. and Sterling, Frances N., *Will Rogers' World*, New York, Evans and Company, 1989
3. Will Rogers' Weekly Article, June 7, 1925.

INTRODUCTION

1. Will Rogers' Weekly Article, July 5, 1925.
2. *Will Rogers' Daily Telegram*, July 1, 1931, Stillwater, Oklahoma, *Will Rogers' Daily Telegrams*, James M. Smallwood, Editor, Oklahoma State University Press, 1979.
3. Will Rogers' Weekly Article, November 24, 1924.
4. *The Wall Street Journal*, February 19, 1993, "White House Gives Details of President's 5–Year Plan," by David Wessel, Staff Reporter
5. *The Wall Street Journal*, October 28, 1991, Review and Outlook, "Our Old Friend, the Deficit".
6. *The Wall Street Journal*, October 30, 1991, "Government Budget Deficit Sets Record in Fiscal 1991; New Mark Seen for 1992," by David Wessel, Staff Reporter.
7. Will Rogers, "Letters of a Self-Made Diplomat," *The Saturday Evening Post*, August 21, 1926.
8. Dr. James M. Buchanan, 1991 Public Lectures, "Ethics and Economic Progress," University of Oklahoma, Norman, October 7–9, 1991.

CHAPTER ONE

1. *The Sunday Oklahoman*, November 10, 1991, "Government Like a Venus fly trap," by Thomas Sowell, Creators Syndicate.

CHAPTER TWO

1. *Will Rogers' Daily Telegram*, February 12, 1932.
2. Will Rogers' Weekly Article, November 2, 1924.
3. *The Wall Street Journal*, July 17, 1991, "Movement To Limit Lawmakers' Terms Revs Up and Heads Toward Congress," by James M. Perry, Staff Reporter.
4. *The Sunday Oklahoman*, December 8, 1991, "Lawmakers Just Love to Spend," by Steven Komarow, Associated Press.
5. *The Wall Street Journal*, October 15, 1991, Leisure and Arts, "Dr. Elayne Boosler Speaks Her Mind," by Larry Wallberg, a free-lance writer based in New York.
6. James M. Buchanan, Ph.D., Lecture, "Why We Should All Pay the preacher: The Economic Origins of Ethical Constraints," delivered at the University of Oklahoma, Norman, October 9, 1991.
7. *The Wall Street Journal*, October 16, 1991, Editorial, "A New Political Ball Game".
8. *The Wall Street Journal*, November 1, 1991, Review and Outlook, "Congress's Sweetheart Justice".
9. Will Rogers Weekly Article, August 5, 1923.
10. *The Atlantic Monthly*, July, 1993, "It's not the economy, stupid," by Charles R. Morris, a principal in Devonshire Partners, a technology consulting firm, page 62.
11. Ketchum, *Will Rogers, His Life and Times.*
12. *The Wall Street Journal*, November 6, 1991, "Liberals for Term limits," by John H. Fund, WSJ Editorial Writer.
13. *The Wall Street Journal*, September 20, 1991, "Washington State's Term-Limit Fever," by Janet R. Beales, Assistant Editor for the Fortune Encyclopedia of Economics.
14. Alan Ehrenhalt, *The United States of Ambition*, New York, Times Books, 1991.
15. Will Rogers' Weekly Article. April 12, 1925.
16. *The Wall Street Journal*, September 27, 1991, "congressional Democrats Put Self-Help First, Boding Ill for Party's '92 Presidential Nominee," by Jeffrey H. Birnbaum, Staff Reporter.
17. Will Rogers' Weekly Article, March 27, 1932.
18. *The Daily Oklahoman,* October 9, 1991, "8 Years Plenty for Congress' Boodlers," by Patrick J. Buchanan, Tribune Media Services.

19. *The Wall Street Journal*, November 7, 1991, "Voters Show Anger at Incumbents, High Taxes But Reject Washington State Bid to Limit Terms," by James M. Perry, Staff Reporter.
20. *The Wall Street Journal*, October 25, 1991, Asides, "Political Harassment".
21. *The Sunday Oklahoman*, November 10, 1991, "Government Like a Venus fly trap," by Thomas Sowell, Creators Syndicate.
22. Ketchum, *Will Rogers, His Life and Times*
23. *Congressional Staff Directory, 1991*, Staff Directories, Ltd., Mount Vernon, Virginia.
24. *The Saturday Oklahoman and Times*, November 16, 1991, Editorial, "Perfect Candidate Profile".
25. Will Rogers' Daily Telegram, July 5, 1934
26. *The Daily Oklahoman*, November 11, 1991, "Boren Gains Ground In Reform of Congress," by Chris Casteel, Washington bureau
27. *The Oklahoman*, January 2, 1992, Column, "David Boren Fights the Confusion," by Patrick B. McGuigan, Chief Editorial Writer.
28. *The Daily Oklahoman*, November 11, 1991, "Boren Gains Ground in Reform of Congress," by Chris Casteel, Washington bureau.
29. *The Daily Oklahoman*, January 2, 1992, Editorial, "David's Impatience".
30. *congressional Staff Directory, 1991.*
31. *The Sunday Oklahoman*, November 17, 1991, "Boren Mulls Political Options, Life Outside U.S. Senate," by Chris Casteel, Washington bureau.
32. *The Daily Oklahoman*, February 13, 1992, Editorial, "A Need For Housecleaning".
33. *The Wall Street Journal*, February 13, 1992, Review and Outlook, "Anti-Incumbent Fever".
34. *The Wall Street Journal*, June 2, 1993, Asides, "Real Campaign Reform".

CHAPTER THREE

1. Will Rogers' Weekly Article, August 22, 1929.
2. *The Daily Oklahoman*, October 10, 1991, "Ethics Panel Discusses Curbs on Taking Gifts," by Paul English, Capitol bureau
3. Will Rogers' Weekly Article, March 22, 1925.
4. *The Daily Oklahoman*, December 10, 1991, Editorial, "Cup of Coffee?"
5. Letter from Common Cause, January 7, 1992.
6. Will Rogers' Daily Telegram, January 13, 1935.
7. Letter from Common Cause, January 7, 1992.

8. Will Rogers' Weekly Article, June 8, 1924.
9. *The Wall Street Journal*, November 22, 1991, Review and Outlook, "'But for the Grace of God'".
10. *The Daily Oklahoman*, November 21, 1991, "Cranston's Dealings Called Repugnant," Washington, Associated Press.
11. *The Daily Oklahoman*, January 22, 1992, Editorial, "Gaps Between Those Fangs".
12. *The Daily Oklahoman*, January 10, 1992, "Finance Rules Get Overhaul In Ethics Panel," by Paul English, Capitol bureau.
13. *The Daily Oklahoman*, January 30, 1992, "Ethics Rules OK'd, Sent To Legislature, Panel Urges Quick Approval," by Paul English, Capitol bureau.
14. *The Wall Street Journal*, November 12, 1992, "Clinton's Team Is Sometimes Moved by Lobbyists Despite Its Vows to Be Tough on Favor-Seekers," by Jeffrey H. Birnbaum, Staff Reporter.
15. Will Rogers' Daily Telegram, September 30, 1929.
16. *The Wall Street Journal*, December 8, 1992 "Clinton's Transition Is Full of Informal Advisers Who Aren't Required to Meet Strict Ethics Rules," by Jeffrey H. Birnbaum, Staff Reporter.
17. *The Wall Street Journal*, December 14, 1992, "Clinton's Latest Cabinet-Level Choices".
18. *The Wall Street Journal*, November 5, 1992, "Influence of Lobbyists Groups Likely Won't Diminish," by Jill Abramson, Staff Reporter
19. *The Wall Street Journal*, February 3, 1993, "Clinton's Plan for Campaign, Lobbying Reform Encounters Resistance From House Democrats," by Jeffrey. H. Birnbaum, Staff Reporter, and *The Wall Street Journal*, May 17, 1993, "Campaign Reform That Incumbents Love To Hate," by Albert R. Hunt, Washington bureau Chief.
20. Larry Makinson, *Open Secrets: The Dollar Power of PACs in Congress*, Washington, D.C., congressional Quarterly Inc., 1990, page 5.
21. John L. Jackley, *Hill Rat: Blowing the Lid Off Congress*, Washington, D.C., Regnery Gateway, 1992, pages 68, 126.
22. Will Rogers' Weekly Article, December 2, 1923.

CHAPTER FOUR

1. Will Rogers' Daily Telegram, March 31, 1935.
2. *Internal Revenue Service Annual Report*, 1990.
3. *The Wall Street Journal*, June 16, 1993, Tax Report.
4. *The Daily Oklahoman*, January 20, 1992, Editorial, "The Tax Collection Rip-off".
5. *The Wall Street Journal*, May 14, 1993, Editorial, "Try the Flat

Tax," by W. Kurt Hauser, president of an investment counsel firm in San Francisco and a member of the Board of Overseers of the Hoover Institution.

6. *The Wall Street Journal*, December 9, 1992, Tax Report.
7. Robert E. Hall and Alvin Rabushka, "A Simple Income tax with Low Marginal Rates," Hoover Institution, 1982, Stanford University.
8. Will Rogers' Weekly Article, October 19, 1924.
9. *The Wall Street Journal*, February 11, 1992, Labor Letter, "Employers Bristle at IRS nondiscrimination pension rules."
10. *The Wall Street Journal*, December 10, 1992, "Brady Expected To Outline Plan For Tax System," by Rick Wartzman, Staff Reporter.
11. *Internal Revenue Service Annual Report*, 1990.
12. *The Wall Street Journal*, December 11, 1991, Tax Report, "Tax help trickles down to more workers, as benefits grow more complex."
13. Will Rogers' Weekly Article, November 2, 1924.
14. *The Wall Street Journal*, January 2, 1992, Editorial, "Incentive Pay for Politicians," by Joseph A. Grundfest, Associate Professor of Law, Stanford University.
15. *The Federal Reserve System, Purposes and Functions*, Seventh Edition, 1984
16. *The Daily Oklahoman*, November 20, 1991, "Here's a Platform on Which to Run...for Your Life," by James J. Kilpatrick, Universal Press Syndicate.
17. *The System Purposes and Functions, Seventh Edition*, 1984.
18. *The Wall Street Journal*, May 7, 1993, Editorial, 298 "Return of the Tax Olympiad".
19. *The Daily Oklahoman*, September 28, 1991, "The U.S. Taxpayers Party Nightmare for bureaucrats," by Joseph Sobran, Universal Press Syndicate.
20. Ibid.
21. *The Wall Street Journal*, January 9, 1992, "The Death of Capitalism," by Herbert Stein, former chairman of the president's Council of Economic Advisers and fellow of the American Enterprise Institute.
22. *The Daily Oklahoman*, February 18, 1992, "Advisers Warn Families to Fight To Cut Tax Burden," by Stacy Martin, Staff Writer.
23. *The Wall Street Journal*, January 7, 1993, "Budget Office, Using Unlikely Script, Estimates Tax Bite for Yet-to-Be Born," by David Wessel, Staff Reporter.
24. *The Daily Oklahoman*, January 21, 1992, Editorial, "Time For A Jump Start".

CHAPTER FIVE

1. Ketchem, *Will Rogers, His Life and Times*
2. *The Daily Oklahoman*, June 25 and November 2, 1993, Federal Finances, and July 14, 1993, "Deficit Seen Falling; GOP Wants Figures" (AP). Also, telephone call to the congressional, November 8, 1993.
3. *The Sunday Oklahoman*, December 1, 1991, "Mounting Debt" Photograph, AP Laserphoto.
4. Will Rogers' Daily Telegram, January 9, 1935.
5. Will Rogers' Daily Telegram, February 28, 1935.
6. *The Wall Street Journal*, February 19, 1993, "White House Gives Details of President's 5-Year Plan," by David Wessel, Staff Reporter.

CHAPTER SIX

1. Will Rogers' Daily Telegram, March 15, 192.8
2. *The Wall Street Journal*, May 10, 1993, "Clinton's Campaign-Finance Proposal Takes Aim at Congress and Lobbyists," by Jeffry H. Birnbaum, Staff Reporter, and *The Wall Street Journal*, June 17, 1993, "Compromise by Democrats Clears Way For Vote on Campaign-Finance Reform," by John Harwood, Staff Reporter.
3. *The Daily Oklahoman*, Nov. 9, 1992, Editorial, "There's Plenty of Room for Change," by Thomas Sowell, Creators Syndicate.
4. Ehrenhalt, *The United States of Ambition.*
5. Will Rogers' Daily Telegram, October 8, 1928.

CHAPTER SEVEN

1. Will Rogers' Weekly Article, July 31, 1932
2. *The Wall Street Journal*, July 15, 1991, "Give Students a Reason to work Hard," by Albert Shanker, President, American Federation of Teachers.
3. *The Wall Street Journal*, February 6, 1992, "U.S. Youngsters Score Low in Science, Math, But Testing Methods Questioned," by Jonathan Weil, Staff Reporter.
4. *The Wall Street Journal*, January 7, 1992, "Can Big Money Fix Urban School Systems? A Test Is Under Way," by Dennis Farney, Staff Reporter.
5. *The Wall Street Journal*, October 1, 1991, Politics and Policy, "Determined Principal and Faculty Use Discipline and Peer Pressure to Make a School 'Drug Free'," by Hilary Stout, Staff Reporter.
6. *The Wall Street Journal*, December 4, 1991, Bookshelf, "School choice and Reforms for the Future," by William Tucker, a writer for *Forbes* magazine.

7. Edward B. Fiske, *Smart Schools, Smart Kids: Why Do Some Schools work?*, New York, Simon and Schuster, 1991.
8. *The Wall Street Journal*, September 6, 1991, Editorial, "Fighting the Golden Rule."
9. *The Wall Street Journal*, January 7, 1992, Editorial, "Poland's Liberated Schools."
10. *The Wall Street Journal*, June 2, 1992, Business World,. "Whittle's Lesson Plan for the Public Schools," by Tim W. Ferguson.
11. *The Wall Street Journal*, May 27, 1992, "Whittle's Hiring of Yale President Adds New Credibility to For-Profit School Plan," by Suzanne Alexander, Staff Reporter.
12. *The Wall Street Journal*, June 5, 1992, "Educational Innovation for Profit," by Benno C. Schmidt, Jr., former president of Yale University.
13. *The Sunday Oklahoman*, February 2, 1992, "The Public Ought to Demand Freedom of Choice in Education," by Cal Thomas, Los Angeles Times Syndicate.
14. *The Wall Street Journal*, December 2, 1991, Review and Outlook, Editorial, "A G.I. Bill for Kids".
15. *The Sunday Oklahoman*, December 22, 1991, Around the State, "Academic Gains Apparently Justify Year-round school," *The Norman Transcript*.
16. *The Wall Street Journal*, July 15, 1991, "Give Students a Reason to work Hard," by Albert Shanker, President, American Federation of Teachers.
17. *The Wall Street Journal*, December 16, 1992, "The Education Empire Strikes Back," by Chester E. Finn, Jr., a former assistant secretary of education, on leave from Vanderbilt University to serve as a founding partner and senior scholar of the Edison Project.
18. *The Daily Oklahoman*, October 30, 1991, Editorial, "Some Sobering Statistics".
19. *The Wall Street Journal*, March 15, 1993, Editorial, "Quantifying America's Decline," by William J. Bennett, secretary of education from 1985 to 1988, is co-director of Empower America.
20. *The Saturday Oklahoman and Times*, December 12, 1992, "Networks OK Rules on Violence".
21. *The Wall Street Journal*, June 9, 1993, "Hollywood Executives Plan To Curb Violence on TV," by a *Wall Street Journal* Staff Reporter.
22. *The Wall Street Journal*, October 28, 1991, People Patterns, "Where the Growth Is Among Households".

23. *The Daily Oklahoman*, Editorial, December 23, 1991 "Flouting Moral Standards".
24. *The Wall Street Journal*, April 1, 1992, "Character Development: A School's Primary Task," by Joseph W. Gauld, president, Hyde Foundation.

CHAPTER EIGHT

1. Will Rogers' Weekly Article, September 20, 1925
2. *Statistical Abstract of the United States*, 1990
3. *Newsweek*, January 6, 1992, "The Newest War," by Charles Lane with Douglas Waller in Washington, Brook Larmer in South America, Peter Katel in Miami and Brook Larmer in the Chapare.
4. *The Wall Street Journal*, December 27, 1991, "Heroin: The Next Act in the Colombian Drug Drama," by Juan Daniel Jaramillo Ortiz, a Columbian lawyer and economist who writes for *El Nuevo Siglo* in Santa Fe de Bogota.
5. *The Wall Street Journal*, February 14, 1992, The Americas. "Peru's Ex-Drug Czar on Cocaine: The Supply Side," by Hernando de Soto.
6. Domestic Cannabis Eradication/Suppression Program, 1990.
7. *The Wall Street Journal*, April 16, 1992, "The Case for Fujimori's Coup," by Walter Palomino Villamonte, a Peruvian and an instructor in economics at St. Augustine College in Chicago.
8. *The Wall Street Journal*, October 9, 1992, The Americas, "Celebrations and Reflections After Peru's Capture of the Century," by Alonso Cueto, a Peruvian writer.
9. *The Wall Street Journal*, April 27, 1992, "To Avoid Repeats of Peru, Legalize Drugs," by Robert J. Barro, a professor of economics at Harvard University.
10. *The Wall Street Journal*, May 6, 1992, Letters to the Editor, Crawford, "Decriminalize Drugs, End the War," by Manuel S. Klausner, Los Angeles
11. *The Daily Oklahoman*, November 27, 1992, "Peru Seeks Clinton's Help In Fighting Coca Business," by Rowland Evans and Robert Novak, Creators Syndicate.
12. *The Daily Oklahoman*, December 2, 1992, "Peruvians Vote in Spite of Intimidation," by Jeane Kirkpatrick, Los Angeles Times Syndicate.
13. Will Rogers' Weekly Article, September 20, 1925.
14. A mailing from Coalition To Stop Gun Violence, 100 Maryland Avenue, N.E., Washington, D.C. 20002, 1993.
15. *The Wall Street Journal*, December 5, 1991, Technology and Health, "Study Links Drop in Firearm Deaths To Handgun Law," by Ron Winslow, Staff Reporter.

16. *The Wall Street Journal*, October 18, 1991, "Assault Weapon Ban Is Rejected By the House," by Jeffrey H. Birnbaum, Staff Reporter.
17. *The Wall Street Journal*, December 12, 1991, Counterpoint, "Gun control Is Constitutional," by Robert A. Goldwin, resident scholar in constitutional studies at theAmerican Enterprise Institute.
18. *The Wall Street Journal*, May 26, 1992, Politics and Policy, "Arms, and Clashes Over the Right to Bear Them, Turn California Politics Into a Heated Gunfight," by James M. Perry, Staff Reporter.
19. Neely, Richard, *Take Back Your Neighborhood*, Donald I. Fine, Inc., 1991.
20. *The Daily Oklahoman*, October 31, 1991, "Curbing Crime; Peaceful Streets," by Patrick B. McGuigan, Chief Editorial Writer, *The Oklahoman.*
21. *The Daily Oklahoman*, December 17, 1992, Editorial, "Crime Pays?"

CHAPTER NINE

1. Sterling and Sterling, *Will Rogers' World.*
2. *The Wall Street Journal*, August 30, 1991, "More Employers Offer Early Retirement To Help Shrink Blue-Collar work Force," by Gregory A. Patterson, Staff Reporter.
3. Will Rogers' Weekly Article, January 18, 1931.
4. *The Wall Street Journal*, July 28, 1992, Bookshelf, "Pitfalls of Helping Poor," by William Tucker, an author who is writing a book on the evolution of the family, and Marvin Olasky, *The Tragedy of American Compassion*, Washington, D.C., Regnery Gateway, 1992.
5. *The Daily Oklahoman*, January 8, 1992, "Boren Wants To Hire Recipients of Welfare," by Mick Hinton, Capitol bureau .
6. *The Wall Street Journal*, December 29, 1992, "Clinton Faces Daunting Task in Turning Welfare Rhetoric Into a Coherent Policy," by Laurie McGinley, Staff Reporter .
7. *The Sundav Oklahoman*, January 12, 1992, Editorial, "Where the Money Goes".
8. *The Saturday Oklahoman and Times*, January 18, 1992, Column, "Fatherless Families No. 1 Problem," by Don Feder, Creators Syndicate.
9. *The Daily Oklahoman*, December 4, 1992, Editorial, "Wisconsin's Better Idea".
10. *The Daily Oklahoman*, December 17, 1992, " Welfare System Reform Studied: Time Limit on AFDC Urged," by Mick Hinton, Capitol bureau.

11. *The Wall Street Journal*, December 11, 1991, "Surging Welfare Costs, Struggle to Control Them Join Health-Care Expense as Hot Political Issue," by Susan C. Faludi and Marilyn Chase, Staff Reporters.
12. *The Wall Street Journal*, April 23, 1992, "Study of Welfare-Reform Effort Finds Positive Signs in a California Program," by Timothy Noah, Staff Reporter
13. *The Wall Street Journal*, April 14, 1992, "What Should We Do About the Poor?" an editorial which appeared in the April issue of *First Things*, a monthly publication of the New York-based Institute on Religion and Public Life.
14. *The Wall Street Journal*, June 14, 1993, Editorial, "A Conservative Welfare State," by Irving Kristol, an American Enterprise Institute fellow, co-edits *The Public Interest* and publishes *The National Interest.*

Chapter Ten

1. Negative Population Growth, Inc., Post Office Box 1206, Teaneck, New Jersey 07666
2. Robert C. Hardy, *One Hundred Years of Upstart Unitarianism in the Bible Belt*, Oklahoma City, First Unitarian Church, 1991
3. Ibid.
4.. Zero Population Growth, 1400 Sixteenth Street, NW, Washington, D.C. 20036, Letter from Paul R. Ehrlich, Honorary President, November, 1991.
5. Ibid.
6. *The Wall Street Journal*, September 13, 1991, Environment, "Overpopulation Takes Center Stage in 1990s," by Frank Edward Allen.
7. Lindsey Grant, "Reconciling Texas and Berkeley: The Concept of Optimum Population," First of a Series, The NPG Forum, November, 1989.
8. *The Wall Street Journal*, December 3, 1992, Demographics, "Census bureau Lifts Population Forecast, Citing Fertility, Immigration, Longevity," by Lucinda Harper, Staff Reporter.
9. Donald Mann, President, Negative Population Growth, "What Does NPG Believe?"
10. *The Daily Oklahoman*, November 22, 1991, "Illegal immigration Hurting the United States," by Paul Harvey, Los Angeles Times Syndicate
11. Leon F. Bouvier, "How To Get There From Here: The Demographic Route To Optimal Population Size," Second of A Series, The NPG Forum, 1989
12. *The Wall Street Journal*, September 27, 1991, workplace, "Immigration Law May Help U.S. Firms, But It Also Creates

Some New Headaches," by Lourdes Lee Valeriano and Joann S. Lublin, Staff Reporters.

13. Alden Speare, Jr. and Michael J. White, "Optimal City Size and Population Density for the 21st Century," Eleventh of a Series, The NPG Forum.
14. *The Wall Street Journal*, December 30, 1991, Washington Insight, "U.S. Faces Pressure to Set Policy on Refugees Amid Prospects of an Influx," by Robert S. Greenberger, Staff Reporter
15. *The Daily Oklahoman*, January 11, 1992, Your Views, "World Is Depending On Abortion," by Hazel T. Baker.
16. *The Wall Street Journal*, June 18, 1993, "Italy's Birthrate. the World's Lowest, Is a Vexing Anomaly," by Peter Gumbel, Staff Reporter.
17. *The Daily Oklahoman*, December 17, 1992, "FDA Says Tests Of Abortion Pill May Be Waived," Washington, Associated Press
18. Letter, November, 1992, Association for Voluntary Surgical Contraception, 79 Madison Avenue, New York, NY 10016.
19. Letter, November 24, 1992, Population Communications International, 777 United Nations Plaza, New York, N.Y. 10017.
20. Ibid.
21. *The Wall Street Journal*, June 24, 1993, Counterpoint, "To Cut Spending, Freeze Immigration," by Daniel James.

CHAPTER ELEVEN

1. *The Wall Street Journal*, January 10, 1992, "From the Armed Forces to the Teaching Force," by Patricia Hines, Deputy Assistant Secretary for Training and Education, Department of the Army.

CHAPTER TWELVE

1. Will Rogers' Gulf Radio Broadcast, April 14, 1935.
2. *The Daily Oklahoman*, January 24, 1992, "Scaremongers' Lies May Actually Endanger Public," by Paul Harvey, Los Angeles Times Syndicate
3. *The Atlantic Monthly*, January, 1992, "The Butterfly Problem," by Charles C. Mann and Mark L. Plummer.
4. Ibid.
5. Ibid.
6. *The Atlantic Monthly*, January, 1992, "Stopgap Measures," by Susan Winckler
7. *The Atlantic Monthly*, January, 1992, "The Case for Human Beings," by Thomas Palmer.

8. *The Wall Street Journal*, January 6, 1992, "Timber Town Is Bitter Over Efforts to Save The Rare Spotted Owl," by Charles McCoy, Staff Reporter.
9. *The Daily Oklahoman*, December 15, 1991, "Scientists to Study Owls," Medford, Oregon, Associated Press.
10. Will Rogers' Weekly Article, December 20, 1925.
11. *The Atlantic Monthly*, October, 1991, "The Mismanagement of the National Forests," by Perri Knize.

CHAPTER THIRTEEN

1. Will Rogers' Daily Telegram, September 6, 1928.
2. Will Rogers' Daily Telegram, March 1, 1931.
3. *The Saturday Oklahoman and Times*, December 28, 1991, Associated Press, "Personal Bankruptcies Rise 24 Percent in Nation."
4. *The Wall Street Journal*, November 15, 1991, Editorial, "New Spin on Jimmynomics".
5. *The Wall Street Journal*, November 21, 1991, "credit card Lawmakers Agree to a 9-Month Study," by a *Wall Street Journal* Staff Reporter.
6. *The Wall Street Journal*, November 21, 1991, "Economists Say Rise in Credit-Card Debt Shows Lower Rates Won't Spur Spending," by Steven Lipin, Staff Reporter.
7. *The Daily Oklahoman*, January 6, 1992, "credit card Junkies Are Drowning in Debt," by Paul Harvey, Los Angeles Times Syndicate.
8. *The Wall Street Journal*, November 14, 1991, "Stores Offer Enticements to Encourage Shoppers to Charge Holiday Purchases," by Francine Schwadel, Staff Reporter; *The Wall Street Journal*, December 16, 1992, "Credit-Card Use Surges as Consumers Charge Holiday Gifts at Record Pace," by Peter Pae, Staff Reporter; *The Wall Street Journal*, November 25, 1992, "Credit-Card Issuers Give Consumers Holiday Incentives," by Peter Pae, Staff Reporter.
9. Will Rogers' Daily Telegram, October 9, 1930.
10. *The Wall Street Journal*, December 26, 1991, "Credit Junkies: Many Keep On paying High Rates on Cards, Through Bad Planning," by Peter Pae, Staff Reporter.
11. *The Wall Street Journal*, February 11, 1993, "The Depression of the 1990s-It's Already Here," by James Dale Davidson, co-author of *The Great Reckoning* (Simon and Schuster) and a principal of Strategic Advisors Corp., Baltimore.
12. CaerLaerPublications, *WealthAngles*, Baltimore, 1992 and *The Daily Oklahoman*, January 6, 1992, "credit card Junkies Are Drowning in Debt," by Paul Harvey, Los Angeles Times Syndicate.

13. Will Rogers' Daily Telegram, July 9, 1930.

CHAPTER FOURTEEN

1. Will Rogers' Daily Telegram, November 4, 1931.
2. *The Wall Street Journal*, December 3, 1991, "Richmond, Va's Loss of Major Store Imperils Bid to Salvage Its Downtown," by Lucinda Harper, Staff Reporter.
3. *The Wall Street Journal*, November 16, 1992, "Developed to Reinvigorate Downtowns, Many Urban Malls Are Disappointments," by Laurie M. Grossman, Staff Reporter.
4. Ibid.
5. Robert C. Hardy, *HERO: An Oral History of the Oklahoma Health Center*, Oklahoma City, Oklahoma Health Sciences Foundation, 1985.
6. *The Daily Oklahoman*, December 3, 1991, Editorial, "Density Not Sole Crime Cause".
7. *The Daily Oklahoman*, February 21, 1992, "City's Downtown Vacancies Top Company's Survey," by Stacy Martin, Staff Writer, and *The Sunday Oklahoman*, June 6, 1993, Real Estate Notes, "Downtown Vacancies Highest in Nation".
8. Research Department, Oklahoma City Chamber of Commerce

CHAPTER FIFTEEN

1. Will Rogers' Weekly Article, July 13, 1930.
2. *The Daily Oklahoman*, November 24, 1992, Editorial, "Clinton's Health Plan".
3. *The Daily Oklahoman*, December 22, 1992, Health Watch, "Most surveyed favor universal health care," Harris survey for Prevention magazine
4. *The Wall Street Journal*, June 10, 1993, Editorial, "Dead on Arrival—Clinton Health Plan," by Joseph Bast, president of the Chicago-based Heartland Institute and co-author of "Why We Spend Too Much on Health care."
5. *The Wall Street Journal*, June 17, 1993, "Adviser on Health care Calls Clinton's Plan 'Pretty Much Done'," by a *Wall Street Journal* Staff Reporter.
6. *The Wall Street Journal*, October 3, 1991, "U.S. Health care Spending Increased 10.5 percent in 1990".
7. *The Wall Street Journal*, December 11, 1991, "Average U.S. Family Is Spending 11.7 percent of Income on Health care, Study Finds," by Hilary Stout, Staff Reporter.
8. *The Wall Street Journal*, December 3, 1991, "Feeling Better: Canada Seems Satisfied With a Medical System That Covers Everyone," by G. Pierre Goad, Staff Reporter.

9. Robert C. Hardy, *How Many Physicians Does Oklahoma Need?,* Oklahoma Health Sciences Foundation, June 1973
10. *The Wall Street Journal,* December 3, 1991, "Feeling Better: Canada Seems Satisfied With a Medical System That Covers Everyone," by G. Pierre Goad, Staff Reporter
11. *The Daily Oklahoman,* December 22, 1992, Labor Letter, "Fewer Doctors in Canada Eye Greener Pastures."
12. *The Atlantic Monthly,* August, 1991, "Healthy Competition," by Regina Herzlinger, Nancy R. McPherson Professor of Business Administration, Harvard Business School.
13. Summary of S.2817, The National Health care Act of 1992, Legislative Update, Office of Government Relations, National Association of Social workers, October, 1992.
14. *The Wall Street Journal,* July 23, 1991, "A Government Health Plan for Free-Marketer," by Laurence S. Seidman, Professor of Economics, University of Delaware.
15. *The Wall Street Journal,* January 22, 1992, "Closed Market: Laws of Economics Often Don't Apply in Health-Care Field,," by David Wessel and Walt Bogdanich, Staff Reporters.
16. *The Wall Street Journal,* November 12, 1991, "Gammon's Law Points to Health-Care Solution," by Milton Friedman, the Nobel laureate in economics, is a fellow at the Hoover Institution.
17. *The Daily Oklahoman,* February 19, 1992, "Health Reform Gets Attention, AMA Chair Says," by Karen Klinka, Staff Writer.
18. *The Wall Street Journal,* February 7, 1992, "Bush Unveils Health Plan Based on Tax Breaks that Critics Fault as Too Modest and Inflationary," by Walt Bogdanovich and Hilary Stout, Staff Reporters.
19. *The Wall Street Journal,* January 3, 1992, "'Play of Pay' Health-Care Plan is Bound to be a Loser," by Stuart M. Butler, Director, Domestic Policy Studies, Heritage Foundation.
20. *The Wall Street Journal,* January 28, 1992, "Give Employees Medical IRAs and Watch Costs Fall," by J. Patrick Rooney, Chairman, Golden Rule Insurance Company, and *The Daily Oklahoman,* January 31, 1992, Editorial "Health care IRAs?"
21. Will Rogers' Weekly Article, July 17, 1927.
22. *Newsweek,* November 30, 1992, "Facing the Powers That Be: The Medical Lobby Lineup," by Gregg Easterbrook.
23. Robert C. Hardy, *HERO: An Oral History of the Oklahoma Health Center,* Oklahoma Health Sciences Foundation, 1985.
24. *The Daily Oklahoman,* December 24, 1992, "How Big is Big? Oklahoma Hospitals Keep Expanding: Duplication Blamed for Costly Care," by Ted Bridis, Associated Press Writer.

25. *The Atlantic Monthly,* March, 1992, "What Market Values are Doing To Medicine," by Arnold S. Relman, M.D., Professor of Medicine and Social Medicine, Harvard Medical School, senior physician at the Brigham and Women's Hospital, Boston.
26. Congressman Glenn English, "Results of the 2nd Health care Survey," Spring, 1992, Newsletter to 6th Congressional District, Oklahoma.

CHAPTER SIXTEEN

1. Will Rogers' Weekly Article, October 14, 1934.
2. *The Saturday Oklahoman and Times*, December 28, 1991, Editorial, "Lessons From 1929".
3. *The Saturday Oklahoman and Times*, December 28, 1991, Column, "Protectionists Are Ignoring History as Well as Economics," by Mona Charen, Creators Syndicate.
4. *The Daily Oklahoman*, January 2, 1992, Canberra, Australia, Associated Press, "Bush Tells Aussies Ag Subsidies to Continue".
5. *The Wall Street Journal*, January 20, 1992, The Outlook, "Managed trade May Serve a Purpose," by Alan Murray.
6. *The Saturday Oklahoman and Times*, December 28, 1991, Column, "Protectionists Are Ignoring History as Well as Economics," by Mona Charen, Creators Syndicate.
7. *The Daily Oklahoman*, January 21, 1992, Column, "We're to Blame for Trade Problems," by Don Feder, Creators Syndicate.
8. *The Wall Street Journal*, January 27, 1992, The Outlook, "Protectionist Calls Belie Competitiveness," by Alfred L. Malabre, Jr. and *The Daily Oklahoman*, February 21, 1992, Foreign Trade: U.S. Trade Balance, 1970–1991, Associated Press/Carl Fox.
9. *The Wall Street Journal*, April 21, 1993, "U.S. Service Exports Are Growing Rapidly, But Almost Unnoticed," by Ralph T King, Jr., Staff Reporter
10. *The Wall Street Journal*, December 30, 1991, Editorial, "Crib Note on Trade".
11. Robert L. Bartley, *The Seven Fat Years and How To Do It Again*, New York, The Free Press, 1992, page 200.
12. *The Wall Street Journal*, December 14, 1992, "U.S. High-Tech Firms Have Begun Staging Little-Noticed Revival," by G. Pascal Zachary, Staff Reporter.
13. *The Wall Street Journal*, May 24, 1993, Special Section on Technology, "Who's A Genius?" by Laurence Hooper, page R–18.
14. *The Wall Street Journal*, December 23, 1992, "Fighting NAFTA: Free-Trade Pact Spurs A Diverse Coalition Of Grass-Roots Foes," by Bob Davis, Staff Reporter.

15. *The Wall Street Journal*, June 16, 1993, Editorial, "Good-Looking Clinton".

CHAPTER SEVENTEEN

1. Sterling and Sterling, *Will Rogers' World.*
2. William E. Simon, *A Time For Truth*, New York, Readers Digest Press, McGraw-Hill Book Company, 1978.
3. *The Wall Street Journal*, January 20, 1992, "January Surprise: Bush Plans To Unveil A 90-Day Moratorium on New Regulations," by Bob Davis, Staff Reporter.
4. *The Wall Street Journal*, January 30, 1992, "Heads of Agencies Asked to Weed Out Unnecessary Rules," by Bob Davis, Staff Reporter.
5. *The Wall Street Journal*, January 20, 1992, "January Surprise: Bush Plans To Unveil A 90-Day Moratorium on New Regulations," by Bob Davis, Staff Reporter.
6. *The Daily Oklahoman*, February 5, 1992, Editorial, "'Regulation Gone Awry".
7. *The Wall Street Journal*, January 9, 1992, "Democratic Runners Seem Readier Than Bush To Flex Federal Muscles to Shape U.S. Business," by David Wessel, Staff Reporter.
8. *The Wall Street Journal*, Review and Outlook, "Regulatory Reversal".
9. *The Wall Street Journal*, March 2, 1992, Global View, "America's Real Trade Enemy Is Washington," by George Melloan.
10. *The Daily Oklahoman*, December 15, 1992, Editorial, "The High Cost of Regulation".
11. *The Wall Street Journal*, March 9, 1993, Business World, "Airline Asks Government for Room to Keep Rising," by Tim W. Ferguson.

CHAPTER EIGHTEEN

1. Will Rogers' Weekly Article, July 23, 1933.
2. *The Daily Oklahoman*, January 27, 1992, "Senior Sector Jumps By 22 percent, Study Says," by J. E. McReynolds, Staff Writer.
3. James M. Buchanan, Ph.D., Lecture, "Why We Should All work Harder; The Economic Value of the work Ethic," delivered at the University of Oklahoma, Norman, October 7, 1991.
4. *The Wall Street Journal*, February 14, 1992, Bookshelf, "More work, Less Play Is Rule of the Day," by John Coston, a Journal news editor in New York, and Juliet B. Schor, *The Overworked American: The Unexpected Decline of Leisure*, Basic Books, 1992.
5. Will Rogers' Weekly Article, December 28, 1924.

6. *The Wall Street Journal*, February 7, 1992, "Employee Ennui: If the U.S. work Ethic is Fading, 'Laziness' May Not Be the Reason," by Bob Davis and Dana Milbank, Staff Reporters.
7. Will Rogers' Daily Telegram, July 9, 1930.
8. James M. Buchanan, Ph.D., Lecture, "Why We Should All Save More: The Economics of the Saving Ethic," delivered at the University of Oklahoma, Norman, October 8, 1991.
9. *The Daily Oklahoman*, January 16, 1992, Editorial, "Encouraging Nest Eggs".
10. Will Rogers' Weekly Article, January 8, 1933.
11. James M. Buchanan, Ph.D., Lecture, "Why We Should All Pay the preacher: The Economic Origins of Ethical Constraints," delivered at the University of Oklahoma, Norman, October 9, 1991.
12. Will Rogers' Weekly Article, October 10, 1926.

CHAPTER TWENTY

1. Will Rogers, Speech at luncheon for Post and Gatty, Tulsa, Oklahoma, Tulsa World, July 14, 1931.
2. *The Atlantic Monthly*, April, 1989, "The Last Wise Man:" "Sketches From A Life," by George F. Kennan.
3. Will Rogers' Weekly Article, December 6, 1931.
4. Will Rogers' Weekly Article, *New York Times*, December 24, 1922
5. Will Rogers' Weekly Article, January 10, 1926.
6. Will Rogers' Weekly Article, June 8, 1924.
7. Will Rogers' Weekly Article, *New York Times*, December 31, 1922
8. Ibid.

Index

A

B

C

D

E

F

G

H

I

J

K

L

M

N

O

P

Q

R

S

T

U

V

W

Y

Z